Wireless Home Networking Simplified

Jim Doherty

Neil Anderson

Illustrations by Nathan Clement

Cisco Press
800 East 96th Street
Indianapolis, IN 46240

Wireless Home Networking Simplified

Jim Doherty and Neil Anderson

Copyright© 2007 Cisco Systems, Inc.

Published by:
Cisco Press
800 East 96th Street
Indianapolis, IN 46240 USA

Printed in the United States of America   2 3 4 5 6 7 8 9 0

Second Printing: November, 2007

ISBN: 1-58720-161-5

Library of Congress Cataloging-in-Publication Data
Doherty, Jim, CCNA.
  Wireless home networking simplified / Jim Doherty, Neil Anderson.
      p. cm.
  ISBN 1-58720-161-5 (pbk.)
  1. Home computer networks. 2. Wireless LANs. I. Anderson, Neil, 1965- II. Title.
  TK5105.75.D66 2006
   004.6'8--dc22
2006036500

Warning and Disclaimer

This book is designed to provide information about building, using, and living with wireless home networks. Every effort has been made to make this book as complete and as accurate as possible, but no warranty or fitness is implied.

The information is provided on an "as is" basis. The authors, Cisco Press, and Cisco Systems, Inc. shall have neither liability nor responsibility to any person or entity with respect to any loss or damages arising from the information contained in this book or from the use of the discs or programs that may accompany it.

The opinions expressed in this book belong to the authors and are not necessarily those of Cisco Systems, Inc.

Feedback Information

At Cisco Press, our goal is to create in-depth technical books of the highest quality and value. Each book is crafted with care and precision, undergoing rigorous development that involves the unique expertise of members from the professional technical community.

Readers' feedback is a natural continuation of this process. If you have any comments regarding how we could improve the quality of this book, or otherwise alter it to better suit your needs, you can contact us through e-mail at feedback@ciscopress.com. Please make sure to include the book title and ISBN in your message.

We greatly appreciate your assistance.

Trademark Acknowledgments

All terms mentioned in this book that are known to be trademarks or service marks have been appropriately capitalized. Cisco Press or Cisco Systems, Inc. cannot attest to the accuracy of this information. Use of a term in this book should not be regarded as affecting the validity of any trademark or service mark.

Publisher
Paul Boger

Cisco Representative
Anthony Wolfenden

**Cisco Press
Program Manager**
Jeff Brady

Executive Editor
Kristin Weinberger

Managing Editor
Patrick Kanouse

Development Editor
Dayna Isley

Senior Project Editor
San Dee Phillips

Copy Editor
Bill McManus

Technical Editors
Doug Foster
Bradley Mitchell

Team Coordinator
Vanessa Evans

Cover Designer
Louisa Adair

**Interior Design and
Composition**
Mark Shirar

Indexer
WordWise Publishing
Services, LLC

Proofreader
Katherin Bidwell

Americas Headquarters
Cisco Systems, Inc.
170 West Tasman Drive
San Jose, CA 95134-1706
USA
www.cisco.com
Tel: 408 526-4000
800 553-NETS (6387)
Fax: 408 527-0883

Asia Pacific Headquarters
Cisco Systems, Inc.
168 Robinson Road
#28-01 Capital Tower
Singapore 068912
www.cisco.com
Tel: +65 6317 7777
Fax: +65 6317 7799

Europe Headquarters
Cisco Systems International BV
Haarlerbergpark
Haarlerbergweg 13-19
1101 CH Amsterdam
The Netherlands
www-europe.cisco.com
Tel: +31 0 800 020 0791
Fax: +31 0 20 357 1100

Cisco has more than 200 offices worldwide. Addresses, phone numbers, and fax numbers are listed on the Cisco Website at www.cisco.com/go/offices.

About the Authors

Jim Doherty is the vice president of marketing at CipherOptics, where he leads the outbound marketing teams. Prior to joining the CipherOptics team Jim held leadership positions with Symbol Technologies and Cisco. Jim has more than 15 years of technical marketing and engineering experience and has led various marketing campaigns for IP telephony, routing and switching, and network security solutions. Jim is the coauthor of the *Networking Simplified* series of books published by Cisco Press. Jim is a former Marine Corps sergeant; he holds a B.S. degree in electrical engineering from N.C. State University and an M.B.A. degree from Duke University.

Neil Anderson is the senior manager of enterprise systems engineering with Cisco. Neil has more than 20 years of broad engineering experience including public telephone systems, mobile phone systems, Internet, and home networking. At Cisco, Neil's focus is on large corporate customers in the areas of routing and switching, wireless, security, and IP communications. Neil is the coauthor of the *Networking Simplified* series of books including *Home Networking Simplified*, *Home Network Security Simplified*, and *Internet Phone Services Simplified*. Neil holds a B.S. degree in computer science.

About the Technical Reviewers

Doug Foster works in the area of packet voice, video, and data convergence. With 30 years of experience for companies such as Cisco, John Deere, and Alcatel and for private business, Doug has some interesting firsthand stories to tell about the evolution of the Internet. He has architected and helped install international networks, such as the migration of John Deere's worldwide SNA business network into a multiprotocol intranet in the mid-1980s. As a result of that work, Doug was asked by the U.S. Department of Defense to speak at Interop '88 on "How John Deere builds tractors using TCP/IP." This was nearly a decade before most businesses began to leverage the value of the Internet and eCommerce applications. Most recently, Doug worked for Cisco as one of its first enterprise voice consultants. Doug has a bachelor of science in mechanical engineering from Iowa State University and lives in Cary, North Carolina, with his wife, Cindy. When not busy with family— daughters, Erin and Amber; son-in-law, Jeremy; and grandson, Jake—or business (Convinsys, Performance Podcasts, and Idea Mechanics), Doug devotes his free time to writing his first book (*Convince Me!*) and to sea kayaking.

Bradley Mitchell works as a freelance writer on the About.com wireless/networking site. He has produced online content at About.com on home computer networking, wireless, and related topics for six years. Bradley is also a senior engineer at Intel Corporation. Over the past 12 years at Intel, he has served in various capacities for research and development of software and network systems. Bradley obtained his master's degree in computer science from the University of Illinois and his bachelor's degree from M.I.T.

About the Illustrator

Nathan Clement declared himself an illustrator four years ago. Nathan holds a bachelor of fine arts degree in art and writing, which launched a surprise career in publishing, design, and art direction. His major roles have been owning a printing company, designing books in-house at Macmillan Computer Publishing, and serving as art director for an ad agency. Through these little adventures, he decided to get back to his art roots and keep both feet planted firmly in both the publishing and design worlds as an illustrator. He has been pleased to illustrate four previous books in the Cisco Press *Networking Simplified* series and has done work for Que Publishing, Macromedia Press, Peachpit Press, Prentice Hall, and *ESPN The Magazine*. He lives with his wife, Greta, a nurse practitioner, in Indianapolis and also pursues children's book illustration with paint and brushes. Contact Nathan at nathan@stickmanstudio.com.

Dedications

From Jim Doherty:

I would like to dedicate this to my good friend and coauthor Neil Anderson. Working together across ten years, two companies, and six books has been both fun and rewarding, and I'm better off for having been a part of it.

From Neil Anderson:

I would like to dedicate this book to my great and talented coauthor Jim Doherty. I could not ask for a more creative and humorous friend and coauthor. It's been a kick to work with you Jim on our common passion.

Acknowledgments

Jim and Neil would like to thank the following people:

Our families, for putting up with yet another book, and our extended families and friends whose phones calls and e-mails about wireless convinced us that this book was still needed.

Our publisher and the fine team at Cisco Press and Pearson Education. We would especially like to thank our editor, Dayna Isley, who we lied to about our schedule at every turn; our production manager, Patrick Kanouse, the team's sole survivor from our first book; our project manager, handler, and den mother, Kristin Weinberger; San Dee Phillips, our project editor (who we just tortured with our poor grammar); and the entire editorial and production team.

As always we want to thank our illustrator, Nathan Clement at Stickman Studios (www.stickman-studio.com/). What can we say, you did it again.

A special thanks to our technical reviewers, Bradley Mitchell and Doug Foster, who work hard on our reader's behalf to keep us honest and accurate.

Another special thanks to some kind folks at Linksys: Stuart Hamilton, Uzi Entin, and Brenton Elmore.

And last but not least, the following people who helped us with technical questions along the way: Brian Cox, Lou Ronnau, Jason Frazier, Steve Ochmanski, and Bruce McMurdo.

Contents at a Glance

Contents

Introduction

We assume that if you read the front cover you know what this book is about, but there's a bit more to it than that. With the explosion of popularity in wireless networking, there is a proportional number of people who do not understand the technology, and a similar number of people who think they understand it (but don't) and are all too willing to dispense advice. Usually it ends poorly, and you get stuck with a network that does not work.

This book is written for all of you out there who want to get the benefits of wireless networking but don't feel like you have the technical background to set it up yourselves. We are confident that if you read this book and follow the steps we lay out, you will have a much better understanding of the technology and, most importantly, a working wireless network. We will try to do this without you having to get a technical degree just to deploy your home network.

What to Expect

We've divided this book into five parts, each of which describes a major part of the process of building and using a wireless network. These sections describe

- How wireless works

- What you need to know

- How to set it all up

- What to do if it doesn't work

- What other cool things you can do with it

Each section is described in greater detail in the following sections.

Part I, "How Does It Work?"

Part I starts by explaining the basics in Chapter 1, "How Wireless LANs Work." We think it's worth mentioning that a basic working knowledge of wireless networking should be of interest to you if you are about to set up your own wireless network, and at a minimum it will help you make some better-informed decisions. In Chapter 2, "Wireless Standards: What the Letters Mean," we cover the main wireless standards. There are a number of choices with regard to the frequency, speed, range, and costs of each of the main standards, and we cover all of them here. We finish this section with Chapter 3, "Selecting the Right Wireless Standard for Your Network." There are a lot of choices out there. This chapter will help you cut through the confusion.

Part II, "What You Should Know"

In Part II we focus on what you should know before setting up your wireless network. This is where we put all the information in Part I to good use.

Chapter 4, "Planning Your Wireless Network," covers how to plan your network to meet the needs of today and bridge the gap to tomorrow. Chapter 5, "Wireless Security: What You Need to Know," covers the very important topic of wireless security. Don't skip this chapter.

Finally, in Chapter 6, "What to Buy," we explain how to figure out what equipment you need to buy. It's important to wait until this point in the book to actually buy gear, especially if you are starting from scratch. Trust us, this will save you money in the long run.

Part III, "How Do I Set It Up?"

In Part III we get to work and build your network. Chapter 7, "Wireless Router Setup," covers setting up your wireless router. This is the heart and soul of your network. In Chapter 8, "Wireless NIC Setup," we help you set up your wireless network interface card (called a NIC). This is the piece that allows your computer to be "wireless." Once everything is up and running, Chapter 9, "Wireless Security Setup," covers the implementation of wireless security in a step-by-step manner, because we need to keep the bad guys off our network.

Part IV, "Honey, This Stupid Wireless Thing Is Not Working"

Into every life a little rain must fall. Part IV covers how to troubleshoot a network that does not want to work the way it ought to. Chapter 10, "Troubleshooting: I Can't Connect at All," focuses on what to do when you can't get a computer to connect to the wireless network. Sometimes you can connect but the coverage is lousy. Chapter 11, "Troubleshooting: I Can Connect Sometimes," covers what to do in these cases. Chapter 12, "Troubleshooting: I Can Connect, but It's Slow," wraps up the section with steps to take when your connection seems slower than it ought to be.

Part V, "Bells and Whistles"

For those of you who want to take a step beyond a basic wireless network, Part V covers some bells and whistles you can add. Chapter 13, "Wireless Video and Entertainment," provides information on how to set up wireless-based entertainment options on your network. Chapter 14, "Wireless to Go," shows you how to take your wireless on the road and connect to hotspots. We close the section and the book with a summary in Chapter 15, "The Future of Wireless Networking," on what we think the future holds for wireless networking.

Housekeeping Stuff

This book focuses on the Windows operating systems and all screenshots were taken from computers running Windows XP. If you are not running Windows XP, you can still follow the recommendations and tips for the chapters where changes or setups are made, or where directory paths are followed. The general steps still hold true, but the directory paths and filenames may change. Your user manual or help files should help get you where you need to go for operating systems other than Windows XP.

We also had to make some decisions regarding what type of gear and programs to install as examples. Most of the gear we recommend here is from Linksys. In the spirit of full disclosure, our current (Neil) and former (Jim) employer is the parent company of Linksys. That said, we believe that Linksys has the most complete and easy-to-use wireless portfolio.

We hope you find this book useful, usable, and entertaining. Good luck, and happy networking.

PART I

How Does It Work

We'll start the book with a few chapters on how wireless works. Nothing too deep or complicated; just a high level overview to provide some information that we think will help you to decide which type of wireless home network you want, where you want to use it, and how you put it together.

Chapter 1, "How Wireless LANs Work," is a primer on how wireless networking works. We'll cover how the pieces talk to each other and how the network sends and receives data to and from the Internet.

Chapter 2, "Wireless Standards: What the Letters Mean," untangles all the different wireless standards. We cover what the letters mean, how they are different from each other, and what the pros and cons of each are. We also tell you what happened to the "missing" letters.

We wrap up Part I with Chapter 3, "Selecting the Right Wireless Standard for Your Network," which provides some guidance on how to determine which wireless standard you should choose. A lot depends on your circumstances, but we will give you our recommendations to at least help narrow down the choices.

How Wireless LANs Work

Albert Einstein was quoted as saying "You see, wire telegraph is a kind of a very, very long cat. You pull his tail in New York and his head is meowing in Los Angeles. Do you understand this? And radio operates exactly the same way: you send signals here, they receive them there. The only difference is that there is no cat."

That, in a nutshell, is how a wireless computer network works. In a wired network, data is sent and received between computers and routers using pieces of cable called *Ethernet*.

In a wireless network, air replaces the cables, and the same computer-to-computer communications are transmitted and received over the air using radio waves, very similar actually to how your mobile phone communicates.

This chapter discusses how wireless networks work and some of the challenges that had to be overcome to make them operate. If it gets too technical, just remember one thing: wireless networking is just a way to send stuff like web pages to and from your computer without a cable.

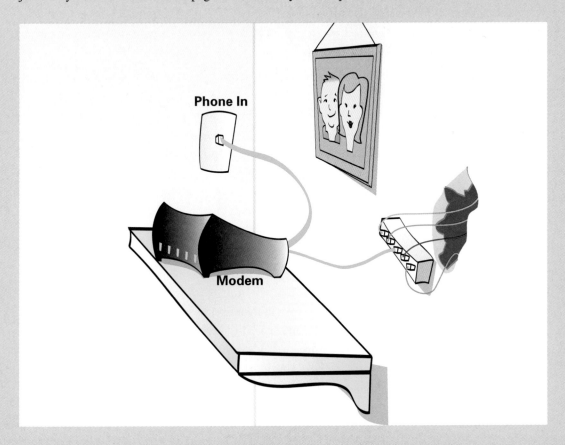

Why Wireless?

For those of you still on the fence about going wireless, we start this chapter off by trying to convince you that it is worth the time, effort, and money to go wireless, especially because it only takes a little of each to get started. The biggest reason for making the switch to wireless boils down to a single word: flexibility.

Wireless technology provides us with a great deal of flexibility when it comes to what devices we put on the network, how many devices we use, and where we put those devices. Let's look at an example. Suppose a family wants to connect to the Internet using broadband cable (this example works with any type of broadband). This family has three computers in the home, one for each parent and one for their teenager, and all family members want to connect to the Internet at the same time. First, they must determine where the cable jacks are located in the home and decide which one they want to connect to the cable modem. Is a cable jack close to where one of the computers will be used? If not, that's a problem. They have to either put a computer where they don't want one or string a long cable across a room.

After they decide which cable jack to use, they have to figure out how multiple computers can get access to it, because there is only a single cable modem. This means they either need to have a single device connected to the Internet at a time or need to buy a device (such as a router) that allows multiple computers to connect to the Internet simultaneously. They also have to decide how to connect all the computers in the house to the router.

At this point, the family has some options:

- Run cables through the walls. If the family were building a new house, they could have it wired throughout for Internet access, but this can be expensive. If they live in an existing home, they could hire an electrician to run cables, but that is really expensive and messy. If they rent, neither of these is an option.

- String cables all through the house. This is cheap, but it's messy and the family members will be tripping over cables all the time.

- Move all the computers to where the router is. This is not a very practical option.

- Go wireless.

Now, some folks may be a little dubious about using a "new" technology, but the ability to provide wireless networking actually has been around for a long time. The reason you have heard about it only recently is that its use was never really necessary previously. The need to provide high-speed network access to multiple, somewhat mobile, computers only emerged with the widespread availability of broadband Internet and inexpensive computers.

The bottom line is that wireless networking is reasonably affordable and easy to install. If you were to build a wired network, by the time you purchased wired network adapters for all your computers, a router to connect them, and all the cables, the price would be close to what a wireless system would cost. Considering the convenience and the absence of clutter, the wireless network is a bargain. Keep in mind that with most wireless routers, you also get four ports for wired access, so with a wireless network you get the best of both worlds.

Before We Get to the Wireless Bit, What the Heck Is a LAN?

The chapter title says we will teach you how wireless LANs work, so it is probably a good idea to start off with a brief description of what a LAN is—nothing overly technical, just some background information that may come in handy later.

A local-area network, or LAN, is just what you think it might be, based on the name: a network connecting computers in a small or localized area. This area can be a house, a small office, or a floor of a building in a big office.

LANs form the basic building blocks of large-scale computer networks. LANs connect to other LANs to form larger corporate or institutional networks. These networks connect to larger networks that span large geographic areas. In some cases the larger networks cover a metropolitan area, called MANs. Still larger are networks covering multiple cities, states, countries, or even spanning the globe. Networks of this size are called WANs, or wide-area networks.

This structure provides a connection hierarchy that is very scalable. In fact, the Internet is the result of multiple WANs connected to each other, which in effect connects hundreds of thousands of LANs together along with the computers associated with those LANs. Think of your home network as one of those many networks.

When people first started connecting computers for networking, they used many different configurations and communication methods (or protocols). Some LANs were connected using a ring topology, where each computer is connected in a line, as shown in Figure 1-1. Communication from one computer to another is passed along the ring until it reaches the intended recipient.

Figure 1-1   Ring Topology

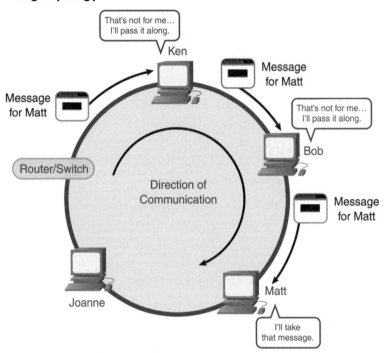

Other topologies included stars, meshes, dual rings, and buses. These configurations are illustrated in Figure 1-2.

Eventually, the topology that was (primarily) settled on was the bus topology. A bus topologoy has all the computers connected to a common cable, which is referred to as the bus. The common "cable" connecting all the computers today is located inside the router or switch, but it works the same way. Other topologies are still in use but most of the time LANs are connected using a bus topology.

 Note: Routers and switches are similar in that they both provide a way to connect multiple computers together. The main difference is that switches typically connect only computers together, whereas routers additionally connect the home network to another network, such as the Internet. For a more thorough discussion on routers, switches, and other types of home networking equipment, pick up a copy of *Home Networking Simplified* (Cisco Press, 2005).

Figure 1-2   Common Network Topologies

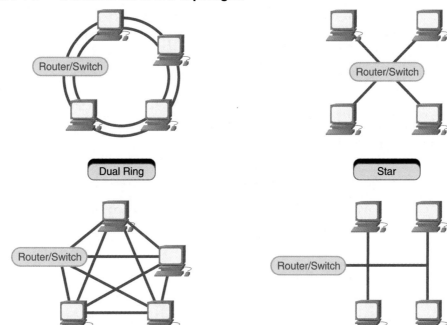

Using the bus topology, one computer communicates with another computer by putting its message out on the bus. What is interesting here is that all the computers on the LAN receive the message. Contained in the message, however, is information about who the intended recipient is. Each computer receiving the message looks to see whether or not it is the intended recipient. If it is, it processes the message. The set of rules governing this type of communication is called the *Ethernet protocol*. If it is not, it ignores the message.

Figure 1-3 shows how this process works. When a message comes in from the WAN (for example, let's assume an e-mail comes in for Bob), all the computers on the LAN are notified of an incoming message. Matt's, Ken's, and Joanne's computers ignore the message because it is not intended for them. Bob's computer sees that it is the intended recipient and processes the message.

The same thing happens when a message is sent out. Let's say Ken wants to look at a web page. His computer sends out a request to view the contents of a web page (this is what happens when you type a URL or click a web link). In this case all the computers, including the switch or router, receive the request. Matt's, Joanne's, and Bob's computers see that the request is not intended for them so they discard it. The switch or router sees the requests and determines that the request is for a computer that is not on the LAN, so it passes the request over to the Internet service provider (ISP). This is illustrated in Figure 1-4.

Figure 1-3   LAN Communication: Incoming Message

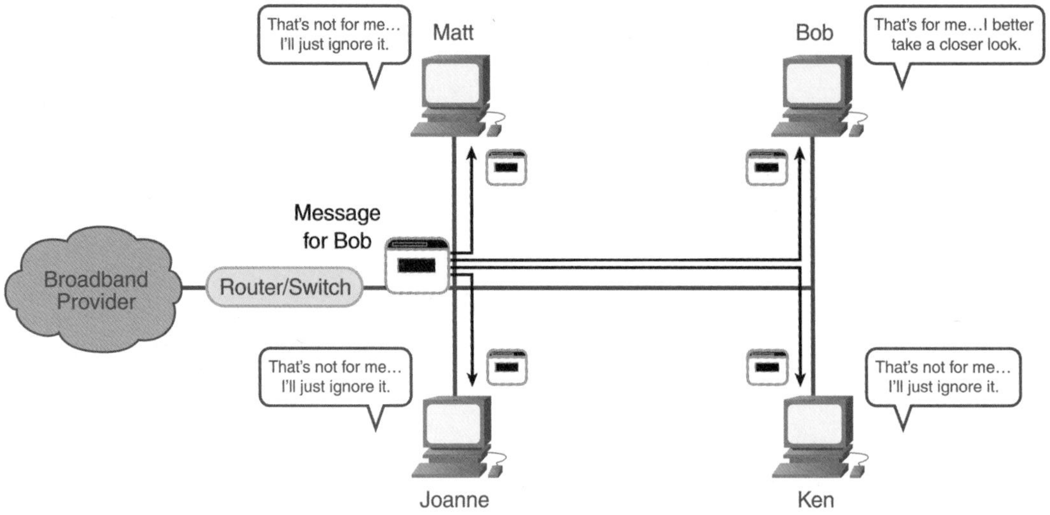

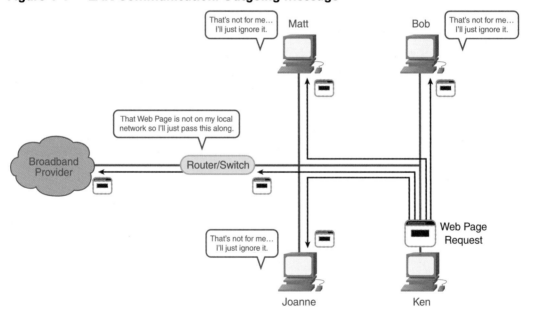

Figure 1-4   LAN Communication: Outgoing Message

While we have simplified this quite a bit, this is pretty much how communication works on a LAN. There are some pretty complex addressing (identification) schemes that are used and there are different protocols, or rules, for different types of communication, but most of them are beyond the scope of this book. The important point is this: Any communication to or from a computer on the LAN is seen by all other computers on that LAN, but is ignored by all but the intended recipient.

This means that if someone wants to "snoop" and monitor someone else's communication, all they have to do is physically connect to the wired LAN and make it so that their computer processes all the traffic rather than just the traffic meant for that computer. The good news is that it is pretty easy to see if someone who does not belong is connected to the LAN. In an office you just have to follow the wires, since they need a cable to connect. In your house, it's the strange guy on the couch with a computer that you did not invite in.

Note: Chapter 5, "Wireless Security: What You Need to Know," and Chapter 9, "Wireless Security Setup," provide a good discussion about wireless network security and the steps you need to take to make your wireless network pretty secure. For an additional source of information about more general home network security, pick up a copy of *Home Network Security Simplified* (Cisco Press, 2006), which covers ten easy things you can do to make your home network more secure.

Okay, Now the Wireless Part

The wired Ethernet protocol and LANs had been around for a long time before wireless networking became practical. In fact, the world had pretty much standardized on wired Ethernet long before any of the wireless networking companies were even formed (the technology was there, but, as we mentioned earlier, there was no commercial need). In addition, the number of computers using wired Ethernet had exploded, and other devices were being connected to the network as well.

This meant that if someone wanted to have computers communicate over a wireless connection, they were going to have to create a standard that worked with, or at least be compatible with, the wired Ethernet standard. The millions of existing computers were not going to change the way that they communicated just because some nerds wanted to check their e-mail while sitting on the toilet. (Okay, we can't prove it, but we suspect this was one of the driving forces behind the whole wireless thing.)

Note: Other types of cableless connections include, infrared, Bluetooth, and powerline. Just to be clear, these are not what we refer to as a "wireless network." Most of these technologies are point-to-point, meaning computer to printer, or mobile phone to headset. They have very limited capabilities for multidevice networks. When we say "wireless networking" throughout the rest of this book, we are referring to Wi-Fi.

Challenges for Wireless Communication

To make wireless communication practical, the engineers had some problems to overcome, despite the fact that the basic technology had been around for a long time. Some of the key problems to overcome were the following:

- **RF signaling**—RF stands for radio frequency. Transmission of radio signals is tightly regulated in pretty much every country. There are open ranges of frequencies where you can transmit without a license so long as the power is low, and restricted bands which require a license and carry heavy fines for unauthorized transmissions. Because of this, wireless networks work on the "open" frequency bands, but this leads to a few other issues.

- **Interference**—Because many other devices use the open frequency bands (including cordless phones and baby monitors), anything using these bands is prone to interference from other devices.

- **Power and range**—The rules for the open frequency band limit the power of transmissions. The problem here is that the lower the power, the shorter the range. Engineers had to develop a way to make sure the range was wide enough to cover your house, to make going wireless worth the cost.

- **Data rates**—Data rate is another way of saying speed. People had become accustomed to the speed of broadband Internet. If switching to wireless meant that it would take an hour to download a single e-mail attachment again (as with dial-up), then no one was ever going to use it. So wireless had to be about as fast as wired.

- **Interoperability**—If seven different companies solve these problems in seven different ways, the technology will not be very usable or commercially viable. To ensure that everyone can make some money, standards are needed to make sure that stuff from different manufacturers works together.

The Solution

The solution for wireless communication was something called 802.11, also known as Wi-Fi (pronounced "why fie"). We go into some detail about 802.11 in Chapter 2, "Wireless Standards: What the Letters Mean?" but for now just look at it as the name of the solution that some smart folks came up with that enables computers to communicate with each other over a wireless connection, without messing up the way computers were already talking to each other. We'll look at this in two parts: first the wireless part, and second how it works with the wired Ethernet protocol.

For all its magic, the technology that drives wireless communication is no more than a fancy walkie-talkie in a really small package. The wireless device—whether it is a card you plug in or electronics that are built right into the computer—is a transmitter and receiver, sending and receiving radio signals. Unlike the kids' walkie-talkies, however, these radios are capable of sending and receiving data at very high rates, from 10 Mbps at the low end to over 100 Mbps at the high end. Just a few years ago, these kinds of speeds were only possible using a cable to connect computers. The really good news is that the range of these wireless devices is good enough that you can put the wireless router in your home and provide access throughout most of your home and probably into areas of your yard. This is all done with minimal power consumption so that the battery on your wireless laptop does not drain too fast.

So now that we have computers that are capable of communicating over a radio link instead of a cable, let's look at how the smart folks made it compatible with the existing wired Ethernet protocol. As it turns out, there was really no way to make wired Ethernet wireless without changing every existing network in the world. To overcome this, the 802.11 team (comprised of engineers from many companies, universities, and other organizations) figured out that the best way to solve the problem was to take the bits of information being sent via Ethernet and stuff them into the wireless signal, which was then transmitted and received using the radio technology mentioned earlier. On the receiving end, the Ethernet packet was then pulled out of the wireless signal and passed onto the computer, at which point all the normal rules for Ethernet applied.

Let's look at this a different way. Imagine that you and your friend have developed a system for passing notes back and forth to each other during a class in which you sit next to each other. You have developed a shorthand system so that the notes are small but still contain all the information you need to communicate. Now imagine that you find yourselves in another class but you are now seated on opposite sides of the room. You still want to communicate with each other, but you really don't want to develop a new system with which to communicate (such as sign language) because using two methods would really be a pain. Your friend gets a great idea and cuts a hole into a tennis ball and stuffs the note into it. She then throws the ball to you. You catch the ball, pull the note out, and write a response. You then take your note and stuff it into the ball, which you then throw back.

This is basically what the wireless LAN (802.11) protocol does with Ethernet communication. 802.11 wireless LANs act as a way to carry the same wired Ethernet conversations that computers are used to, but over the air instead of over a cable. Pretty neat.

Putting It All Together

Now, back to the network discussion. When computers are connected to a LAN, they are physically connected to each other, which is the basis for their association to that LAN.

With a wireless LAN, the computers have to find a way to connect, or associate, themselves to the LAN, because they are not physically connected. The way they do this is by tuning themselves to the wireless router using the name of the router (the wireless router's name is called the Service Set Identification number, or SSID). When you tell your computer to connect to an access point, the computer tunes to the access point's frequency and asks permission to join the LAN. If the access point is open, any computer asking to join the LAN will be allowed to do so. If the LAN has encryption security enabled, the computer needs to know the encryption key to even ask permission to join.

 Note: In addition to *wireless router*, you may also see the terms *base station* or *wireless access point*, and all three pretty much mean the same thing in home networks. Well stick with *wireless router* for the rest of this discussion.

Once a computer has connected, or associated, itself to the access point, it becomes part of the LAN. And, as we mentioned before, if a computer is on a LAN, it then has access to every bit of communication that takes place on that LAN. Now the computer can send and receive information to and from other computers on the LAN or to and from the Internet by transmitting over wireless to the wireless router (or access point). The wireless router acts as the central communication routing point, much like the wired cable in the LAN example earlier.

Unlike a wired LAN, you cannot tell who is on your wireless LAN by following wires or casually looking around, as illustrated in Figure 1-5.

Figure 1-5   Wireless Network Environment

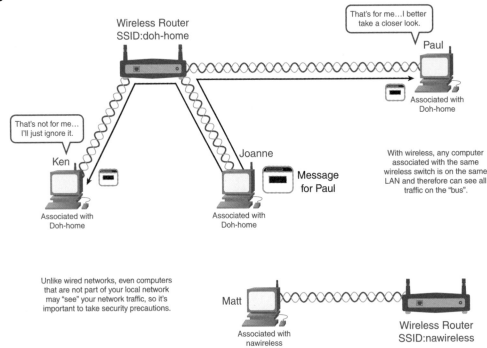

This is really the big risk with wireless: Someone can connect to your network without being in your house or being physically near your router. Now, it's not all bad, because there are some really simple actions you can take to prevent people from connecting to your LAN and your network, and we will show you how to take those actions in Chapter 9.

Summary

In a nutshell, all the computers on a LAN see all the network traffic regardless of who the intended receiver is. The computers just ignore all the stuff that's not intended for them.

In a wireless network, the same protocols or communication rules are used, the packets are just "stuffed" into a wireless carrier and then "unpacked" on the receiver end, and everything works the same way it does in a wired network. The big difference here is that any wireless computer in the range of the wireless signals can "see" the traffic even if it is not part of the LAN. This makes wireless very convenient, but it also makes the need for security very, very important.

The rest of this book takes you through all the considerations for wireless networking, including the standards, what equipment you need, how to apply security, and how to put it all together.

Where to Go for More Information

One of the best places on the web to learn about networking, wireless, and pretty much anything else you can think of is HowStuffWorks: www.howstuffworks.com.

Linksys also provides on its site some good information about wireless networking and how it works: www.linksys.com.

Wireless Standards: What the Letters Mean

If you have already done some research about, or gone window shopping for, wireless networking stuff, you probably noticed that each piece of wireless gear has a letter (or letters) associated with it. The letters are usually A, B, G, N, or some combination such as A+G. In addition, the letters are usually prefaced by the words "wireless," "wireless standard," or "802.11." So it is possible that while shopping for a router, you could see boxes that say any of the following:

- Wireless B

- 802.11g

- Wireless A+G

- Wireless Standard N

You might also see boxes that include each manufacturer's own terminology, such as "SRX Technology," "MIMO," "Range Extension," "Speed Booster," "pre-N," or any number of other descriptions or marketing ploys.

You may have scanned the products on the shelves and left the store without purchasing anything because you had absolutely no idea what in the world you needed. This chapter helps you cut through all the confusion and explains what the letters mean, where they come from, and which ones work together.

The Standard 802.11 and the IEEE

Regardless of how the letters on the wireless equipment are presented, they all fall under a standard referred to as *IEEE 802.11*.

IEEE stands for the Institute of Electrical and Electronic Engineers. While this may not sound like a very exciting group of people, the IEEE is the worldwide standards body for all sorts of technologies, and it has greatly contributed to advancement of technologies ranging from the Internet, to the phone system, to DVDs, and much, much more. The IEEE standards ensure that nearly all devices, technologies, and parts (within the realm of electronics anyway) are standardized and agreed upon. Without such a standards body, it would be extremely difficult for all vendors to make gear that works together. Just think about how much of a pain it would be, for instance, if every stereo speaker manufacturer used different types of cables and connectors. This type of standardization also allows for very rapid innovations and price reductions because everyone with an interest in a technology works to further a single standard instead of multiple competing ones.

When a new technology comes along, the IEEE puts a workgroup together made up of engineers from multiple companies (often competing ones), government bodies, and universities to develop the standards for that technology. These workgroups are each given an identifier based on the nature of the technology. The workgroup that determines the standards for wireless networking is workgroup 802.11, which is also the name of the standard.

Once the workgroup develops the base standard, all subsequent additions, variations, or modifications are given a letter designation off the base standard. This is where 802.11a, 802.11b, and so forth come from. Because most people would not have a clue about what 802.11 is, most people just say "wireless standard," which is really the same thing.

The IEEE developed and approved the original wireless standard (802.11, without any other identifiers) in 1997. This standard was limited in that it had a maximum throughput of about 2 megabits per second (Mbps), which was pretty slow. There were other issues as well that impacted wide adoption, such as price and the fact that most people were still on dial-up access, which does not support the need for a wireless network with multiple computers behind it. 802.11 did get the whole wireless networking thing going, though, and was followed by a number of improvements.

802.11a

In 1999, two years after the original standard was developed, the IEEE published the standards for revisions A and B, both of which were different "flavors" of the original wireless standard. Wireless standard A was the faster of the two revised wireless types. It was a bit more costly to develop and therefore had much slower adoption than the B standard, which was used by most of the companies making wireless devices for home networking. Because of this, many people think that standard B came out before standard A. Given the fact that engineers develop these standards, that assumption is just silly. (If you are wondering, the convention is to use lowercase letters with 802.11 and uppercase letters when alone, for example, 802.11a and the A standard.)

 Note: In the spirit of full disclosure, the authors made the statement that B came out before A in one of our previous books. It has also come to our attention that during the review of that book, one of our technical reviewers did in fact catch this error, and we ignored him. Sorry Bradley.

The A standard provides up to 54 Mbps, which is plenty fast for most home networking applications, including Voice over IP (VoIP) programs, such as Skype, running on your PC. In fact, if you have high-speed Internet access (which you really ought to if you are considering any type of wireless networking), even the slowest of the modern wireless standards provides more throughput (bandwidth) than the fastest home networking connection (cable, satellite, or even small business data service). The type of wireless standard you use generally does not affect the performance of your Internet access.

The 802.11a standard operates in an unregulated frequency range (5 GHz). *Unregulated* means that any product can use the range so long as the transmission power is not too strong. Because of this, your 802.11a-based router may get some interference from cordless telephones, baby monitors, and other electronics; however, we have found that there does seem to be less interference from these types of devices in the 5-GHz band than in the 2.4-GHz band, where 802.11b and 802.11g wireless networks operate. This will change as time goes on and more and more devices are made for the 5-GHz band.

The bad news is the equipment for the A standard tends to be a bit more expensive than the equipment for the other standards, and because the system uses a higher frequency range, the signal does not pass through walls or other obstacles as easily as the signals from the standards using lower frequencies (trust us, it's a physics thing). This means that in general the range of an 802.11a router will not be as good as other standards such as 802.11b and 802.11g, all other factors being equal. Table 2-1 provides a summary of the wireless A standard.

Table 2-1   **802.11a Summary**

Feature	Description
Frequency	5-GHz range
Throughput	54 Mbps
Pros	Fast Less interference from other electronic devices such as cordless phones (for now)
Cons	Range is limited More expensive than B or G Difficult to find compatible hotspots
Compatibility	Not compatible with 802.11b, 802.11g, or 802.11n

802.11b

802.11b was developed at the same time as the A standard. Because it was less expensive to develop, 802.11b is the standard that most vendors first developed for home networking. As a result, 802.11b is also the first standard that enjoyed widespread adoption and is still widely used in home networking and Internet hotspots (Internet cafés and public wireless locations) today. This standard operates at 2.4 GHz and offers up to 11 Mbps of performance.

802.11b is the slowest of the main wireless standards but it is also the least expensive and most widely deployed. Keep in mind, though, that the speed of the B standard (11 Mbps) is still faster than most forms of high-speed Internet access, so the only limitation will be the applications you run within your network. So, although this standard would not work well for sending high-definition video over your wireless network within your home, it should be just fine for downloading video clips from YouTube (www.youtube.com).

802.11b has a range of about 150 feet (maximum) in open air before signal degradation becomes noticeable. The frequency used by the B standard is also unregulated, and you will find that many devices that use radio transmission (baby monitors, cordless phones, Bluetooth, and others) also use this frequency band and may interfere with your wireless router signal. We'll talk about this a bit more in Chapter 3, "Selecting the Right Wireless Standard for Your Network."

Table 2-2 provides a summary of the wireless B standard.

Table 2-2   802.11b Summary

Feature	Description
Frequency	2.4 GHz
Throughput	11 Mbps
Pros	Least expensive of the wireless standards Most widely deployed Range is good Used by most hotspots
Cons	Slowest of the wireless standards Prone to interference from other devices
Compatibility	Compatible with 802.11g and 802.11n Not compatible with 802.11a

802.11g

The 802.11g standard was developed in 2003 and borrowed from the best of the two previous standards (A and B). Wireless G offers the speed of the A standard (54 Mbps) but still operates on the unregulated 2.4-GHz frequency band, which provides the cost and range benefits of the B standard. Since its inception, the G standard has proven to be very popular and is very quickly replacing the B standard. The equipment cost for this standard is a bit more than for the B standard but less than for the A standard. The G standard is starting to become widely available in hotspots, and many computers that come with built-in wireless capabilities (which is most of them these days) come with G capability. This standard is also backward compatible with the B standard, so if you find yourself near a router using the B standard, your G-capable computer can communicate with it (the opposite is also true).

Some additional proprietary upgrades to the G standard make it even faster (up to 108 Mbps). Linksys has two flavors of speed enhancement. The first is called *Speed Booster*, which, as you might have guessed, boosts the speed (although Linksys only claims 54 Mbps+). The other enhancement is called *SRX*, which stands for Speed and Range eXpansion. Linksys claims that its top-of-the-line version of SRX provides 10x speed and 3x range enhancement. We have not done laboratory tests to measure this but the SRX routers do provide a noticeable improvement in both speed and range.

 Note: We do not recommend buying and deploying such proprietary extensions of the 802.11g or other standards. They have several limitations, including two important ones:

■ You do not get the additional performance unless your wireless router and wireless NICs are both using the proprietary scheme. Buying an SRX router, for example, and using plain old 802.11g wireless NICs means you get 802.11g performance and no SRX enhanced performance.

■ Proprietary extensions can lead to incompatibilities with standard equipment.

Therefore, we recommend you stick with one of the standards and be wary of proprietary manufacturer extensions.

Table 2-3 summarizes the wireless G standard.

Table 2-3   802.11g Summary

Feature	Description
Frequency	2.4 GHz
Throughput	54 Mbps
Pros	Very good speed Available at most hotspots Good range Less expensive than A
Cons	More expensive than B Prone to interference from cordless phones and other electronics
Compatibility	Compatible with 802.11b and 802.11n Not compatible with 802.11a

802.11n

The newest standard is designated as wireless standard N, scheduled to have final approval by the IEEE in 2007 (originally it was 2006, but it was not ratified). Prior to the final approval, several vendors have begun to offer products for this standard based on the initially released specifications. Users who buy the products now should be OK even if there are changes to the standard in the mean time (which, if there are any, are likely to be minor and would only require an additional software or firmware download).

The N standard achieves much higher speeds than the G standard using a technology called multiple inputs, multiple outputs (MIMO). MIMO does exactly what you might expect: It uses several radio-based connections (in both directions) to achieve very high (100 Mbps+) speeds (also called bandwidth, throughput, or capacity) and extended ranges. In addition to using multiple radio streams, MIMO also takes advantage of reflected signals (radio signals that "bounce" off of walls, ceilings, or other obstructions) to enhance the strength of the signal and, therefore, improve the transfer rates and range. This feature also greatly reduces "dead spots" within the operating range of the router, meaning that it can cover more of your house with fewer signal problems.

Wireless standard N provides the bandwidth necessary to run applications such as streaming high-definition video signals, digital music or interactive multiplayer video games, within your home over your wireless network.

The N standard is also backward compatible with the G and B standards, so you will not have to replace the wireless cards in all your PCs in the event that you buy an 802.11n router to stream high-definition video from a single computer or device. Table 2-4 provides a summary of the wireless N standard.

Table 2-4   802.11n Summary

Feature	Description
Frequency	2.4 GHz
Throughput	100 Mbps+
Pros	Very high data-transfer speeds Greater coverage range No dead spots in coverage
Cons	Still new so you may not find many hotpots that offer it (although if you have N on your computer, it will work with an 802.11g system) The most expensive of the wireless standards (at the time of this writing, but eventually it will be as cheap as the others)
Compatibility	Compatible with 802.11b and 802.11g Not compatible with 802.11a

Combinations

You may see some wireless routers or devices that offer multiple wireless standards such as A+B. These devices work on only one standard at a time with any given device. In other words, if you have a computer that uses the G standard, it can use only that standard. You will not get the benefits of both standards on any single device. Chapter 3 covers how to choose a standard in detail.

What Happened to the Other Letters?

At this point you may be wondering what happened to the other revisions. As it turns out, the revisions to the 802.11 standard do not always involve new wireless standards. In many cases the revisions are updates to the communication protocols, which, by themselves, do not warrant a new wireless standard. For a complete list of the other revisions, check out Appendix C, "802.11 Additional Revisions," which is provided for information purposes only. These updates have limited relevance for the home networking crowd.

Summary

The 802.11 standard specifies how wireless works and communicates with both devices and the network. Although there are many 802.11 specifications, only four have any relevance to the purchasing decisions of the home user (standards A, B, G, and N). How you choose the right standard for your situation is the subject of Chapter 3.

It is also important to note that we most likely have not seen the last of new wireless standards. Because wireless is such a relatively new technology, there are bound to be more improvements.

Finally, because wireless networks use radio transmitters at particular frequencies that are authorized by governments, do not assume that the wireless router you purchased in your country can safely be used in another country. Research the standards for the country you wish to visit to make sure it uses the same frequencies as the wireless equipment you purchased.

Where to Go for More Information

Wi-Fi Planet is a good site for general information about wireless networking, providing a plethora of articles and tutorials. For this chapter, we referenced the tutorial "802.11 Alphabet Soup" by Jim Geier at www.wi-fiplanet.com/tutorials/article.php/1439551.

Linksys also provides a great deal of information about the various wireless standards at www.linksys.com. Click **Network Basics** on the Learning Center drop-down menu and then click the **Wireless Standards** tab on the left side of the page to access the information.

Selecting the Right Wireless Standard for Your Network

If you have looked around at your local technology store for wireless networking equipment, you probably noticed the array of wireless designations. With several broad-based standards available and even more vendor extensions, it's no wonder people leave the store confused and probably empty handed.

This chapter helps you choose which wireless standard is right for you. The decision does not have to be difficult at all. We try to boil the facts down and make it easy.

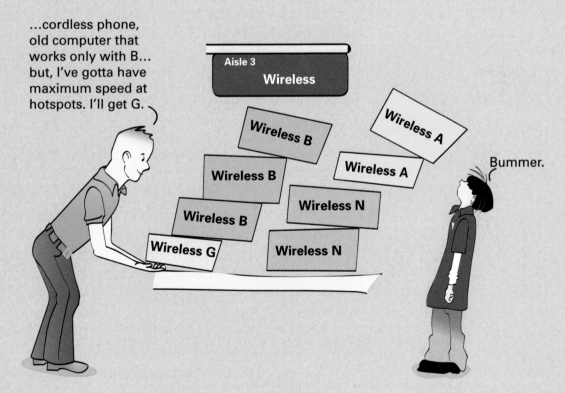

What to Consider When Choosing Your Wireless Standard

So how do you sort through the many wireless options that are available to you and decide what's best for your home network? First, you must keep in mind that there are two sides to this decision process:

- What to choose for the wireless access point/router that will "host" your wireless network

- What to choose for wireless network interface cards (NICs) that will allow the computers on your home network to "join" the network wirelessly

The previous chapters covered the various wireless standards that exist and the advantages and disadvantages of each. Knowing the frequencies and other facts about the various standards is all well and good, but you still need to make a decision that will work well for you not only now, but also for at least a couple of years so that you can recoup the investment you made. In our opinion, you need to weigh the following six primary factors:

- **Compatibility**—How well will all your wirelessly connected stuff work together?

- **Speed**—How fast is fast enough?

- **Range**—How far from the router can I get a wireless signal?

- **Security**—What level of security is supported?

- **Cost**—How much?

- **Future proofing**—Will the technology be obsolete the day after I buy it?

As it turns out, compatibility and speed are intimately related. The following sections explore all six factors, followed by our bottom-line recommendations.

Compatibility

Whatever wireless standard you choose, it's very important that the wireless router and wireless NICs are compatible. Otherwise, your wireless network will not work at all or, at best, will work rather poorly.

There are three primary factors to consider for compatibility:

- What are the relationships between the standards, and which standards are compatible with each other?

- How does multi-standard, or dual-band, equipment fit into the picture?

- Are the proprietary extensions offered by manufacturers, like SRX, something you should consider?

We examine these questions in the following sections.

Relationships Among Wireless Standards

The first really important point to understand is the relationships among the wireless A, B, G, and N standards, introduced in Chapter 2, "Wireless Standards: What the Letters Mean." As previously mentioned, NICs need to be compatible with the wireless router you purchase or your router won't be of much use to anyone. Fortunately, the relationships are pretty straightforward:

- A NICs are compatible *only* with A routers.

- B NICs are compatible with B, G, and N routers.

- G NICs are compatible with B, G, and N routers.

- N NICs are compatible with B, G, and N routers.

Likewise, the relationships work in both directions such that a G router is compatible with B, G, and N NICs.

The key point to remember is that the lowest standard (in terms of speed) shared by the router and the NIC dictates the performance of the interaction between the two devices. This means that N and B devices work together, but only at the B level of performance. Figure 3-1 and Figure 3-2 illustrate this concept.

Figure 3-1   B NIC on Different Routers

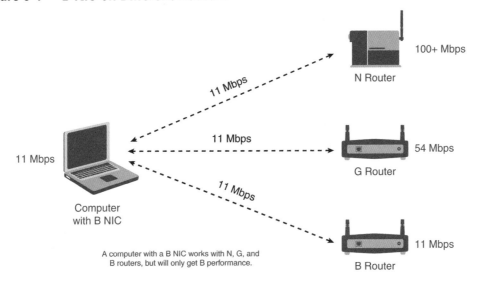

Figure 3-2   G Routers with Different NICs

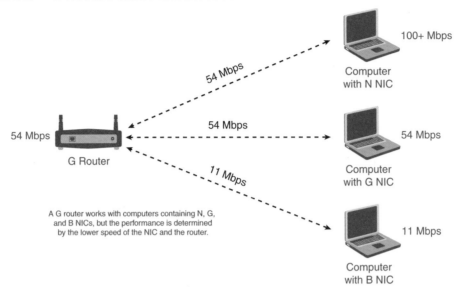

Table 3-1 summarizes the compatibility between standards and the performance you will have when combining NICs and wireless routers.

Table 3-1   Wireless Standards Compatibility Summary

	A Router	B Router	G Router	N Router
A NIC	A performance	Not compatible	Not compatible	Not compatible
B NIC	Not compatible	B performance	B performance	B performance
G NIC	Not compatible	B performance	G performance	G performance
N NIC	Not compatible	B performance	G performance	N performance

Dual-Band Products

Another point to consider is that some manufacturers provide *dual-band* (also known as *dual-standard*) wireless NICs and routers, meaning that the product supports two bands. As discussed in Chapter 2, 802.11a operates in the 5-GHz band, while 802.11b, 802.11g, and 802.11n all operate in the 2.4-GHz band. The designation of a router or NIC as *dual-band* means that it supports at least one wireless standard in each band, meaning 2.4 GHz and 5 GHz.

By definition, G routers and NICs are dual-standard, because they are backward compatible with the B standard. So, *dual-band* almost always refers to the wireless A standard, plus another standard like B, G, or N. Thus, you will see products labeled A+B and A+G. You will likely see some A+N routers as well. The same holds true for wireless NICs. You can have NICs that are single-band only, such as B or G, or dual-band, such as A+G.

Proprietary Extensions

The next complication is that some vendors provide proprietary extensions to their products to make them run even faster. For example, we mentioned in Chapter 2 that Linksys provides a Speed Booster version of its wireless G products that improves the transmission speed beyond the standard 54 Mbps. Linksys also provides an SRX series of wireless G products that doubles the speed to 108 Mbps. Other vendors have similar product extensions. You need to understand three things about such extensions:

- They are (or should be) backward compatible with the base standard.

- The extended speeds typically work only when you are using both that vendor's NICs and its routers with that particular extension. So, to get the benefits of SRX, you need to have both an SRX router and an SRX NIC.

- If you already own or intend to purchase a laptop with a built-in NIC, it most likely is not going to support such proprietary extensions.

Remember this when you are thinking of buying products with such extensions. Make sure they are compatible with the base standard, at a minimum. You should also make sure that you have the correct NIC for any manufacturer-based extensions. It would be a waste to pay the extra money for the Linksys SRX router, for example, if your NIC supports only the base G standard.

Speed

The second consideration when choosing your wireless standard is resulting speed. Later in the chapter, in the section "Comparing the IEEE WLAN Standards," Table 3-2 gives an indication of the performance you will receive when you use a type of wireless NIC with a type of wireless access point/router. In general, the maximum performance the different wireless standards offer follows:

- **802.11a**—54 Mbps

- **802.11b**—11 Mbps

- **802.11g**—54 Mbps (up to 108 Mbps with extensions)

- **802.11n**—100 Mbps+

However, these speeds are the "stated" numbers, which are often only achieved in a lab setting. Once you have a router in your house, any number of factors can come into play that impact the speed you actually get. These factors include the distance between the router and the computer, the building materials in your home, interference from cordless phones and other devices, and, in some cases, even sunspots. Okay, that last one is pretty rare, but it can happen, and the basic point is that many factors—most of which are out of your control—affect the actual speed of the router.

Also, at the risk of being redundant, remember that the lower of the NIC and router speeds dictates the speed. For example, a NIC for the 802.11b standard will certainly function with a wireless router for the 802.11g standard, but it will only operate at the 11-Mbps rate, not the higher 54-Mbps rate of the G standard. Similarly, a NIC for the 802.11g standard will work just fine with a wireless router for the 802.11b standard. It will just operate at the slower 11-Mbps rate of the B standard.

Note: It is important to realize that even the slowest of the wireless standards often provides greater bandwidth than even the fastest residential high-speed Internet connection at the time this book was written. Average broadband provides download speeds (from the Internet) between 1 and 2 Mbps, and upload speeds (to the Internet) between 256 kbps and 1 Mbps). Even very high-speed broadband provides download speeds up to 6 Mbps and maximum upload speeds of around 2 Mbps (and at a price premium).

Even the lowest-speed wireless standard, 802.11b, operates at 11 Mbps and, factoring in the wireless overhead, delivers about 6 Mbps. This can pretty easily keep up with most broadband connections.

The point is, before you go and spend a lot of money on the very fastest wireless router, be sure that you really need the speed you are paying for.

Range

In general, the range of most current wireless routers on the market is adequate for the average house or apartment, so it's not really something to be very concerned about.

If you do have a large house or area you want to cover with your wireless router (maybe you want to lie by the pool or mount your laptop to your John Deere riding mower), then you may want to consider range as a factor.

Wireless B and G offer about the same range. Wireless A operates in the 5-GHz range and therefore signals last a shorter distance. Wireless N is specifically designed to provide up to four times the range of wireless B and G, and therefore offers the longest range on the market today. Keep in mind, though, that the closer you get to the maximum range, the lower the speed will be and, in some cases (such as with B), the speed at the edge of the range will be quite slow.

Security

Most new wireless routers on the market support the full range (or nearly so) of wireless security options available. There are two primary security-related factors to look for:

- What types of encryption are supported?

- Does the wireless router also provide a firewall?

Encryption comes in a number of "flavors" including (from least to most secure) WEP-64, WEP-128, WPA, and WPA2. Similar to wireless standard and speed, encryption that can be used is determined by the lower of the encryption supported between the router and NIC. You want WEP-128 at a minimum, but WPA or WPA2 is preferred. See Chapter 5, "Wireless Security: What You Need to Know," and Chapter 9, "Wireless Security Setup," for a more thorough discussion on wireless security types and recommendations.

Note: Unlike the wireless standard performance, with encryption the lowest available standard determines the type of encryption for all devices on the network. In other words, if you have a NIC that is limited to WEP-64 on your network, all the devices on the network must be set to encrypt at the WEP-64 standard regardless of any higher encryption standard that they are capable of.

The other factor to consider is whether the wireless router you buy contains a built-in stateful packet inspection (SPI) firewall. *Stateful* means that the firewall looks inside the packet to make sure it is part of a valid communication session. Basically it keeps hackers from "tricking" your computers into talking with their computer. This provides a good level of security between your home network and the Internet, and we highly recommend it.

By the way, the type of encryption and whether or not a firewall is included are completely independent of the wireless standard supported by the router. In other words, all types of encryption are possible with all the wireless standards. It's just a matter of determining what types of encryption are supported by the wireless router and NIC you have or are considering buying.

Cost

Costs have come way down for wireless networking, to the point that it is almost the same cost to put up a wireless network as a wired one. Wireless NICs can be more expensive than wired NICs, but costs are falling rapidly. The latest (and fastest) wireless standard (at this time N) tends to be the most expensive option, followed by the next fastest speed (A and G at this time), and finally the slowest wireless standard (at this time B). The gap is rapidly closing as prices come down across the board; however, you pay a price premium for faster speed.

It is getting pretty difficult to find wireless B equipment still for sale because it has been replaced for the most part by wireless G equipment.

Additional Considerations

When making your decision, you need to consider a couple of other points, including

- What types of wireless NICs do you already own versus what you must go out and purchase? Many new laptops (and even some desktops) are sold with built-in wireless NICs.

- Do you want to be able to use wireless network access outside your home in a publicly provided wireless network (hotspot)?

The last thing you want to do is purchase a wireless router only to find out that you need to replace a wireless NIC that came with your laptop because it is not compatible. Similarly, you will be quite frustrated if you buy a wireless NIC for your laptop, intending to use it at hotspots, only to find out you bought the wrong standard.

 Note: Wireless NICs come in various form factors, including PCI for installing in desktop computers, PCMCIA and Express Cards (plug-in cards) for installing in laptop computers, and USB for connecting to any computer or device with a USB port. Choose whichever makes sense for your network, computers, and budget.

Comparing the IEEE WLAN Standards

With the preceding considerations in mind, it's time to make a choice between wireless standards. Table 3-2 provides an easy-to-read, side-by-side comparison of the four standards. This table should help you figure out which standard is right for you.

Table 3-2   IEEE WLAN Standards Comparison

	A	B	G	N
Speed	Up to 54 Mbps	Up to 11 Mbps	Up to 54 Mbps (faster with proprietary extensions)	100 Mbps or faster
Cost	$$$	$ (Finding new equipment for sale is difficult. You may have to purchase via alternative channels such as eBay.)	$$	$$$$
Frequency	Uncrowded 5-GHz band. Can coexist with 2.4-GHz networks without interference.	More crowded 2.4-GHz band. Some conflict may occur with other 2.4-GHz devices, such as cordless phones, microwaves, and so on.	More crowded 2.4-GHz band. Some conflict may occur with other 2.4-GHz devices, such as cordless phones, microwaves, and so on.	More crowded 2.4-GHz band. Some conflict may occur with other 2.4-GHz devices, such as cordless phones, microwaves, and so on.
Range	Shorter range than 802.11b and 802.11g. Typically, 25 to 75 feet indoors.	Typically, up to 100–150 feet indoors, depending on construction, building material, and room layout.	Typically up to 100–150 feet indoors, depending on construction, building material, and room layout. Much farther with extensions such as Linksys SRX.	150–400 feet is claimed although this has not been widely verified on the high end.
Hotspots	Very few hotspots support the A standard.	Most hotspots support the B standard.	The number of public hotspots supporting the G standard is growing rapidly, allowing wireless connectivity in many airports, hotels, public areas, and restaurants.	Very few hotspots support the N standard, but your N NIC will work with G or B hotspots.

Table 3-2   IEEE WLAN Standards Comparison

	A	B	G	N
Key Benefits	Good alternative if the 2.4-GHz band has too much interference.	Widely supported.	Good mix of speed and broad support.	Blazing-fast speed for high-end networking applications.
Shared Internet Connection	✓	✓	✓	✓
Multiplayer Gaming over Internet	✓	✓	✓	✓
Multiplayer Wireless LAN Games			✓ (with speed extensions)	✓
VoIP	✓	✓ (Performance can be an issue in some cases.)	✓	✓ (over Wireless)
Streaming Audio			✓	✓
Streaming Video			✓ (with speed extensions)	✓
Large Homes		✓ (Keep in mind that speed greatly suffers at the edge of the usable range.)	✓ (with speed extensions)	✓

Recommendations

Based on the information in Table 3-2, here are our bottom-line recommendations:

■ If you just want Internet access, are on a tight budget, or do not anticipate a large amount of internal traffic (from a wireless juke box, for example), either the B or G standard is a good choice. Choose B only if you already have B-only NICs for most of your computers.

■ B equipment may be hard to find for sale in retail locations because it has been mainly replaced by G equipment in the market, so if you can't find B, go with G.

■ If you plan on using hotspots or getting on other people's networks, G offers the best bet for compatibility and speed.

■ If you anticipate a large amount of internal traffic, plan on setting up a wireless gaming system, or want a little bit of future-proofing, N is the best choice. Purchasing G with an extension such as SRX will give you similar performance, but as N begins to gain popularity (and it will), a proprietary G extension will limit your flexibility.

We do *not* recommend the A standard unless you happen to have a specific reason to avoid using B, G, or N. For example, if you are getting known interference from 2.4-GHz cordless phones, or if you live in an apartment and you are surrounded by G routers, A might be an option. Keep in mind, though, that cordless phones are now also being offered in the 5-GHz range, which can potentially interfere with wireless A networks.

For the purposes of helping the broadest group of readers, we will hedge our bet just a bit and show the setup and configurations for both an N and a G router throughout the remainder of this book.

Summary

There are several important factors to consider when choosing your wireless standard, including compatibility, security levels supported, and the performance you expect.

B, G, and N devices are compatible with each other and offer the most opportunity for compatibility outside your network as well, at wireless hotspots.

Standard A equipment works only with other A equipment. Unless you have an explicit need for wireless A, avoid building out an A network.

If you have typical requirements for speed and range, a G network usually is sufficient. If you need extra speed inside your home for streaming video, heavy gaming, or other wireless applications, or you need significant extra range, then an N network is probably a better bet.

Where to Go for More Information

To learn more about wireless A, B, and G standards, check out Bradley Mitchell's article on About.com titled "802.11 Standards—802.11b 802.11a 802.11g": http://compnetworking.about.com/cs/wireless80211/a/aa80211standard.htm.

Space.com has an interesting article about interference from sun spots: www.space.com/scienceastronomy/solarsystem/sunspot_detail_021113.html.

PART II

What You Should Know

Now that we have provided you with information on how this wireless networking stuff works, we provide the information you need to plan out your wireless network and get ready to set it up.

In Chapter 4, "Planning Your Wireless Network," we provide you with a method for figuring out how and where you will be using your wireless network. This is a pretty simple step but it is important because it could keep you from buying products you don't need, or at least keep you from making multiple trips to the electronics store.

Chapter 5, "Wireless Security: What You Need to Know," provides some critically important information regarding wireless security. If you are not yet convinced that you need wireless security, this chapter should change your mind. Even if you are a believer in security, you might want to give this a quick read through because there have been quite a few updates in this area in the last couple years.

Part II finishes with Chapter 6, "What to Buy." Lots of gadgets out there claim to improve your wireless networking experience. This chapter provides you some guidance on what is necessary, what is cool, and what should be avoided.

Planning Your Wireless Network

The first step in building your wireless network is to sit down and do some planning. Sure, it's fun to run out and start buying stuff, but a little time spent up front will save you a lot of frustration and rework time later.

Wireless Network Topologies

Before laying out the wireless network, we need to discuss the basic concept of wireless network topologies. There are essentially two types of wireless networks:

- Peer-to-peer (also called *ad hoc*)

- Peer-to-access point (also called *infrastructure*)

A peer-to-peer (or ad hoc) wireless network does not have a central point of access or control. Every computer on an ad hoc network is considered an equal "peer," having the same rights and access as any other computer on the wireless network. In other words, all the computers communicate directly

with each other, without going through an intermediary device. Any computer with a wireless network adapter (also called a network interface card [NIC]) may connect to any other wireless NIC.
Figure 4-1 shows an example.

Figure 4-1   Peer-to-Peer Wireless Network

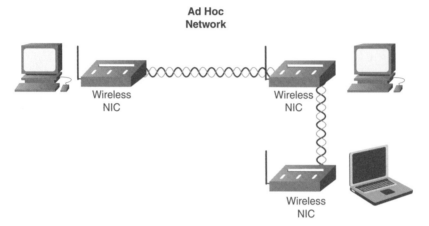

In a peer-to-access point (or infrastructure) wireless network, a central wireless "base station" provides the rendezvous point for all the wireless NICs on the network. In this case, each computer on
the network always communicates only with the base station, or wireless access point, and never
directly with other computers on the network. Figure 4-2 shows an example.

Figure 4-2   Peer-to-Access Point Wireless Network

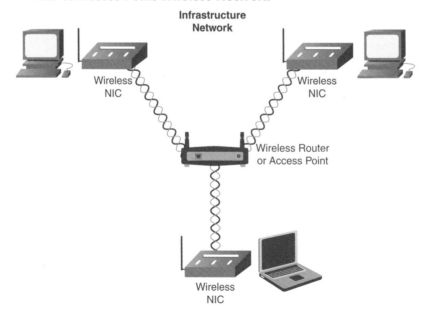

Although you can set up a peer-to-peer wireless network and use a computer with a wired Internet connection to provide Internet access to your other computers, we are not big fans of that style of wireless network, for the following reasons:

■ Because no central authority determines who can join the wireless network and who cannot, security becomes a real concern.

■ One of the computers must be designated as the owner of the high-speed broadband Internet service and provide gateway access for all the other computers on the home network, which can end up being very restrictive.

■ Because of the reason just mentioned, if the Internet gateway computer is not turned on, all other computers on the home network will not be able to access the Internet.

A peer-to-peer network offers a small cost advantage because it is not necessary to purchase a wireless router or access point, but in the end we feel strongly that it is just not worth the money you save.

Note: We assume that you will take this advice, and the "how to" sections of this book are based on this assumption. You should know, however, that even if you do use the infrastructure type of networking, you need to manually disable the ad hoc networking capability on your wireless-enabled computers. Failure to do so presents a significant security risk. Chapter 9, "Wireless Security Setup," provides a step-by-step guide on how to turn this feature off.

Sketching a Network Layout

In our opinion, the best way to start planning your wireless network is to create a drawing or sketch of the area (floor plan) in which it will be used. You don't need architectural drawings, just a simple floor plan (all floors and a rough idea of the room sizes). If you plan to (or want to) use your computer outside (for example, near a pool or on a patio in the backyard), you should include that area in the drawing as well.

Once you have the sketch completed, you need to figure out where you want (or need) to place the wireless router and where your computers and other devices that will be wireless are going to be used. If for some reason the location of your broadband modem (and therefore your wireless router) must be in a specific location, put a mark in that room on your drawing. If you have some flexibility with the location of your modem and router, put the same mark in the rooms where you have the appropriate port for Internet access (cable, DSL, or other). Figure 4-3 shows an example completed sketch. We used a red circle with an *I* in it to denote where we could put an Internet connection. You can use whatever marks you like; keep a legend on the side of the paper so you know what you meant.

Next, put a mark in the rooms where you are likely to have a desktop computer, or other wired device such as a storage server, or network printer. In Figure 4-3, we used a blue diamond with a *C* in it to denote where we want to have a wired network connection, like a desktop computer.

Finally, put a mark in the rooms or areas where you can conceive of using a laptop computer and other wireless devices, including video cameras, printers, video game consoles, and so on. (This would include bathrooms, which we admit to using our computers in.)

In Figure 4-3, we used a green square with a *W* in it to denote where we want to have a wireless network connection, like a laptop.

In addition, if you have a cordless phone system that operates in the 2.4-GHz band (it should be written on the phone somewhere), you may want to mark the location of the phone's base station on the sketch. As we mentioned before, these phones can cause interference with your network if the wireless router is too close. In Figure 4-3, we used a pink moon with a *P* in it to denote where we currently have a cordless phone base station.

Figure 4-3   Sample Sketch of a House

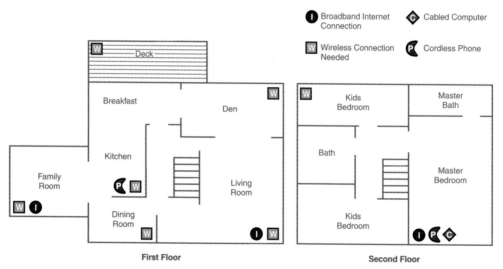

From the sketch, you can make some decisions about where you will put your wireless router, which computers will have wired connections, and which computers will have wireless connections.

Suppose, for example, that you have two desktop computers (a spouse's and a son's), one personal laptop (a daughter's), and one work laptop (yours). Suppose you also happen to have cable outlets in three areas of the house (master bedroom, living room, family room).

You need to have at least one computer with a wired connection (at least during initial setup and sometimes when changes are required). In this example, the family decides to have the high-speed broadband service installed to the outlet in the master bedroom. The wireless router can be placed next to the cable modem and the "Spouse" desktop computer. All three of these devices will be cabled together with Ethernet cables.

Because the daughter's laptop and the son's desktop computer are in other bedrooms of the house, and not easy to run Ethernet cables to, these computers will have wireless connections. The last computer is the work laptop, which is used primarily in the den, but could also be used in the living room, breakfast nook, and on the back deck. Wireless is definitely the way to go for this laptop as well. By jotting these requirements into the sketch, we have what's shown in Figure 4-4.

Figure 4-4   Adding Wired and Wireless Computers to the Sketch

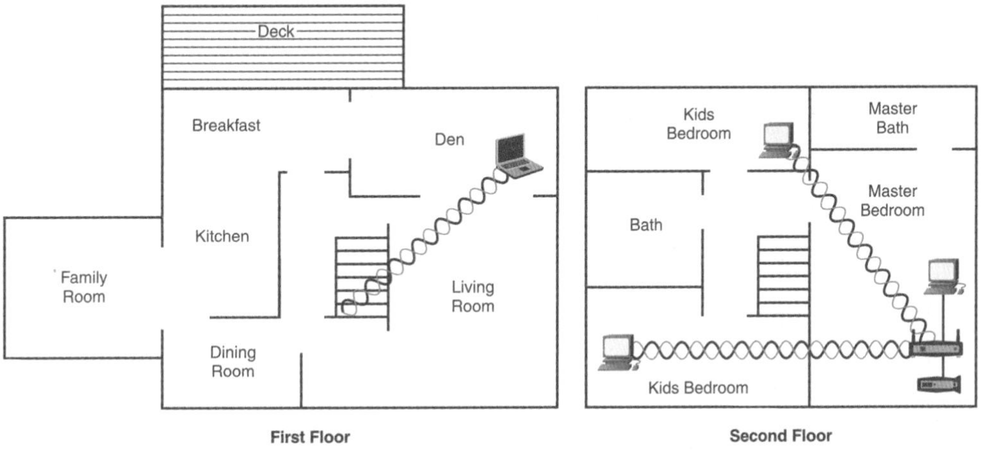

For your network, determine the best location for the modem and wireless router based on your planned usage. Usually, the most central point of the house where you can set up a modem and router is the best option. If you live in a huge house, you may need a signal repeater or range extender, or a high-gain antenna. We will cover these types of devices in Chapter 6, "What to Buy," and recommend that you try a basic router first to see if the performance is adequate.

Chapter 11, "Troubleshooting: I Can Connect Sometimes," also contains some good advice on where to site your wireless router. We recommend reading that chapter before you finalize your network plan. By spending a little extra time up front understanding the trouble you could have, you could end up saving a lot of time and frustration later.

For now, mark the best available spot for your broadband modem and wireless router with an *X*. In this example, we chose the master bedroom because it has an available broadband connection jack, has a wired desktop computer (important for administration), and is fairly centrally located.

Thinking Your Network Plan Through

One of the most common errors we see with friends and family setting up a network is that even when they do plan out the usage as shown in the previous section, they typically only consider how they will use the network the day it is installed. Consider, though, all the advances that have been made in both computing and networking in just the past few years. New capabilities are being added all the time, and what was considered "advanced" yesterday is pretty much the norm today, so much so that putting a network together without the new technologies seems odd. For example, a few years ago it was not really possible to have a wireless printer on your network. Now it's quite easy to set one up and well worth the small effort. Because of this, it's important to sit down with some blank sheets of paper and think about what you have today, what you are likely to have six months from now, and what you would love to have two years from now, in your home network.

Determining the Networking Capabilities of Your Computers

If you are not sure what type of capability your computers have, you need to figure that out to understand what, if anything, you need to purchase.

Everything we build from here on out will be connected to the network. As a result, every device we want to add to the network is going to need a NIC or equivalent network adapter. *NICs* are cards that enable a PC, laptop, printer, or other device to talk to other PCs, laptops, and so on. There are two distinct types of NICs:

- **Wired**—Uses cables to connect to the network

- **Wireless**—Uses the air to connect to the network, much like your cell phone

Keep in mind that most new PCs and laptops come with built-in NICs, and many new laptops have built-in wireless capabilities.

Let's start with the easy one first—wired—and then move on to wireless.

Looking for a Wired NIC

Pretty much every PC out there today (unless you have a really old one) has a wired NIC with an Ethernet port. The wired NIC has a slot for an Ethernet plug that looks like a fat phone cord plug. This slot is almost always located on the back of a PC, but could be on the side of a laptop as well. You may also have a plug-in card for your laptop that has the port in it. We're guessing, though, that less than 1 in 100 computers or laptops will not have the port hard mounted on the computer. Figure 4-5 shows what the wired NIC port looks like.

 Note: Be careful that you do not confuse a modem jack with an Ethernet jack. The modem jack is the same as a phone jack on your wall. The Ethernet jack is a bit wider. Another way to tell them apart is that if you look into the jack, modems typically have two or four pins or contacts, whereas Ethernet jacks have eight.

Looking for a Wireless NIC

Determining if you have a wireless NIC is not as easy because in many cases there's nothing to actually see. If you have purchased your computer any time after 2003, there is a good chance you have built-in wireless capability.

Figure 4-5   Wired NIC Port

If you have Windows XP, you can quickly check your computer's wireless capability by performing the following steps (you can also follow the steps in older versions of Windows, but the path might be slightly different):

Step 1   Click the **Start** button and then click the **My Computer** icon. (Depending on your setting, you may need to right-click the **My Computer** icon and choose **Open** from the menu.)

Step 2   Click the **View System Information** option, as shown in Figure 4-6.

Figure 4-6   My Computer Window

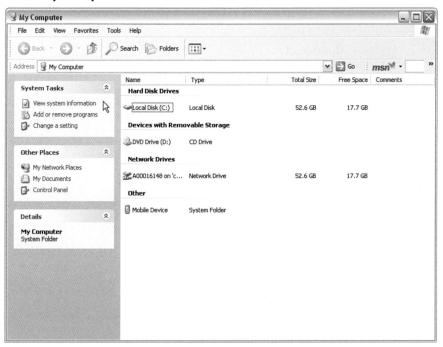

Step 3   Click the Hardware tab in the System Properties window and then click Device Manager, as shown in Figure 4-7.

Figure 4-7   System Properties Window

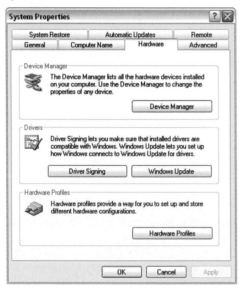

Step 4   In the Device Manager window, click the plus sign (+) next to the Network Adapters icon, as shown in Figure 4-8.

Figure 4-8   Device Manager Window

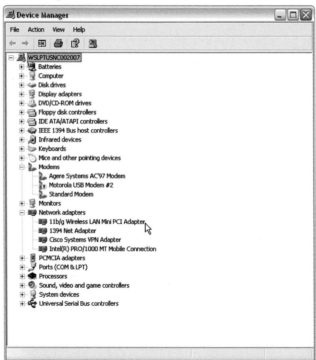

Step 5   Look at the list of network adapters and see if any of the options say "wireless" or "WLAN" (for wireless LAN). If any of the devices shown have either of those words in the description, you have some form of wireless capability on your PC. This screen also tells you what type of wireless you have, whether it's A, B, G, N, or some combination thereof. As you can see in Figure 4-8, the computer shown has B and G capability.

Note: If your computer doesn't run Windows XP, or if after following these steps you are still not sure whether the computer has built-in wireless, check the product documentation that came with the computer (or online).

Determining Your Immediate Needs to Create a Wireless Network

Table 4-1 shows a worksheet we found useful for planning a network. Fill it out twice: once for today and once for what you think your home network may look like one to two years from now. You can complete the table either on a piece of paper or, better yet, in a spreadsheet program. The example shown in Table 4-1 is based on our houses. It may seem like a lot, but trust us, the first time your 12-year-old daughter comes to you complaining that she can't connect to her teacher's website from the back porch to download her homework, all will become apparent.

Table 4-1   Planning Your Network: Example Worksheet

Computer or Device	Need	Have	Type to Buy
Today			
Desktop PC (Spouse)	Wired NIC and wireless NIC	Wired NIC	
Desktop PC (Son)	Wireless NIC	Wired NIC	
Laptop 1 (Work)	Wireless NIC	Wired NIC Wired B/G NIC	
Future			
Laptop 2 (Daughter)	Wireless NIC	None	
Xbox video game console	Wireless NIC	None	

At this point, you need to consider several other factors in your planning:

- What type of Internet access do you have today? Will it have bandwidth (transfer speed) adequate for your needs? For this exercise, let's assume that you are going to use the wireless G standard. We'll show how to set up both a G and an N system in the chapters that follow, but most people should pick one system, as described in Chapter 3, "Selecting the Right Wireless Standard for Your Network," and stick with it.

- Where is the Internet access physically located in your house? Is it convenient?

- Do family members need to share resources, like printers?

- Do you have computer-savvy neighbors or family members who can help?

Completing Your Plan

You should now have a good idea of where you expect to use your computers, where you are going to put your router, and what the wireless capability is for all your computers. Use the method of determining the wireless capability on all of your computers and complete the planning table you began earlier.

Don't worry too much yet about understanding all the details in this chapter. We will explain more as we build out our network. For now, just have a look at the worksheet we put together, shown in Table 4-2. This is an example where we have two desktop PCs and two laptop computers, each identified by its primary user. We also have a video camera and a video game system that we want to include on the network. Later, we will consider options for each of the items we don't yet have and make the best choice based on our needs. After you inventory your equipment, you may want to create a table similar to what's shown in Table 4-2 for your own needs.

Table 4-2   Network Readiness

Computer or Device	Need	Have	Type to Buy
Today			
Desktop PC (Spouse)	Wired NIC and wireless NIC	Wired NIC	None
Desktop PC (Son)	Wireless NIC	Wired NIC	USB wireless G NIC
Laptop 1 (Work)	Wireless NIC	Wired NIC Wired G/B NIC	None
Future			
Laptop 2 (Daughter)	Wireless NIC	—	Plug-in (PCMCIA) wireless card or USB wireless G NIC
Xbox video game console	Wireless NIC	None	Wireless G game adapter (covered later in the book)

In this case, if you happened to have a wireless card that operates on the B standard, you could use it in any of the computers. Just keep in mind that you will only get the B performance for the computer you are using it with.

Summary

This chapter was all about thinking through how and where you want to use your wireless computers so that you don't wind up buying things you don't need. Many of the calls we get from friends and family when they have trouble with their wireless network setup stem from their use of the ever-popular "ready-fire-aim" tactic of running out and buying gear and then trying to hook it all together without starting with a plan. By taking the few extra steps described in this chapter, you should be well on your way to getting your network up and running now and you should have an easier time expanding or upgrading your network later.

Wireless Security: What You Need to Know

At this point you should have a good idea of which type of wireless standard will work best for you, and how and where you plan on using or accessing your wireless network. Now it's time to think about security. This is one of the most important considerations regarding your wireless network, yet, sadly, most people don't take the little bit of time required to protect themselves from hackers and identity thieves. We urge you to take the time to understand and implement security on your wireless network. This chapter focuses on the types of security (and the risks of not enabling it). Chapter 9, "Wireless Security Setup," shows you how to implement the different types of security on your network and wireless enabled devices.

 Note: Wireless security involves taking additional precautions beyond using a firewall. Even if you currently have a firewall, you still need to enable wireless security. For a more detailed treatment on the ten things everyone should know about home network security, please see *Home Network Security Simplified* (ISBN: 1158720-163-1).

Why Should I Worry About Wireless Network Security?

Controlling access to who is on your network is one of the most critical components of overall network security. Access to a wired network is easy to control, because people have to be physically inside your house to plug a computer into the router. With a wireless network, people just have to be in the proximity of your house. Physical barriers such as windows and doors do not control access in this case, so we have to take other steps to block intruders.

The security issue with a wireless network stems from the fact that the signal is omnidirectional. Unlike a wired network, where signals are fairly well contained, the wireless signal goes everywhere in all directions (including up and down, for those of you in multistory buildings) for 100–300 feet or more. Anyone who wants to gain access to your signal need only put a receiver (a computer with a wireless card) inside the signal range.

Note: Why would someone want to access your wireless network? Well, there are lots of reasons. One of your neighbors could "leech" onto your network just to receive free Internet access. Although irritating, this is not all that harmful in itself, if all they are doing is browsing the Internet on your dollar. However, *war-drivers* (hackers who drive around looking for unsecured wireless networks) or professional hackers could use the access to obtain your personal information. For example, eavesdropping while you are conducting an online purchase could expose your credit card information.

One of the most unusual illicit uses of unsecured home wireless networks also offers perhaps the strongest reason yet to secure your wireless network. Recently, several instances have surfaced where people conducting illegal activities used unsecured home networks for the anonymity that they can provide. One fellow parked in a neighborhood, easily gained access to an unprotected home wireless network, and downloaded huge amounts of illegal child pornography. He was caught and arrested, but it was due to a traffic violation, not the downloading (the police noticed the pictures on the computer after they pulled him over). If someone commits illegal activity in this manner, that activity can easily be traced to your broadband subscription, in which case you could end up having to explain to the authorities that it was not you or other family members conducting the illegal activity.

We are always amazed when we drive through a neighborhood and check how people have deployed their wireless networks. On a sample drive through a single neighborhood using cheap equipment that's easy for the average person to get and use, we easily found 114 wireless routers, only 45 (roughly 40 percent) of which were protected in any fashion. From such a scan, potential intruders can easily obtain a survey of the available wireless networks, their SSIDs, channel numbers, and, most importantly, which networks have been secured and which have been left wide open (roughly 60 percent). In Figure 5-1, the networks with a circle and a padlock inside are those that are at least using encryption. The networks with a circle without a padlock are wide open. Anyone can sit on the street near these houses (or businesses), associate to the access point, and access the Internet or try to break into the rest of the home network.

The state of your wireless router when you take it out of the box is wide open. You can get your wireless router up and running fast, but if you do not take a few minutes to secure your router (and it really only takes a few minutes), you could be asking for trouble.

Figure 5-1 Scanning for Available Wireless Networks in a Neighborhood

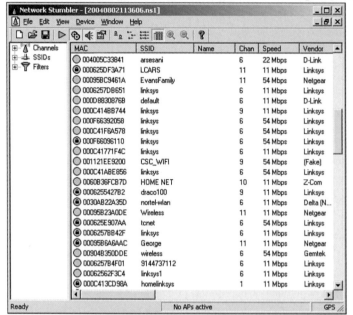

What Do I Do to Secure My Wireless Network?

You can take three really simple steps to dramatically increase the security of your wireless network. It is not foolproof wireless security, but it will keep you from being an easy target and it will keep most of the riffraff out.

As Figure 5-1 showed, there are plenty of easy targets out there, so all you need to worry about in most cases is the curious neighbor or someone specifically looking to access a network with no protection at all. The steps described in this section will not keep out a really serious hacker, but if you have reason to worry about a hacker specifically targeting you (as opposed to someone hacking at random), then you can hire a security specialist or, better yet, just don't use wireless. For the vast majority of you, though, read on.

Figure 5-2 shows varying degrees of wireless home network security and the vulnerabilities related with the networks.

So what are the three things you need to do to improve your wireless network security?

- Don't advertise your network (turn off SSID broadcast).
- Scramble (encrypt) your wireless signal using encryption.
- Don't use ad hoc networking.

Figure 5-2   Security Examples

Wireless Settings
Enabled SSID Broadcast
Default SSID (e.g., linksys)
No Encryption

Wireless Settings
Disable SSID Broadcast
Changed SSID (e.g., fluffycat)
No Encryption

Wireless Settings
Disable SSID Broadcast
Random SSID (e.g., kr90oLMZ)
128-Bit WEP Encryption

Wireless Settings
Disable SSID Broadcast
Random SSID (e.g., Fh560S0eeXt)
WPA2 Encryption

Security Issues
Wireless routers come from the store this way. Anyone with a laptop can get on this network, and most hotspot programs will make it easy. Don't do this.

This person is asking for trouble!

Security Issues
This network will keep most nonhackers off the network, but all your information (including e-mail online shopping data) is sent in cleartext for anyone to see.

This person is still vulnerable.

Security Issues
This network is secure enough for most people, including encrypting all data sent and received. There are more secure options, but this is the minimum you should do.

Secure enough for most people, but a dedicated hacker could take you down.

Security Issues
This network has the most security possible today and is fairly equivalent to business-class security. If you need more than this, hire a professional.

Very secure.

Don't Advertise Your Wireless Network

Every wireless router is given a name that allows clients (that is, wireless-enabled computers) to find and associate to it. This name is called the *service set identifier (SSID)*. The first step you can take to greatly improve the security of your wireless network is to not broadcast the SSID!

Most wireless routers have the broadcast SSID setting turned on when you take them out of the box. This feature announces the name of your network to every wireless-capable computer within range. Although this makes it easy for you to connect to your network, it makes it easy for the rest of the neighborhood, too. Turn this feature off (we show you how in Chapter 9). In addition, knowing the name of a network (even if the broadcast function is turned off) gives you the power to get on that network, so you should choose a random SSID name.

Any SSID that is easy for you to remember is probably easy to figure out, so avoid SSIDs that include your name, the word "home," the word "network," or anything related to *your name-home-wireless-network*. We suggest that you rename the SSID to something personal (but not easily guessed) or use a random combination of numbers and upper- and lowercase letters. Don't worry about having to memorize this, because you can just write it down and keep in a drawer or a folder where you can access it later if you need it. Remember, however, that although this step will keep out the nosy neighbors and provide your router with some level of anonymity, it will not by itself protect your network.

In Chapter 7, "Wireless Router Setup," and Chapter 9, you will see in more detail how to set up the wireless router and how to secure it, including choosing an SSID, so don't worry if you have not thought of one yet.

Scramble Your Signal

Another step you can take to improve the security of your network is to turn on encryption. This section describes wireless encryption technologies, how to select one for your wireless network, and how to choose an encryption key.

What Is Encryption?

If you are unfamiliar with encryption, the concept is pretty simple. Remember being a kid and making up a list like this:

A B C D E F G H I J K L M N O P Q R S T U V W X Y Z
1 2 3 4 5 6 7 8 9 10 11 12 13 14 15 16 17 18 19 20 21 22 23 24 25 26

Then your friend wrote you a note like this:

9

12 9 11 5

3 8 5 5 19 5

You pulled out your handy-dandy decoder table and translated it to "I like cheese." Congratulations, you were doing encryption.

We are obviously oversimplifying, but encrypting your wireless network is actually a similar concept. You are going to choose a key for your wireless network. That key is known to both the sender and receiver—for example, your computer and the wireless router. Every time you send information between each other, you use the key to encode it, you transmit it, and then you use the key again to decode the message back to its real information.

In the previous simple example, the only reason you and your friend knew what each other were saying was that you both had the same decoder. As long as only you and your friend have the key, you can talk without anyone else eavesdropping on your conversation.

In the case of wireless encryption, instead of a single letter-to-number translation, a mathematical formula is calculated using the original information and the key. The result is a highly encoded piece of information that is very difficult to decode without knowing the key. In general, the longer the key, the harder it is to break. Think of an encryption key like a PIN code that has 16 or 32 digits instead of 4. (How the mathematical formulas work are beyond the scope of this book. If you are interested, pick up a book on cryptography.)

There are several standards available for wireless network encryption, including the following two most common ones:

- **Wired Equivalent Privacy (WEP)**—WEP provides a simple and fairly effective means for keeping your information private and your network secure from those wishing to access it without your knowledge or approval. WEP is the most widely available encryption standard and is offered with several different key lengths, including 64, 128, 152, and even 256 (bits). You may also see references to 40 and 104, but these are exactly the same as 64 and 128. WEP is good enough to keep any nonhacker from seeing your information but it is by no means a bulletproof encryption method.

■ **Wi-Fi Protected Access (WPA)**—WPA is a newer and more sophisticated method of encryption. We recommend that you use WPA if it is available on your gear because it provides better protection than WEP. The two common types of WPA are Temporal Key Integrity Protocol (TKIP) and Advanced Encryption Standard (AES). The TKIP version is often referred to as WPA, while the AES version is often referred to as WPA2 and provides near business-level security for home networks.

The major difference between WEP and WPA is that with WEP your encryption key remains the same until you change it, whereas WPA automatically changes the key periodically for you. Changing the key makes it more difficult for someone to discover the key, and even if they do, the key is only useful for a very short time, because it will change again.

Some home networking products (wireless computers, NICs, and wireless routers) support all of the encryption options, while others support a smaller subset. This is important because both the computer and router need to be talking with the same encryption method and key to understand each other.

Choosing an Encryption Key

So how do you choose an encryption key? There are two ways, one very simple, and one not so simple. The simple way is to use the key generator that is built into the home networking products. (Linksys products offer a key generator in every wireless card and router Linksys sells.) Essentially, you just create a passphrase, which is like a password, enter it into the NIC or router (using the administration tool), and click a Generate Key button. Examples are shown later, in Chapter 9.

The rules for selecting a passphrase and choosing a password are the same: Never use names, pets, or words. Make up a random series of 8 to 63 lowercase letters, uppercase letters, and numbers. Do *not* try to spell words or use clever encoded phrases such as *weLUVr2Dogs* (Chapter 9 has more on creating strong passwords). The key generator will take the passphrase and translate it into a series of numbers (0–9) and letters (A–F). Don't worry about understanding the number system, but this is the encryption key. Write down both the passphrase and generated key; you are going to need it several times.

 Note: Passphrase generators are proprietary, so each vendor's key generator works only with its router/NIC. You can still use WEP/WPA with routers and NICs from different vendors, but you will need to type in the encryption keys manually. In addition, Windows XP does not support the concept, so you have to always manually enter the key itself (for WEP).

Table 5-1 summarizes the different encryption methods mentioned previously. It is important to note that these encryption methods typically cannot be mixed together on the same network, so pick the highest level of security that all your wireless network devices can support.

Table 5-1 **Available Wireless Encryption Methods**

Encryption Method	Security	Recommendations
64-bit WEP (sometimes referred to as 40-bit WEP)		Minimum level of encryption. We recommend 128-bit WEP. However, if you have some older devices, they may only support 64-bit WEP.
128-bit WEP (sometimes referred to as 104-bit WEP)		Very commonly used and offers a high degree of security. A professional hacker with enough money and time can "crack" the code, but this is secure enough for most people.
WPA (sometimes referred to as WPA-TKIP)		Adds a degree of security beyond WEP. The secret key is changed periodically to reduce the opportunity for "cracking." Typically available with a software upgrade for older devices.
WPA2 (sometimes referred to as WPA-AES)		Adds a new encryption algorithm (AES) to WPA, which makes it even more secure. May or may not be available for older devices.

VERY IMPORTANT: **We can't stress enough that any time you create something such as an encryption passphrase, password, or WEP key, you need to write it down in your notebook. If you lose it, you may have to reset the wireless router to the factory defaults and start over.**

The second way to choose an encryption key is make it up yourself using a random combination of numbers (0–9) and letters (A–F). You will need to create an exact number of numbers and letters depending on which key length you are trying to create. For example, a 64-bit key has 10 hex digits; a 128-bit key has 26 hex digits; and so on (the administration screen where you set this up will specify the number of characters). If at all possible, use the built-in key generator from a passphrase. You will pull your hair out trying to create them by hand.

If you have guests who want to use your network, you need to give them your passphrase or security key. If you need to, you can always change the key after they leave. Chapter 9, "Wireless Security Setup," also discusses how to use a USB media key to easily add quests to your network. You can also have them use a direct (wired) connection into the router, which does not require encryption.

Disable Ad Hoc Networking

Your wireless-enabled computer has two basic modes of communication: infrastructure and ad hoc networking. In infrastructure mode, all the computers on the network must communicate through the router. So whether you are talking to the Internet or with another computer on the local network, all your communication traffic goes through the router. This is what most people are and should be doing.

In ad hoc mode, computers can communicate directly with each other without going through a router or any other device. This is great if, for example, you want to share a file with someone quickly. The bad thing is that if you have this mode enabled, someone who knows what they are doing can get access to all your files, possibly without you even noticing it. To avoid this, we strongly recommend that you disable this function using the steps outlined in Chapter 9. If you find yourself in a situation where you need to use this feature, turn it on for the duration of use and then immediately disable it.

Other Tips to Consider

One of the first things you should do is change the administrative password on your router. We cover how to do this in Chapter 7. This is an important step that you should not skip over.

Another good security tip is that you should get in the habit of turning your wireless router (and your modem) off during periods of long inactivity (if you go away for the weekend, for example). If it's not turned on, it can't be hacked.

Summary

Enabling security on your wireless network is critical even if you have a firewall, because a firewall protects you against some threats but does little to protect against wireless access threats. Broadcasting your SSID and leaving the encryption feature disabled is, at best, an invitation to give your neighbors free Internet access and, at worst, an easy path to losing your identity. Encryption is an absolute must on any wireless network. As we demonstrate in Chapter 9, it takes no more than five minutes to set up good wireless security, which could save you years of aggravation trying to get your credit history repaired.

Note: Securing your wireless network is just one aspect of home network security. To learn about the full breadth of necessary steps you should take to secure your home network, pick up a copy of *Home Networking Security Simplified*. It covers the top ten things you should do to secure your home network.

Where to Go for More Information

Check out Bradley Mitchell's article "Top 9 Tips for Wireless Home Network Security" on About.com: http://compnetworking.about.com/od/wirelesssecurity/tp/wifisecurity.htm.

JiWire has an article titled "Complete Guide to Wi-Fi Security" by Tony Bradley and Becky Waring: www.jiwire.com/wi-fi-security-introduction-overview.htm.

Linksys also has some good information about network security at www.linksys.com. Click **Network Security** on the Learning Center drop-down menu and follow the Network Security links on the left side of the page.

The U.S. Justice Department defines the federal law regarding hacking in 18 U.S.C. 1030, "Fraud and Related Activity in Connection with Computers": www.usdoj.gov/criminal/cybercrime/1030_new.html.

Wikipedia has an entry on cryptography and encryption: http://en.wikipedia.org/wiki/cryptography.

CHAPTER 6

What to Buy

The next step in building your network is to determine what you need to buy. Based on the planning diagram and tables you did in Chapter 4, "Planning Your Wireless Network," you should have a good idea of the basic device types you need to get your network up and running.

Determining Network Readiness

We'll follow the example started in Chapter 4. We first need to take inventory of the type of NICs we have already in the different computers we want to participate in the wireless home network. Make a table like that shown in Table 6-1, recording how we need to connect the computer in the Need column, and what we have today in the Have column.

Table 6-1   Network Readiness

Computer or Device	Need	Have	Type to Buy
Today			
Desktop PC (Spouse)	Wired NIC and wireless NIC	Wired NIC	
Desktop PC (Son)	Wireless NIC	Wired NIC	
Laptop 1 (Work)	Wireless NIC	Wired NIC Wireless B/G NIC	
Future			
Laptop 2 (Daughter)	Wireless NIC	None	
Xbox video game console	None	Wireless NIC	

Based on the table, we have wireless capability in one of the laptops (as a reminder, Chapter 4 showed you how to determine if your computer has wireless capability). This leaves us with one laptop and two desktop computers that need additional equipment to support wireless.

In addition to outfitting the computers with the right equipment, you also need a wireless router, which will communicate with all the computers and provide them access to the Internet via the cable or DSL modem.

In addition, you may want to consider some extra bells and whistles (such as game adapters or wireless cameras) at some point, so we'll cover them here as well.

To make this easy, we are going to go with all Linksys gear here. This is not a requirement, because all wireless equipment using the same standard should be compatible regardless of who the manufacturer is. The one exception, noted in earlier chapters, is that proprietary extensions such as Linksys SRX require compatible equipment on both sides. In other words, to get the benefit of SRX, you need both the SRX router and the SRX NIC. We're going to stay away from all that here and keep our example pretty simple.

Another reason we will use all Linksys products is that, by having Linksys on both sides (that is, a Linksys wireless router and Linksys wireless NICs), we can take advantage of some advanced features that make installing and setting up the wireless network easier. These features are not always available if we have a mixed environment (meaning different manufacturers for the router and NICs).

To that end we are going to base everything from here on out on the wireless G standard. This includes the routers, NICs, and, where available, the extra stuff such as game systems. In cases where G is not available, we use B-standard devices, which, as we previously mentioned, will work with the G router, albeit at B performance levels.

Another compelling reason to avoid proprietary extensions such as Speed Booster and SRX is that the preliminary N standard is available now and offers all the benefits of these extensions (and then some) without locking you into proprietary equipment. For those who require (or think they will require in the future) speed and range beyond what G has to offer, we also provide a walkthrough for an N-based system. We cover only the router, though, because the NIC setup is identical.

For the NICs, there are a number of options. In the desktop computers, you can install a card inside the computer, but this involves taking the cover off, which is kind of a pain. We'll show you how to do it for the sake of completeness, but there are better options. One such option is to use a USB wireless adapter, which requires a USB interface. Most computers made over the last 5 years or so have a USB interface. The easiest way to determine if you have a USB interface is to look for the slot on your computer. It could be on the front, side, or back, depending on the make and model. The port is shown in Figure 6-1.

Figure 6-1   USB Interface

If you do go with a USB NIC, you can either get a small box that connects to the USB port via a USB cable or get a NIC that has the same form factor as a memory key or memory stick. Pictures of both are shown later in this chapter in the section "Wireless NIC Options."

Note: There are two kinds of USB: 1.0 and 2.0. The USB NICs we reference work with both USB standards, but both yield better performance with USB 2.0.

If you need to buy a NIC for your laptop, you can also use any of the USB NICs (as with desktop PCs, USB ports have been standard on laptops for several years). That said, we recommend a PCMCIA card for laptops, which is a card that plugs into a slot in your laptop. These cards are specifically made for laptops and don't stick out like USB sticks do, so you can carry your laptop around without too much worry about the card breaking off (which is not an option with a USB key). Note, though, that if you put your computer in a computer bag for transport, it's a good idea to take the PCMCIA card out to prevent the card from breaking off pins.

Note: A newer type of laptop card, called ExpressCard, is now being used. ExpressCards are roughly half the size of the previous generation of PCMCIA cards. At the time of this writing, not many ExpressCards are available, but we expect they will become popular. Whether you buy PCMCIA cards or ExpressCards is up to you; just make sure that whichever you buy matches what you have in your laptop. PCMCIA and ExpressCards are *not* compatible.

Figure 6-2 shows a comparison of a PCMCIA card (bottom) and two ExpressCards (top two).

Figure 6-2   PCMCIA and ExpressCard Comparison

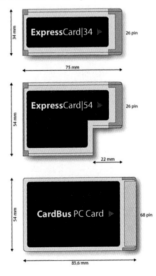

Note: PCMCIA stands for Personal Computer Memory Card International Association. We had to look it up on Google. No one (except maybe for the folks paying dues to that association) would ever actually use the words instead of the acronym, and if you were to go to your favorite electronics store and ask them for a "Personal Computer Memory Card International Association card," they would probably just ask you to leave.

Later, in Part V of the book, we will cover how to connect some other devices to your wireless network, including a wireless gaming system and a wireless video camera. The wireless game adapter is perfect for those of you who like or want to play Xbox Live (or the Sony PlayStation or Nintendo GameCube versions) but have the TV and Xbox in a different room than the router and broadband modem. These game adapters are good for extending your Voice over IP (VoIP) service, such as Vonage, to another room without adding another cordless phone (and more interference) to your house. We will also show you how to install and use a wireless video camera, which is great for monitoring the baby, or the nanny, or your husband, or some combination of those people should your situation require it.

Note: In the event that you have a desktop computer that has neither a wireless card nor a USB port, you can use the wireless game adapter to provide wireless capability to your computer, assuming it has a standard wired NIC installed. If not, you probably have a really old computer and you are either looking at installing a card on the motherboard or taking heroic measures (not covered in this book) to connect that computer to the network.

Some older computers may lack the horsepower to be able to operate a wireless NIC. For example, Linksys wireless NICs are supported only in computers with 200-MHz Pentium processors and higher. Sometimes, though, we have an older computer such as a Pentium 133 MHz that we still want to use. The solution to this problem is to go ahead and install a wired NIC in the computer, and then add a wireless Ethernet bridge (such as the Linksys WET11) to provide the wireless connection. The wireless bridge is "self-contained" and does not need the PC to connect itself to the wireless router. Wireless Ethernet bridges are a little hard to find but can be worth their weight in gold if you absolutely must put an older computer on the wireless network.

So, based on all of the preceding information, we need to finish our table and round out the categories of equipment we need. The completed table is shown in Table 6-2.

Table 6-2   Network Readiness Completed

Computer or Device	Need	Have	Type to Buy
Today			
Desktop PC (Spouse)	Wired and wireless NIC	Wired NIC	USB wireless NIC (G standard)
Desktop PC (son)	Wireless NIC	Wired NIC	USB wireless NIC (G standard)
Laptop 1 (Work)	Wireless NIC	Wired NIC Wireless G/B NIC	None
Wireless router	Wireless router	None	Wireless G Router
Future			
Laptop 2 (Daughter)	Wireless NIC	None	PCMCIA wireless NIC (G standard)

Making Your List, Checking It Twice

Now that we know what types of stuff we need to buy, next we need to actually figure out models and numbers. The shopping list in Figure 6-3 includes the devices we will be using in our examples in the remainder of the book, but we want to make the point again that all of the equipment we are choosing can be substituted with the same equipment from another vendor, so long as you stick with the base N, G, or B standard.

Figure 6-3   Shopping List

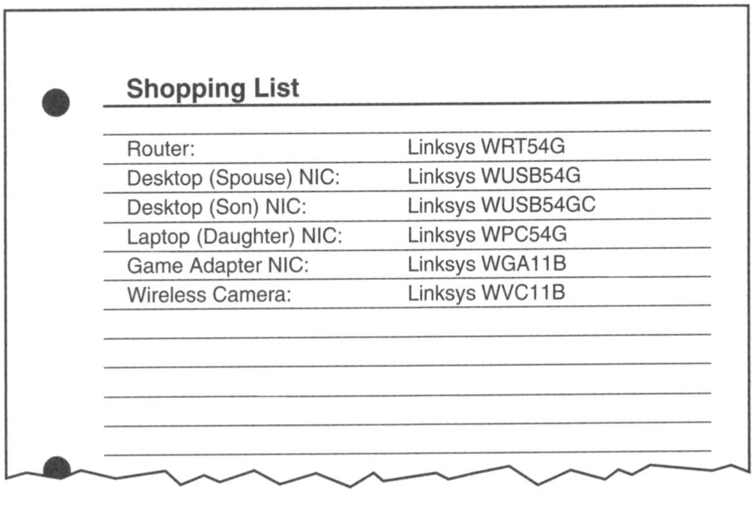

Shopping List

Router:	Linksys WRT54G
Desktop (Spouse) NIC:	Linksys WUSB54G
Desktop (Son) NIC:	Linksys WUSB54GC
Laptop (Daughter) NIC:	Linksys WPC54G
Game Adapter NIC:	Linksys WGA11B
Wireless Camera:	Linksys WVC11B

For a closer look, the following sections summarize the equipment.

Wireless Router Options

Because we will be putting together a G-based network, the router we chose—WRT54G—is the base
G router with no extensions, shown in Figure 6-4. If you plan to have the router sit out in the open
and you want something a little smaller (and nicer looking), you can go with the compact router
(WRT54GC), shown in Figure 6-5.

Figure 6-4   Linksys Wireless-G Broadband Router (WRT54G)

These materials have been reproduced by Cisco Press with the permission of Cisco Systems, Inc.
COPYRIGHT ©2007 CISCO SYSTEMS, INC. ALL RIGHTS RESERVED

Figure 6-5   Linksys Compact Wireless-G Broadband Router (WRT54GC)

These materials have been reproduced by Cisco Press with the permission of Cisco Systems, Inc.
COPYRIGHT ©2007 CISCO SYSTEMS, INC. ALL RIGHTS RESERVED

We will also show you how to set up and install the new N-based router just for kicks. Here we will use the WRT300N router (see Figure 6-6).

Figure 6-6   Linksys Wireless-N Broadband Router (WRT300N)

Wireless NIC Options

For the desktop NICs, we have decided to use USB devices. We will go with a different kind of USB NIC for each, but this is only to show how to set them up rather than for some engineering reason. The devices we picked are the USB box WUSB54G (see Figure 6-7) and the USB stick WUSB54GC (see Figure 6-8). For the laptop, the obvious choice is the G-based PCMCIA card WPC54G (see Figure 6-9). Depending on the location of the "Spouse" PC (or any other PC, for that matter), you can use a standard Ethernet cable to connect the PC to one of the wired ports on the back of the wireless router.

For the desktop, we could have also picked an internal PCI card, such as the Linksys WMP54G (see Figure 6-10).

Figure 6-7   Linksys Wireless-G USB Network Adapter (WUSB54G)

Figure 6-8   Linksys Compact Wireless-G USB Adapter (WUSB54GC)

Figure 6-9   Linksys Wireless-G Notebook Adapter (WPC54G)

Figure 6-10   Linksys Wireless-G PCI Adapter (WMP54G)

Note: As we discussed in Chapter 5, "Wireless Security: What You Need to Know," make sure to consider the wireless security you want to use (WEP, WPA, WPA2, and so on). Most wireless routers and NICs on the market today support all of them, but you need to double-check, especially if you are buying older or used products. If all the wireless NICs in your network support WPA2, except for one that supports only WEP-128, then your entire network will need to fall back to WEP-128 as the least-common denominator.

For example, we will see in Chapter 13, "Wireless Video and Entertainment," that for networking your DVR over a wireless connection, WPA is not supported today, so WEP-128 is the maximum security possible (this could change by the time this book is published and purchased, so check the URLs listed in Chapter 13 for the latest information).

Gear for Travel Bugs and Road Warriors

If you travel a lot and want or need to maintain wireless connectivity in hotel rooms or offices with a high-speed wired connection, a wireless travel router is a good piece of kit to bring along with you, and it does not take up a lot of room in your bag. This is especially convenient if you subscribe to an Internet telephony (VoIP) service such as Vonage. Using a wireless travel router and your VoIP termi-nal adapter (the box your phone connects to), you can bring your office with you wherever you go. Imagine traveling to Singapore and having your office number from Boise ring in your hotel room without it costing you a dime. Cool stuff. We talk more about travel routers in Chapter 14, "Wireless to Go."

The Linksys model number for the Wireless-G Travel Router with SpeedBooster is WTR54GS and it is shown in Figure 6-11. Note that this model has the Speed Booster extension, but because we recommended that you get the standard-G NICs, you will only get standard-G performance out of this router. No worries, though, because it's still plenty fast.

Figure 6-11   Linksys Wireless-G Travel Router with SpeedBooster (WTR54GS)

Extra Stuff

In Chapter 13 we will discuss connecting a video game console, such as Microsoft Xbox, to the wireless network so that we can participate in online gaming over the Internet. For this we chose the Wireless-G Game Adapter, model number WGA54G, shown in Figure 6-12.

In Chapter 13 we will also discuss connecting a wireless video camera to our wireless network. For this we chose the Wireless-G Video Camera, model number WVC54G, shown in Figure 6-13.

Figure 6-12   Linksys Wireless-G Game Adapter (WGA54G)

Figure 6-13   Linksys Wireless-G Internet Video Camera (WVC54G)

Where to Buy Your Gear

You can shop for this stuff in just about any electronics or computer store. Pretty much everything on the shopping list in Figure 6-3 should be available in the larger retail chains and easily available online.

If you are looking for equipment alternatives (whether the same Linksys equipment or the same type of stuff from different vendors), we highly recommend www.cnet.com. From the main page, click the **Reviews** tab and then the **Networking** tab, as shown in Figure 6-14 and Figure 6-15, respectively. Once there, you can drill down by networking type, manufacturer, price, or other categories. You can also search on a specific item such as wireless G routers. The results page gives you a table of all the compatible devices, with CNET.com's rating score, summary review, and price ranges. You can drill down further to detailed reviews. Clicking the Check Prices link will take you to a page that lists the verified prices for many of the stores selling the item. Figure 6-16 shows the results for a search on wireless G routers.

Note: Rebates are quite common for consumer networking equipment such as wireless routers, wireless NICs, and other wireless equipment. But the rebates may not be reflected in such online comparisons, and may be offered by one retailer and not another. So shop around and check the prices on a couple different retail sites to see who has the best price and potential rebates.

Figure 6-14   CNET.com Main Screen

Figure 6-15   CNET.com Networking and Wi-Fi Page

Figure 6-16   CNET.com Search Results for Wireless G Router

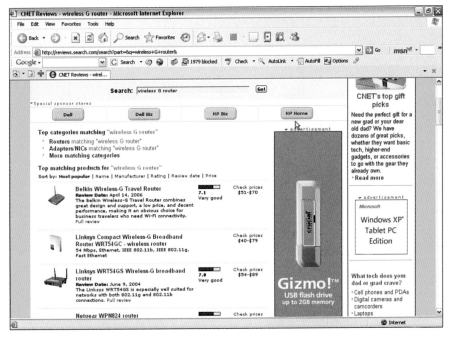

You may have noticed while drilling down into the Networking section that the site also reviews computers, MP3 players, and other electronics, so it's worth bookmarking if you buy tech stuff. There are lots of sites like this, but if we had to pick one, this would be it.

Summary

So that's it for the shopping list. Keep in mind, though, that you do not need to go out and buy all new equipment, especially if you have compatible equipment. For example, if you have a couple of wireless B NICs, you can still set up your network with a wireless G router and use the wireless B NICs.

There is also a healthy market for the "older" standards, so if you are not one of those people who always needs to have the latest and greatest tech gadgets, you can probably get some used wireless B equipment for a good price.

Where to Go for More Information

CNET's website is a good resource: www.cnet.com.

PC Magazine has a pretty good website that includes reviews on many wireless networking products: www.pcmag.com/category2/0,1874,4236,00.asp.

Linksys provides product information at its website: www.linksys.com.

PART III

How Do I Set It Up?

Now that you have gotten an overview of wireless networking, put some thought into planning your wireless network, and purchased the stuff you need to build it, it's time to start putting it together. "Finally," you may be saying to yourself, but trust us, every minute you put into some thought up front will save you hours of frustration later on.

The next step is to start building the network. If it's the first time you have ever built a home network, don't worry, we will keep the steps straightforward and easy to understand. If you are upgrading your network to wireless or extending your wireless network's capabilities, again we will give you the information you need to build a solid and secure wireless network. Even if you have built a wireless network before, you may learn a thing or two (we do just about every time we build one).

Chapter 7, "Wireless Router Setup," shows you how to set up the wireless router, which is the heart of your wireless home network. We'll cover how to connect the router to your broadband service and get the wireless part up and running.

Chapter 8, "Wireless NIC Setup," shows you how to set up the wireless NICs on your computers. We'll cover how to get the computers talking to the wireless router. We also show you several different ways of setting up the wireless NICs, including using Windows XP to set up a laptop with a built-in wireless NIC, as well as using a couple of the Linksys programs that come with add-on wireless NICs.

We wrap up Part III with Chapter 9, "Wireless Security Setup," which shows you how to lock down your wireless network with the essential security. This is a critical step in building your wireless home network that unfortunately many people do not take. We will show you how a couple of very simple steps can make your wireless network secure enough and still usable.

Wireless Router Setup

The wireless router is really the brains, or at least the heart, of your home network. The wireless router provides a number of functions, including

- Enabling several computers to connect to your home network either through a wired Ethernet cable or a wireless signal

- Providing a gateway to your broadband Internet connection so that several computers can share it

- Enforcing security policies to protect your home network from unauthorized access

This chapter provides the steps necessary to set up your wireless router, starting with connecting the wireless router to your broadband service. CHapter 8, "Wireless NIC Setup," then walks you through getting wireless NICs to join the wireless network, to get your wireless home network up and running.

The starting assumption is that you already have a broadband Internet connection set up, either to a single computer in your house or with a wired home router. If you do not, we recommend that you read through *Home Networking Simplified*.

Note: It is possible to build a home network without wireless, using a wired router and Ethernet cables. It's also possible to build a home network without a router at all, using ad hoc networking and Internet connection sharing on one of your computers. Both of these types of home networks have significant disadvantages. The focus of this book is on wireless home networks, which offer many advantages over wired and ad hoc home networks, so we will not discuss these other network types further in this book.

Connecting the Wireless Router

The first step to building your wireless home network is to connect the wireless router. The steps to connect the wireless router depend on what you are starting with. Most often you will be starting with a single computer connected to your broadband cable or DSL service, which is typically how the broadband service is required to be installed initially. In this case, do the following:

Step 1 Power off or unplug the cable or DSL modem. It's a good idea to have the wireless router and PC turned off also at this point.

Step 2 Unplug the Ethernet cable from the back of the PC that is connected to the cable or DSL modem.

Step 3 Connect the Ethernet cable just unplugged to the port on the wireless router marked Internet or WAN.

Step 4 Take another Ethernet cable and plug it into the computer where you unplugged the cable in Step 2.

Step 5 Plug the other end of that same cable into a port on the wireless router marked 1. Figure 7-1 shows how the connections should look.

Figure 7-1   Connecting the Wireless Router

Computer with
Wired NIC

Ethernet
Cable

Cable or DSL
Modem

Before

After

Computer with
Wired NIC

Ethernet
Cable

Wireless
Router

Ethernet
Cable

Cable or DSL
Modem

Step 6   Power on the cable or DSL modem first and then the wireless router.

After a minute or two, the cable or DSL modem should finish booting and connect to the broadband service. On the front of the wireless router, the power LED and the LED for Ethernet 1 should be lit (assuming it's a Linksys, that is). The Internet LED may or may not be lit. Ignore it for now. We need to start setting up the wireless router.

Note: If you are upgrading from dial-up to broadband DSL or cable service and your service is not installed yet, it's probably a good idea to wait until the installation has occurred before proceeding with your wireless router setup. You could still set up the wireless router and wireless on your computers, but very often a good way to test the connection is to try and browse the Internet, which you will not be able to do until the broadband service is up and running.

You may be asking yourself, "Why are we setting up a wireless router and the first step is to connect a computer to it with a wired cable?" The answer is that whenever you are making changes to your wireless home network, you want to do so from a computer connected to your wireless router with a wired connection. Sometimes you will change settings on the wireless network that affect the wireless signals. If you are changing settings from a wireless-connected computer, it is possible to "cut off the limb you are standing on," so to speak, meaning you can disconnect yourself inadvertently and not be able to get back into the wireless router over a wireless connection. For this reason, we strongly recommend changing settings from a wired computer.

Configuring the Wireless Router

Now that you have finished connecting the router and it's powered on, you need to tell the router a few things about the home network you want to set up. Out of the box, the wireless router has some default assumptions about what the network should look like, but you need to tailor a few of the options, including what type of broadband service you have, and give a name to your wireless network.

To set up a wireless router, you can access the settings in a couple different ways. Almost all wireless routers provide a way to use your Internet browser (such as Internet Explorer) to access all the different settings on the router in a very straightforward manner, just as easy as filling out a web page on the Internet.

Linksys in particular is simplifying this process even further. When you purchase your wireless router, the box includes a CD that contains a Setup Wizard. The Setup Wizard allows you to quickly enter a few settings and get up and running fast. The Setup Wizard will not allow you to change some of the more advanced settings on the wireless router, however. When we need to set some of these later, we will use a method other than the Setup Wizard.

Finally, Linksys is taking new steps to make home networks easy to set up and manage with a product called EasyLink Advisor.

The following sections cover all three types of setups: with Linksys Setup Wizard, with an Internet browser, and with Linksys EasyLink Advisor. Keep in mind that even if you set up your wireless router now using the Setup Wizard, for example, at some point you will probably decide you want to customize your settings a bit more than the Setup Wizard or EasyLink Advisor allow. In that case, it will be necessary to use the Internet browser method, so it's a good idea to get familiar with that option now. Table 7-1 summarizes the different setup methods.

Table 7-1   Wireless Router Setup Options

	When to Use	Where It Runs	Which Settings Can Be Configured
Linksys Setup Wizard	First-time setup only	On the PC (with wired connection), used to initially set up the wireless router	Basic settings only
Internet browser	First-time or subsequent changes	Any PC or laptop connected to the network (wired highly recommended)	All settings
Linksys EasyLink Advisor	First-time or subsequent changes	On a single computer designated as your administration PC (with a wired connection)	Many settings

Check the instructions that come with the wireless router you buy to see which method(s) is included for setup.

Note: You may be tempted to go ahead and set up some of the security features of the wireless router. In fact, the Setup Wizard and EasyLink Advisor prompt you to do so. We strongly recommend not doing so yet. If you jump the gun, you may have trouble and then not know whether the problem is caused by a basic connection issue or a security feature. Get the wireless router and your computers connected first (which we will do in this chapter and Chapter 8, "Wireless NIC Setup") and then apply the security settings (which we walk through in Chapter 9, "Wireless Security Setup").

Using the Linksys Setup Wizard

The current software setup utility shipping with most Linksys routers is the Setup Wizard. The steps for setting up the wireless router with this program are as follows (the Linksys WRT54G is shown as an example):

Step 1   Insert the CD containing the Setup Wizard in the CD or DVD drive of your computer.

Step 2   The Setup Wizard should start automatically. If it does not, access the CD drive using My Computer and double-click the **Setup.exe** program file.

Step 3   Click **Click Here To Start** as shown in Figure 7-2.

Figure 7-2   Starting the Linksys Setup Wizard

Note: Some of the figures contain a step number in a big black circle on the dialog box. This step number does not correspond to the steps that follow, so do not pay much attention to them.

Step 4   Several steps will be displayed to guide you through the connection steps that we finished in the previous section. You do not need to repeat these steps. Just click **Next**. The last step is shown in Figure 7-3. We skipped showing all the steps to save some space.

Figure 7-3   Guided Connection of Cables

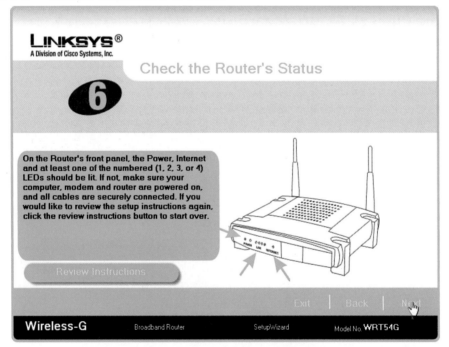

Note: The Linksys Setup Wizard indicates in Figure 7-3 that the Internet LED should be lit. This may or may not be the case. If it is lit, it is because the default out-of-the-box setup happened to match your broadband Internet service settings. It's quite possible the default settings will not match and the LED will not be lit. This is normal, so just move on with the rest of the steps.

Step 5   If you have cable as your broadband Internet service, set the Internet Type to **DHCP**, as shown in Figure 7-4. Click **Next**. Skip Steps 6 and 7.

Figure 7-4   Set Internet Type to DHCP for Cable

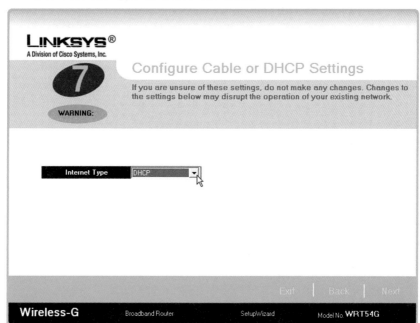

Step 6   If you have DSL as your broadband Internet service, set the Internet Type to **PPPoE**, as shown in Figure 7-5. Enter the username and password for the DSL service from your DSL provider. Click **Next**. Skip Step 7.

Figure 7-5   Set Internet Type to PPPoE for DSL

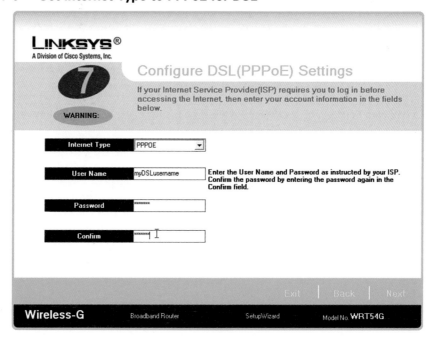

Step 7   If you have DSL or cable as your broadband Internet service, and have a static IP address from your provider (you usually have to specifically request this and pay extra for it), set the Internet Type to **Static IP**, as shown in Figure 7-6. Enter in the fields provided the IP address, subnet mask, gateway, and DNS addresses given to you by your broadband provider. Click **Next**.

Figure 7-6   Set Internet Type to Static IP for a Static IP Address

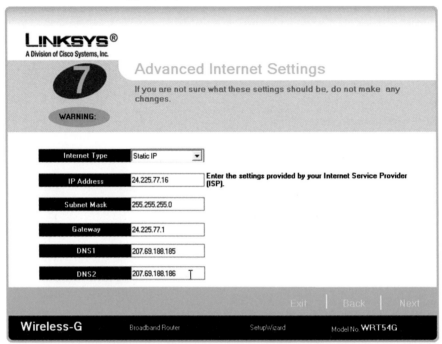

Step 8   Enter a new password for the wireless router, as shown in Figure 7-7. This password is to enable you to protect who can log in to the router and change its settings. Choose a strong password (as described in Chapter 9). Write it down. Click **Next**.

Step 9   The Setup Wizard checks to see if the Internet connection was set up correctly and is working, as shown in Figure 7-8. If it is confirmed to be working, the wizard proceeds with the next step; otherwise, the wizard asks whether you want to try repairing the connection.

Figure 7-7   Change the Router's Administrative Password

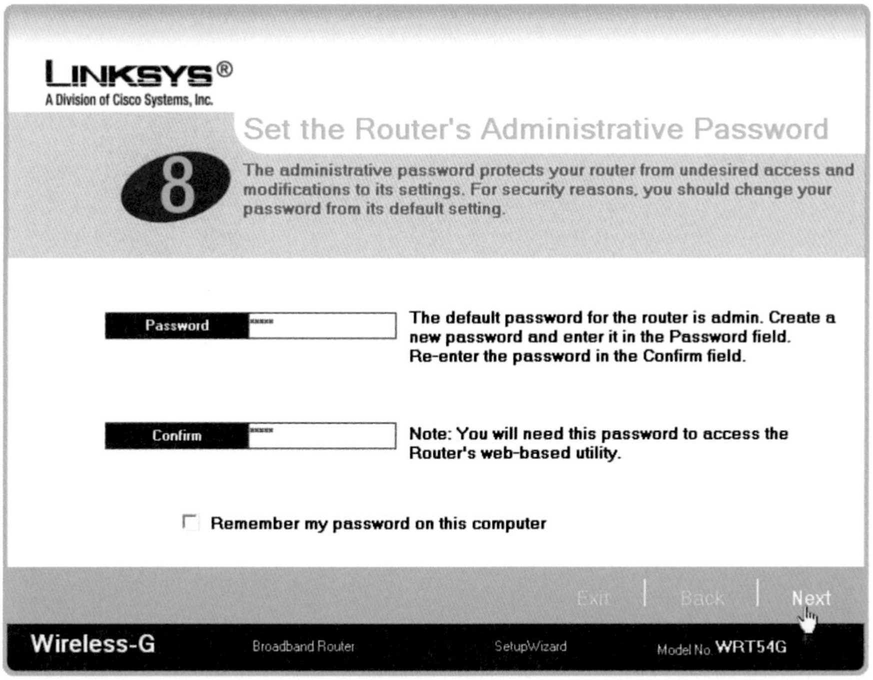

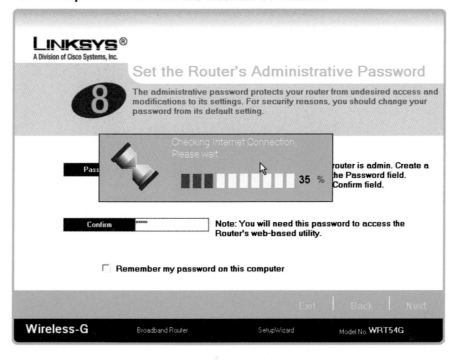

Figure 7-8   Setup Wizard Checks the Internet Connection

Step 10 If the wireless router you are using supports the Linksys SecureEasySetup feature, you may see a screen such as shown in Figure 7-9. Click **Skip**.

Figure 7-9   SecureEasySetup Screen (if available)

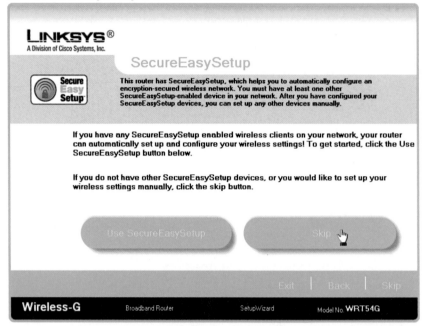

Step 11   Enter the SSID you have chosen for your wireless network, as shown in Figure 7-10 (KF34DC3 in this example). Write it down. Keep the channel at the default setting. Click **Next**.

Figure 7-10   Set the SSID for the Wireless Network

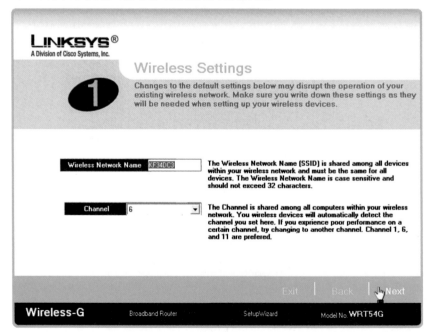

Step 12 Set the Security setting to **Disable**, as shown in Figure 7-11. We will take care of the security settings later (in Chapter 9) after we make sure the network is operating properly. Click **Next**.

Figure 7-11   Leave Wireless Security Disabled for Now

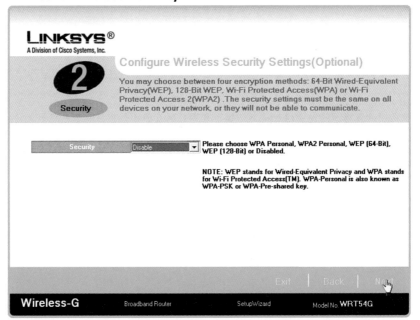

Step 13 Confirm the wireless router settings, as shown in Figure 7-12. Under New Settings, you should see the SSID you have chosen, the default channel number, and that encryption is disabled. Click **Save Settings**.

Figure 7-12   Confirm and Save the Settings

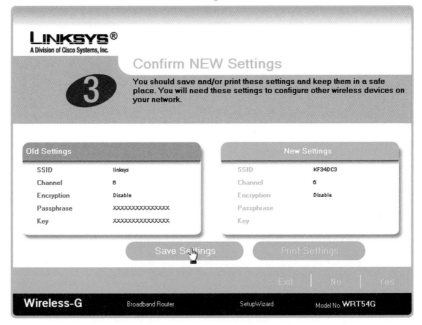

Step 14   As shown in Figure 7-13, that is the end of the setup process. Click **Exit**.

Figure 7-13   Successful Setup

The wireless router should now be set up, connected to the Internet, and broadcasting the wireless signal for your home network.

To test the Internet connection, launch your Internet browser (such as Internet Explorer) and try browsing a web page.

Unfortunately, the Setup Wizard does not provide confirmation that the wireless network is working as planned. We will have to wait until we connect a wireless computer in Chapter 8.

Using an Internet Browser

As mentioned before, the Setup Wizard is a really good approach the first time you set up the wireless router. After that, you are going to want to familiarize yourself with using an Internet browser to change the settings on your wireless router.

Note: If you used the Setup Wizard to set up the wireless router, you do not need to repeat the steps that follow. They essentially do the same thing, just using the Internet browser method instead. As mentioned earlier, using the Internet browser allows you to configure a lot more settings than the Setup Wizard.

The steps for setting up the wireless router with a browser are as follows (the Linksys WRT54G is shown as an example):

Step 1 Start the Internet browser you use (such as Internet Explorer). Type **192.168.1.1** in the Address field, as shown in Figure 7-14, and click **Go**. This is the default IP address of Linksys routers out of the box.

Note: The default IP address used by Linksys wireless routers is 192.168.1.1. Wireless routers from other manufacturers could use a different default, so consult the user guide to see what the default is.

Figure 7-14   Point Your Internet Browser to the Wireless Router

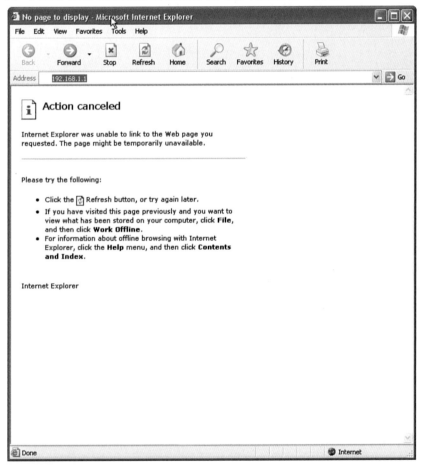

Step 2 You are prompted for the wireless router's username and password, as shown in Figure 7-15. Enter the default for Linksys routers, which is **admin** for the User Name field and **admin** for the password. Click **OK**.

Figure 7-15 Enter the Username and Password for the Wireless Router

Step 3 If you have cable as your broadband Internet service, set the Internet Connection Type to **Automatic Configuration – DHCP**, as shown in Figure 7-16. Click **Save Settings**. Skip Steps 4 and 5.

Figure 7-16 Set Internet Connection Type to DHCP for Cable

Step 4   If you have DSL as your broadband Internet service, set the Internet Connection Type to **PPPoE**, as shown in Figure 7-17. Enter the username and password for the DSL service from your DSL provider. Click **Save Settings**. Skip Step 5.

Figure 7-17   Set Internet Connection Type to PPPoE for DSL

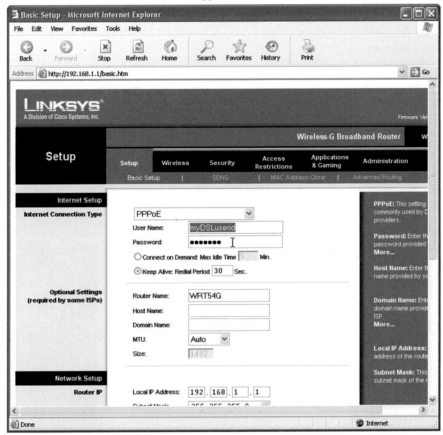

Step 5   If you have DSL or cable as your broadband Internet service and have been assigned a static IP address (typically you must request this for a specific reason and pay extra), set the Internet Connection Type to **Static IP**, as shown in Figure 7-18. Enter in the fields provided the Internet IP address, subnet mask, gateway, and static DNS addresses given to you by your broadband provider. Click **Save Settings**.

Figure 7-18   Set Internet Connection Type to Static IP for Broadband with Static IP Addresses

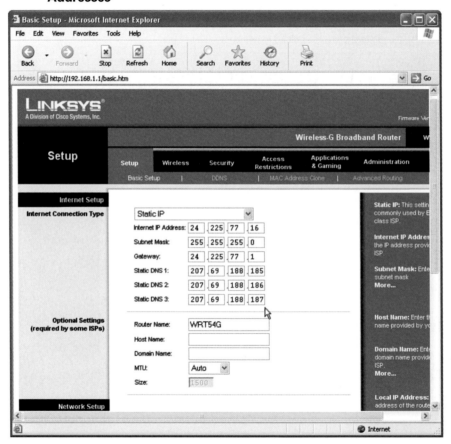

Step 6   Click the **Administration** tab near the top of the browser and then click the **Management** subtab. Enter a new password for the wireless router, as shown in Figure 7-19. This password is to enable you to protect who can log in to the router and change its settings. Choose a strong password. Write it down. Click **Save Settings**. You may be prompted to log in again to the router using the new password.

Figure 7-19   Change the Router's Administrative Password

Step 7 Click the **Wireless** tab and then click the **Basic Wireless Settings** subtab. Enter the SSID you have chosen for your wireless network, as shown in Figure 7-20 (KF34DC3 in this example). Keep Wireless Channel at the default setting. Click **Save Settings**.

Figure 7-20 Set the SSID for the Wireless Network

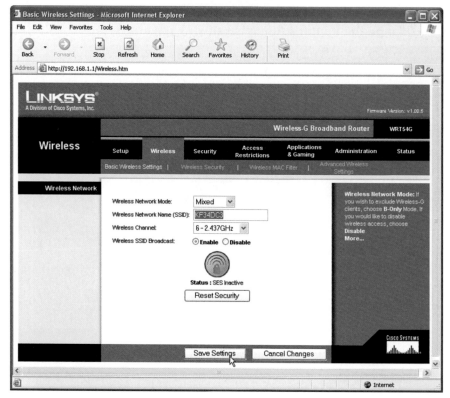

Step 8 Click the **Wireless Security** subtab. Verify the Security Mode is set to **Disabled**, as shown in Figure 7-21. We will take care of the security settings later, in Chapter 9, after we make sure the network is operating properly. Click **Save Settings**.

The wireless router should now be set up, connected to the Internet, and broadcasting the wireless signal for your home network. To test the Internet connection, start your Internet browser (such as Internet Explorer) and try browsing a web page.

To confirm that the wireless network is working as planned, we will have to wait until we connect a wireless computer (in Chapter 8).

Figure 7-21   Leave Wireless Security Disabled for Now

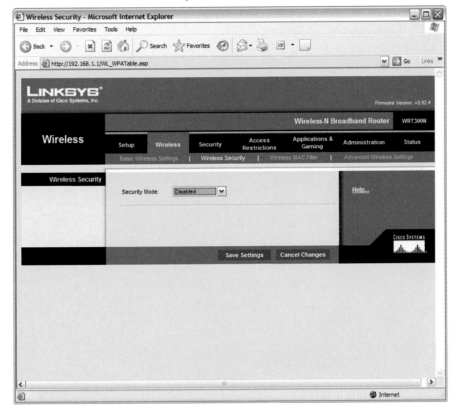

Using Linksys EasyLink Advisor

The newest software setup utility for Linksys routers (at the time of this book's publication) is the EasyLink Advisor program.

EasyLink Advisor is different from the two methods described previously. The Setup Wizard runs one time (for the most part) on a computer connected to the router with a wired connection. The Internet browser can be used any time you want to change settings on the wireless router.

In comparison, EasyLink Advisor is a program that is installed on a designated computer on your home network; one with a wired connection to the wireless router. The program keeps a database of the settings for the router on that computer, and it can be used anytime to monitor the network status, change settings, add new computers and devices, and so on.

The steps for setting up the wireless router with Linksys EasyLink Advisor are as follows (the Linksys WRT54G is shown as an example):

Step 1   Insert the CD containing the EasyLink Advisor software in the CD or DVD drive of your computer.

Step 2   The installation should start automatically. If it does not, access the CD drive using My Computer and double-click the **EasylinkAdvisorWeb.exe** program file.

Note: If you have a personal software firewall program installed on the computer that you are installing EasyLink Advisor on, it may block EasyLink from accessing your wireless router. Click **Allow** when your personal software firewall asks if you want to allow EasyLink to access the Internet (and router), or temporarily disable the software firewall while you are setting up your network.

Step 3   After installation the program will launch, as shown in Figure 7-22.

Figure 7-22   Starting Linksys EasyLink Advisor

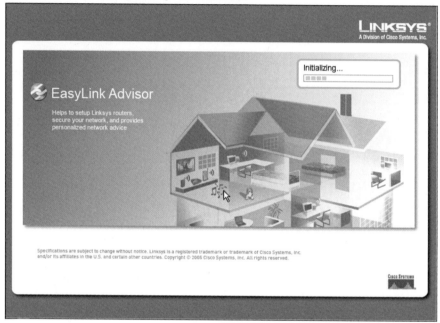

Step 4   EasyLink asks for a network name, as shown in Figure 7-23. Enter a name for your network (we used KF34DC3 in this example). The name cannot contain any spaces or special characters because EasyLink also uses this name for the SSID of your wireless network. Click **Next**.

Step 5   EasyLink scans the network, as shown in Figure 7-24. It first tries to configure the settings for cable broadband, and then, if unsuccessful, prompts you for your DSL username and password.

Figure 7-23   Setting the Network Name

Figure 7-24   EasyLink Scanning Your Network

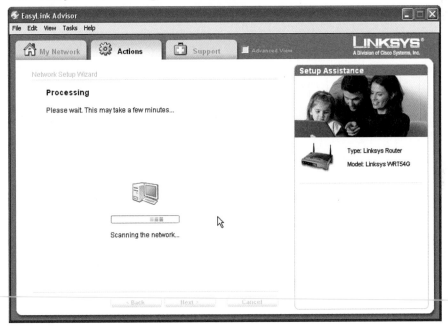

Step 6   EasyLink asks you to visually confirm that the wireless router LEDs are lit appropriately, as shown in Figure 7-25. Check your router and click **Next** after confirming.

Figure 7-25   Visually Confirm the Wireless Router Operation

Step 7   EasyLink asks if you want to turn on wireless security, as shown in Figure 7-26. As in the previous sections, we recommend not turning it on at this point. We will take care of the security settings later, in Chapter 9, after we make sure the network is operating properly. Click the **Turn Off Wireless Security** radio button and click **Next**.

Figure 7-26   Leave Wireless Security Disabled for Now

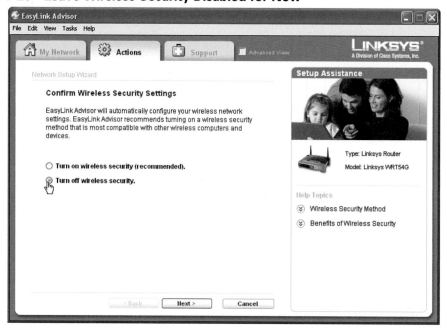

Step 8 EasyLink confirms that the wireless network is set up properly, including the broadband Internet access, as shown in Figure 7-27. Click **Click Here to Test Your Internet Connection with Your Web Browser**, which starts your Internet browser. If you can browse a web page, great. If not, see the troubleshooting suggestions on the right side of the window and also the troubleshooting chapters later in this book (Chapters 10 through 12). Click **Finish** when done.

Figure 7-27   Wireless Network Is Now Set Up

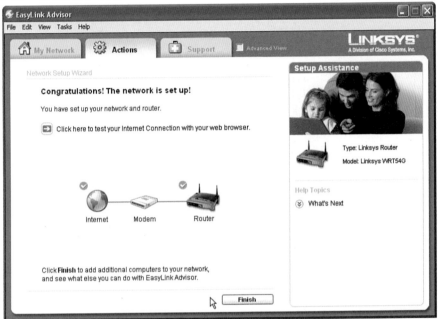

Step 9 Click the **My Network** tab, as shown in Figure 7-28. Starting at the top left, your ISP is displayed, then the broadband modem, followed by your wireless router. Underneath the wireless router you will see the computers (and other devices) connected to your home network. Right now only the computer we used to set up the network is shown.

Note: At the time this book was written, EasyLink Advisor did not provide a means to change the administrator password on the router. We recommend doing so (for security reasons). So if you use EasyLink to set up and manage your home network, we recommend using the Internet browser method to change the password. EasyLink will try to access the router using the default password (admin) and then prompt you for the new password you assigned, so that it can still communicate with the router.

Figure 7-28   EasyLink Graphical View of Your Network

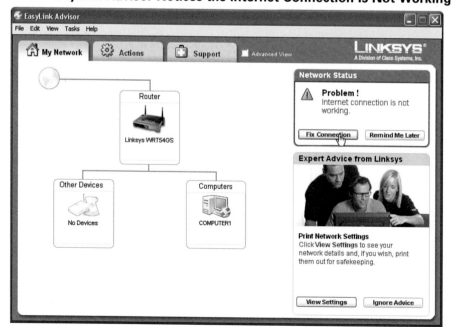

Figure 7-28 shows what the initial network should look like if things are working properly, including connectivity to the Internet. EasyLink Advisor can also help troubleshoot when something is not quite right. If, for example, the Internet connectivity is not working properly, EasyLink tells you, as shown in Figure 7-29.

Figure 7-29   EasyLink Advisor Notices the Internet Connection Is Not Working

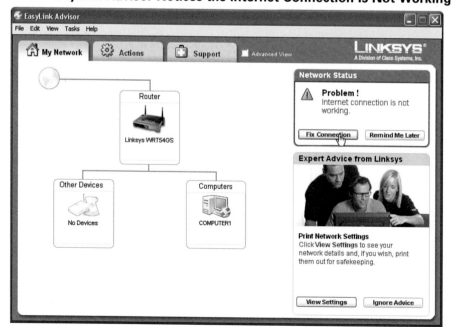

If you click **Fix Connection**, EasyLink Advisor will walk you through different steps to help you find out what is wrong. Figure 7-30 shows an example of EasyLink suggesting to reboot the wireless router and shows the steps to do so.

Figure 7-30   EasyLink Advisor Advises How to Fix the Internet Connection

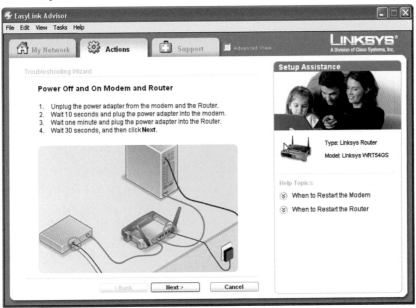

After one of the steps is successful at repairing the Internet connection, EasyLink Advisor shows that the connection is working, as shown in Figure 7-31.

Figure 7-31   EasyLink Advisor Shows the Internet Connection Status Working

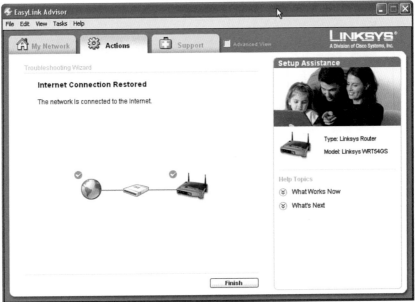

As you can see, EasyLink Advisor provides an easy way to set up your home wireless network. Keep in mind that EasyLink is not just for setup, but also for making ongoing changes and additions to your home network.

Chapter 8 shows how to use EasyLink to add computers to the network, and Chapter 9 shows how to turn on wireless security with EasyLink.

Summary

There are a couple of methods for setting up the wireless router in your home network. It's getting easier and easier to do so.

The Linksys Setup Wizard is an easy way to set up the network initially but does not provide a good way to make ongoing changes.

Using an Internet browser to access and change the router settings provides access to all the settings in the router. At some point you will likely have to change a setting that the other setup utilities do not enable you to change, so it's a good idea to be familiar with this method even if you use an auto-mated program (like the Setup Wizard or EasyLink Advisor) to set up the wireless network.

EasyLink Advisor is both a setup tool and a good way to make ongoing changes and additions to your home network. As Linksys evolves this program, it will provide more extensive capabilities for easy management of your home network.

When you purchase your Linksys wireless router, it will come with a CD containing either the Linksys Setup Wizard or the Linksys EasyLink Advisor. Use whichever one comes with your wireless router. You use the Setup Wizard only once, and then switch to using the Internet browser to make further changes. EasyLink Advisor can be used for both initial setup and ongoing changes; however, there may be settings that you cannot perform with EasyLink Advisor, and in those cases you should just use the Internet browser to set them.

Where to Go for More Information

For more information about Linksys EasyLink Advisor, go to the Linksys main website: www.linksys.com.

Check out Bradley Mitchell's article on About.com titled "Networking with a Router": http://compnetworking.about.com/od/homenetworking/a/routernetworks.htm.

Wireless NIC Setup

Each computer or device that you want to join your wireless network needs a wireless network interface card (NIC). A wireless NIC provides a number of functions, including

- Enabling a computer (or device) to connect to your home network through a wireless signal

- Securing the communications path between the wireless router and your computers and devices connected over wireless

- Providing a way for you to connect your computer to other wireless networks outside your home

This chapter provides the steps necessary to set up your wireless NICs, getting them to communicate with your wireless home network. The starting assumption is that you have already completed the wireless router setup in Chapter 7, "Wireless Router Setup."

Installing the Wireless NIC

There are several types of wireless NICs to consider (as introduced in Chapter 6), including

- **PCI card**—Installs inside a desktop PC

- **PCMCIA or ExpressCard**—Plugs into a laptop

- **Integrated**—Is already built into a laptop

- **USB**—Plugs into the USB port of any computer

If you have a laptop, first check whether it already contains an integrated wireless NIC. If it does, then you are all set. If your laptop does not have a built-in wireless NIC (or if it does but not the wireless standard you want to use), then the best option is to buy a PCMCIA wireless card.

If you have a desktop (or tower) PC, check whether it already contains an integrated wireless NIC, because (although not that common) some are now shipped with one. If not, then you have two options:

- Buy a PCI wireless card that installs inside the computer in an open card slot

- Buy a USB wireless NIC that plugs into any open USB port

USB NICs are handy because you can avoid opening up a computer to install them, but they do provide another box (albeit a little one) to add to a cluttered computer desk. USB is also an option for laptops, but they are a bit unwieldy on the go, so most people opt for a PCMCIA card.

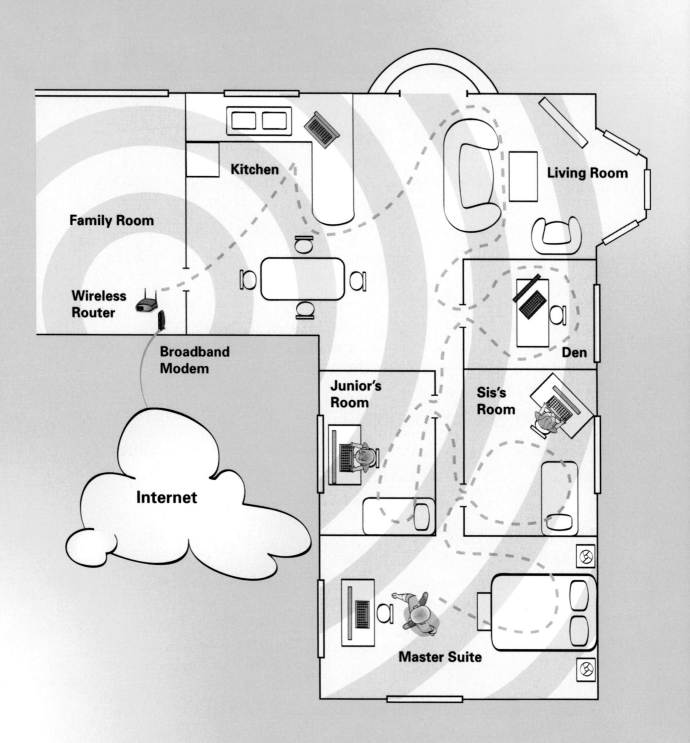

If you have an older PC or an early version of the Xbox, then there's a good chance that you either don't have a USB port or do have one but it is taken up by something else such as a printer. In this case, a wireless Ethernet bridge is a good alternative. It works just like a wireless USB NIC, except that it plugs into your Ethernet port, essentially changing a wired port to a wireless one.

Note: By the way, USB wireless NICs may also be a good option for other devices you want to connect to your wireless network, such as a DVR or video game console. However, make sure that the device supports the specific USB wireless NIC, because they are not as universally supported as they are in PCs. We will discuss some of these options more in Chapter 13, "Wireless Video and Entertainment," which explains how to connect entertainment devices to your wireless network.

The next few sections discuss installing the different types of wireless NICs. Skip to the sections that match the types of NICs you chose for the computers to connect to the network. In general, there are two types of installation procedures:

- Load software from a CD that comes with the NIC and then actually plug the NIC into the PC or laptop

- Plug the NIC into the PC or laptop, and then Windows XP performs an auto-install, possibly asking for the CD that comes with the NIC

Which type you follow depends on the type of NIC and the version of Windows you are running. If you are running a Windows version older than XP (such as 2000, 98SE, and so on), you will likely follow the first type. If you are running Windows XP or Vista, you will likely follow the second type. However, you should look at the quick setup instruction sheet that comes with the wireless NIC to see which is recommended.

Installing a PCI Wireless Card in a Desktop Computer

To install a PCI wireless card in a desktop computer, follow the manufacturer instructions that came with the card you purchased. In general, you will do the following:

Step 1   Shut off and unplug the PC and then open it up. This is typically done by removing the screws on the outer edge of the back of the computer. Once the screws are off, the outer casing should slide off (see the user manual for your computer for how to remove its cover).

Caution: Because of the potential damage that can be caused by static electric discharge, it's a good idea to take precautions so that you don't zap your computer. As long as you don't shuffle across your shag carpet wearing your socks or play with balloons beforehand, you're probably okay. But you should touch a metal doorframe or doorknob to discharge yourself.

Step 2   Plug the new NIC into an available slot (see Figure 8-1).

Figure 8-1   Installing a PCI Wireless Card

Step 3   Close up the computer.

Step 4   Turn on your computer and let your operating system boot.

Step 5   Windows may have all the drivers needed, or it may need to copy some from the CD that came with your NIC. If you are prompted to do so, put the CD into your CD drive.

Step 6   The install program on the CD should start by itself. If it does not, open a directory window and double-click the install or setup icon in the CD directory.

Again, for some installations you will insert the card first, for others you will run a setup utility from a CD first, and then plug in the card. Look at the quick setup instruction sheet that comes with the wireless card to see which you should do. Make sure to consider which Windows version you are using. Many setup instructions will have one set of instructions for Windows XP/Vista and another for older versions of Windows.

Installing a PCMCIA Wireless Card in a Laptop Computer

To install an PCMCIA NIC in a laptop, plug the NIC into an available PCMCIA slot in your laptop. Again, look at the quick setup instruction sheet that comes with the wireless card to see if you should run a setup utility from the CD first or plug the card in first.

The following steps install a PCMCIA wireless card from Linksys (WPC54G) into a laptop running Windows XP:

Step 1   Insert the CD that came with the wireless card in your CD or DVD drive. The setup program should start automatically. If it does not, browse the files on the CD and double-click the install program to start it. Click **Click Here to Start** (see Figure 8-2).

Figure 8-2   Installing a PCMCIA Wireless Card (Linksys WPC54G)

Step 2   When the setup utility prompts you to do so, insert the PCMCIA wireless card into an available slot in the laptop (see Figure 8-3).

Figure 8-3   Plugging in a PCMCIA Wireless Card

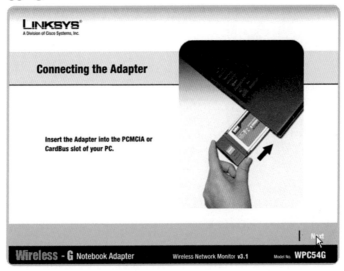

You generally do not need to shut down the laptop, just plug in the card.

Installing a USB Wireless NIC in a Computer

Let's take one example of installing a USB wireless NIC from Linksys (WUSB54G) into a computer running Windows XP. In this case, the setup instructions tell us to plug the USB NIC in first, and then insert the CD if Windows XP asks for it.

Step 1   Connect one end of the USB cable to the wireless NIC (see Figure 8-4) and the other to an open USB port on your computer (desktop, tower, or laptop).

Figure 8-4   Connect the USB Wireless NIC

Step 2   Windows XP detects the new hardware plugged into the computer and starts the process of installing the software. Check the **Install the Software Automatically** check box and click **Next** (see Figure 8-5).

Figure 8-5   Windows XP Detects the New Hardware

Step 3   Windows XP locates the software drivers for the USB wireless NIC (see Figure 8-6). If it cannot locate them automatically, it may prompt you to insert the CD that came with the NIC when you bought it. Click **Next**.

Figure 8-6   Windows XP Locates the Driver Software

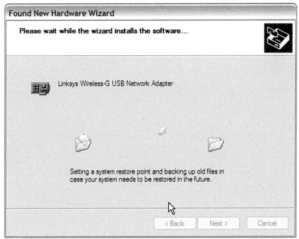

Step 4   The install was successful (see Figure 8-7). Click **Finish**.

Figure 8-7   Installation Is Complete

You generally do not need to shut down the computer, just plug in the USB NIC. Because the wireless USB NIC gets its power from the computer it is connected to through the USB cable, you do not need to worry about a power cord.

Associating the Wireless NIC to the Wireless Router

The next step after installing the wireless NIC is to "teach it" how to find and communicate with your wireless router (that you installed in Chapter 7).

Whenever your wireless NIC is enabled and turned on, it starts scanning for a wireless router to communicate with, much like when you turn on your cell phone and it immediately starts searching for a cell tower to connect to.

It's quite possible (likely, even) that your NIC will be able to see signals from two or more wireless routers. Figure 8-8 in the next section shows an example where we can see the signals from our own wireless router, but also from a neighbor's and from a coffee shop's across the street. So how does the NIC know which is your router?

The answer is the SSID. Remember in Chapter 7 that when we set up our wireless router we assigned it a unique name for our wireless network (KF34DC3 in our example). Each wireless router (and access point) identifies itself using its assigned SSID. So, for our NIC to communicate with our router, we have to tell it which SSID to look for.

Note: One question that comes up is what happens if two wireless routers use the same SSID? The answer depends somewhat on your wireless NIC, but in general the NIC will pick the strongest signal it sees and try to associate to that wireless router. In most cases, "strongest" means the one in your house, but that is not always the case. If your neighbor's wireless router has a stronger signal than yours and you are both using the same SSID, it's very possible your NIC will try to associate with their router, not yours. This is another reason it's very important to pick a unique SSID for your network.

Wireless Profiles

The process of "teaching" NICs how to talk to a wireless router is called managing wireless connections. The process of managing wireless connections is pretty simple for desktop computers and other devices that never leave your home, because you have to manage those connections just once. For laptops, it's a little more complicated, because you may want to connect to your wireless router when you are home, and to other wireless connections when you are not at home (for example, at work, at the airport or a hotel, at a coffee shop, and so on).

If wireless NICs could only remember how to connect to a single wireless router, we would have to reprogram the NIC every time we wanted to connect to a different wireless signal (see Figure 8-8).

Fortunately, we can use any number of wireless connection managers and create a set of wireless profiles. Each profile contains the critical information the NIC needs to know to remember how to connect to a wireless router. Profiles can include the SSID, the type of wireless security being used, the encryption key (see Chapter 9, "Wireless Security Setup"), and other information.

Then, when the wireless NIC encounters wireless signals, it compares the information being advertised by the wireless router with the stored profiles to see if there is a match. In the example shown in Figure 8-9, the wireless NIC has three wireless profiles configured, named Home, Work, and Hotel. The SSIDs for these three wireless networks are KF34DC3, Corporate-G, and StayWithUs, respectively.

Figure 8-8   Wireless NIC Scanning for Wireless Networks

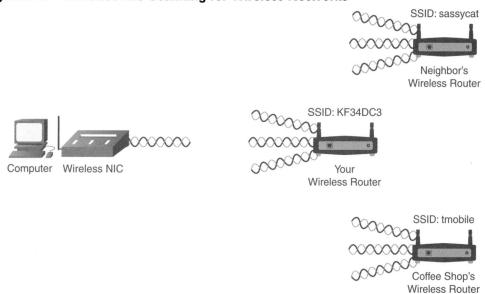

Figure 8-9   Matching Wireless Profiles to Available Wireless Networks

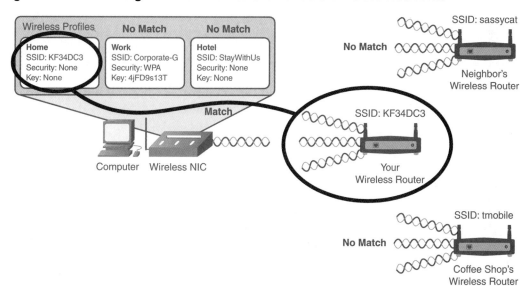

In this example, the wireless NIC scans for signals (much like a cell phone scans for cellular towers) and detects three wireless signals with SSIDs: sassycat, KF34DC3, and tmobile. The wireless NIC matches the profile for the Home network to the wireless router advertising the same SSID and then tries to associate to it.

Associating is kind of like seeing someone who looks familiar at a party. From a distance it looks like Ned Flanders. So you walk over to take a closer look and say, "Aren't you Ned Flanders? Didn't we go to high school together?" Ned answers, "Yes, of course," and you have a lengthy conversation about the good old days…'65 Mustangs, Def Leppard, blonde girls who feathered their hair like Farrah Fawcett. Ah, let's pause a moment to reminisce.

Wireless association is very similar. The wireless NIC sees a signal that has the same SSID as one in its set of profiles. It attempts to associate by starting a conversation with the wireless router, sending certain signals to let the router know the NIC is there and wants to communicate. The wireless router may grant access or may not. In addition to the SSID, if wireless security is enabled, those parameters must match also (including type of encryption, encryption key, and so on). We will cover more on wireless security in Chapter 9.

If the wireless router grants access, it then typically assigns the NIC an IP address to use on the wireless network, at which point we can begin exchanging data. If it denies access for some reason (maybe we are not speaking the same wireless security language or are not authorized to use that wireless signal), the association fails and we must keep trying other wireless router signals until we find one to associate with.

Wireless Connection Managers

Wireless connection managers are programs that let you manage the wireless profiles in your computer, and which one you are currently connected to. If you use your computer only at home, such as a desktop PC or some other device that does not leave your home, you will typically use the wireless connection manager when you first set up your wireless network, and maybe again if you make changes. In this case you will likely also have only a single wireless profile: your home network.

If you own a laptop, chances are you will have several wireless profiles, including your home wireless network and several other profiles for traveling. Chapter 14, "Wireless to Go," covers how to use wireless outside your home.

There are several types of wireless connection managers, including

- Windows Wireless Network Connection utility

- Linksys WLAN Monitor utility

- Other programs such as Boingo

In this chapter we show the Windows Wireless Network Connection utility and the Linksys WLAN Monitor utility. We cover other programs such as Boingo in Chapter 14.

Starting with Windows XP and continuing with Vista (also available via patch updates for Windows 2000), it is possible to manage wireless connections within Windows, and not require an add-on program. This is the long-term direction for wireless NIC management: letting Windows manage the devices just like most other devices in the PC or laptop.

If managing your wireless NIC using Windows is supported, it is probably the best option. For those NICs that you cannot manage with Windows, you need an add-on program from the NIC manufacturer. These cases include

- NICs that use a very new wireless standard or type of wireless security that is not yet supported by Windows

- Wireless NICs from manufacturers that force you to use their specific software

Reference the documentation that comes with the wireless NIC you purchase to see if Windows can be used to manage the NIC or if you must install a program provided by the manufacturer. We expect the vast majority of wireless NICs will use Windows for wireless connection management.

As a final note, you typically use either the Windows Wireless Network Connection utility or a manufacturer's utility, such as Linksys WLAN Monitor, and not both. Most commonly, the two options are mutually exclusive, meaning you cannot use both at the same time.

Using the Windows Wireless Network Connection Utility

Let's look at an example of using the built-in wireless connection manager functionality of Windows XP to manage the USB wireless NIC we installed earlier (Linksys WUSB54G). The steps to associate the NIC to the wireless router are as follows:

Step 1   Choose **Start > Connect To > Show All Connections**. Select the USB wireless NIC on the right side of the dialog box and then click **View Available Wireless Networks** on the left side. (See Figure 8-10.)

Figure 8-10   Locate the Wireless NIC

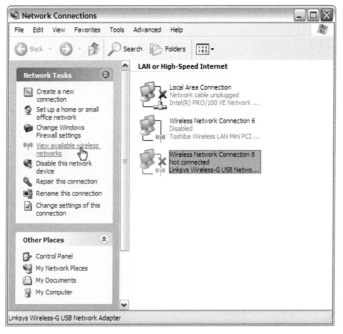

Step 2   You will see a list of available wireless network signals, as shown in Figure 8-11. If you do not, try clicking **Refresh Network List**. Locate your wireless network in the list. The SSID you chose should be displayed (in our example we used KF34DC3). Select it and click **Connect**.

Note: If your wireless NIC is managed using a manufacturer's proprietary utility, such as Linksys WLAN Monitor, and you attempt to use the Windows Wireless Network Connection utility, you will see a message such as "Windows cannot configure this wireless connection." In that case, you need to use the manufacturer's utility or disable that utility and let Windows manage the NIC before proceeding.

Figure 8-11   Connect to the Wireless Router

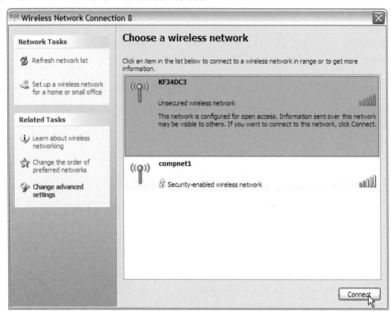

Step 3   You may be prompted that you are connecting to an unsecured wireless network, as shown in Figure 8-12. This is because we have not enabled wireless security yet (which we do not recommend doing yet, but we will do it in Chapter 9). Click **Connect Anyway**.

Figure 8-12   Confirm Connection to an Unsecured Wireless Network

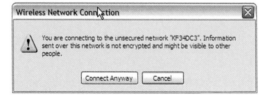

Step 4   The NIC will associate to the wireless router. The status will change to Connected in the dialog box to view available wireless networks, as shown in Figure 8-13.

Figure 8-13   Connected to Wireless Network

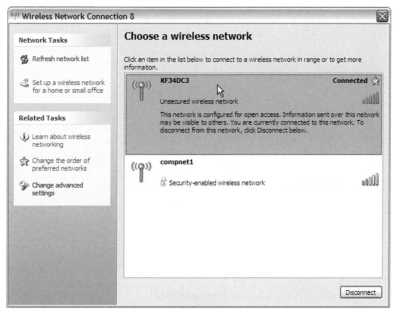

You can test the connection by trying to browse the Internet. Launch your web browser (such as Internet Explorer) and see if you can browse a web page.

Using Linksys WLAN Monitor

Now let's look at an example of using the Linksys WLAN Monitor program to manage the PCMCIA wireless NIC we installed earlier (Linksys WPC54G). The steps to associate the NIC to the wireless router are as follows:

Step 1   Launch the WLAN Monitor utility by double-clicking the icon on the running tasks taskbar (lower right of your screen) or choose **Start > Linksys Wireless Card > WLAN Monitor** and then click **Site Survey**. Locate your wireless network in the list (see Figure 8-14). The SSID you chose should be displayed (in our example we used KF34DC3). Select it and click **Connect**.

Step 2   Click the **Link Information** tab. If the wireless NIC connects properly to the wireless router, you will see green bars in the Signal Strength and Signal Quality boxes on the dialog box, as shown in Figure 8-15. Strength in this case measures the power your NIC is sensing, and quality is a measure of the speed (data rate) you are getting as compared to the maximum amount possible.

Figure 8-14   Perform a Site Survey and Connect

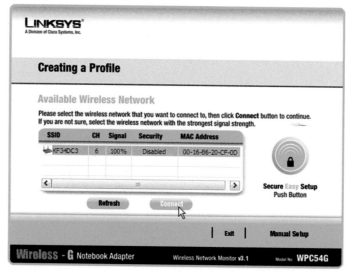

Figure 8-15   Verify Connection to the Wireless Router

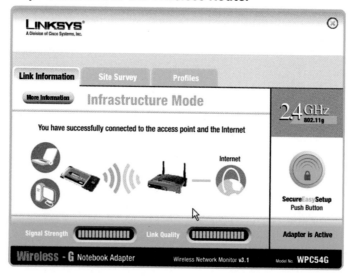

Step 3   Click **More Information**. You will see the status information for the wireless network and a display of the wireless parameters, including the SSID, security, and so on, as shown in Figure 8-16. Click **Save to Profile**. Remember that the name of the profile can be (and probably should be) different from your SSID name.

Step 4   You are prompted for a name for the wireless profile, as shown in Figure 8-17. Enter a descriptive name (we chose "home network" for this example). Click **OK**.

Figure 8-16   Save the Connection as a Wireless Profile

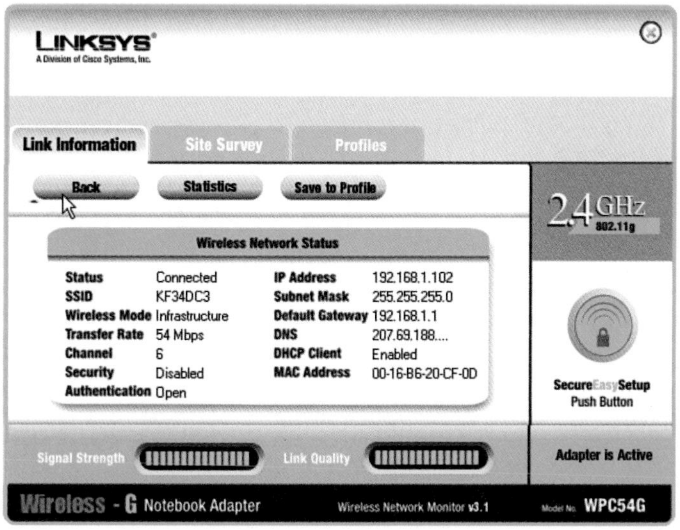

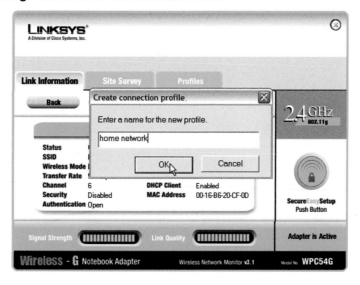

Figure 8-17   Assign a Name to the Wireless Profile

You can test the connection by trying to browse the Internet. Launch your web browser (such as Internet Explorer) and see if you can browse a web page.

Using Linksys EasyLink Advisor

As discussed in Chapter 7 on setting up the wireless router, there is a new software setup utility for Linksys routers (under development at the time this book was written) named EasyLink Advisor. EasyLink provides a simplified way to set up wireless routers.

EasyLink can also aid in the setup of wireless NICs. Before starting, you need a USB memory stick. If the computer is running Windows XP, we can use EasyLink to create a wireless profile on a USB memory stick, and then simply plug that USB memory stick into the computer we want to add, automatically creating the wireless profile. As you'll see later in this section, several steps are involved, but they are all straightforward.

 Note: At the time this book was written, using a USB memory key to add a computer to a wireless network using EasyLink Advisor only works for computers running Windows XP and higher, and only when using the Windows Wireless Network Connection utility to manage wireless NICs. It does not work if a separate program utility is required to manage wireless NICs, including the Linksys WLAN Monitor program or other manufacturers' wireless connection manager programs.

If you are using an older version of Windows (for example, Windows 2000 or 98SE), the EasyLink program helps you print out the wireless profile data you need. Then you have to use the printout to manually set up your wireless NIC using a wireless connection manager program, like the example shown in the preceding section for the Linksys WLAN Monitor program.

The following example uses a Linksys WRT54G wireless router and two computers with wireless NICs, both running Windows XP:

Step 1   On the computer with Linksys EasyLink Advisor installed, launch the EasyLink Advisor program by double-clicking the icon on the running tasks taskbar or by choosing **Start > Programs > Linksys EasyLink Advisor**. Click the **Actions** tab and then click **Add an Additional Computer to This Network**, as shown in Figure 8-18.

Figure 8-18   Adding a Computer with Linksys EasyLink Advisor

Step 2   Select **Wireless**, as shown in Figure 8-19. Click **Next**.

Figure 8-19   Select Wireless to Add a Wireless-Connected Computer

Step 3   If you are using at least Windows XP or higher, select **Yes, It Uses Windows XP**, as shown in Figure 8-20. Click **Next**.

Figure 8-20   Verify It Is a Windows XP Computer

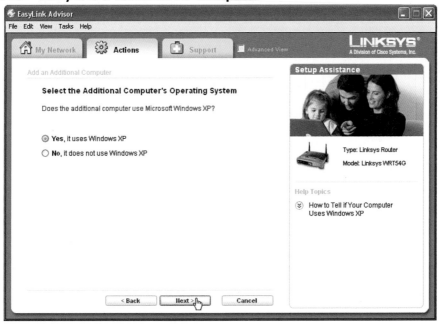

Step 4   EasyLink asks if you want to set up the computer with a network cable, as shown in Figure 8-21. Click **No, I Do Not Have an Extra Network Cable** and then click **Next**.

Figure 8-21   Bypass the Network Cable Setup

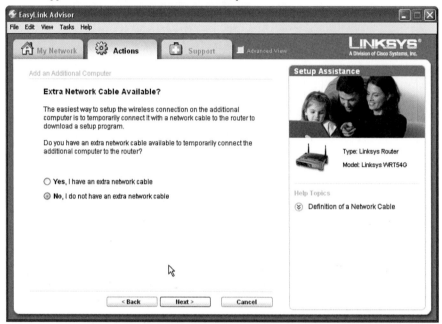

Step 5   Click **Yes, I Have a Removable Media Device**, as shown in Figure 8-22. Plug a USB memory stick into an open USB port on the computer running EasyLink and click **Next**.

Figure 8-22   Choose to Set Up Using a Removable USB Memory Key

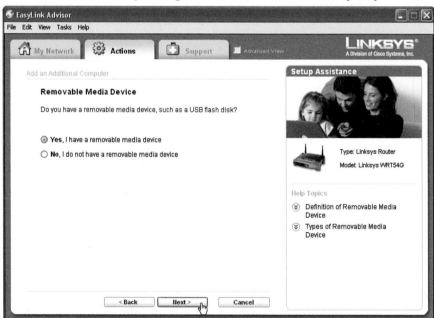

Step 6   EasyLink confirms the location you want to save the wireless profile to (on the USB memory key, in this example E:/), as shown in Figure 8-23. Confirm that EasyLink has the right location and then click **Next**.

Figure 8-23   Confirm the Save Location on the USB Memory Key

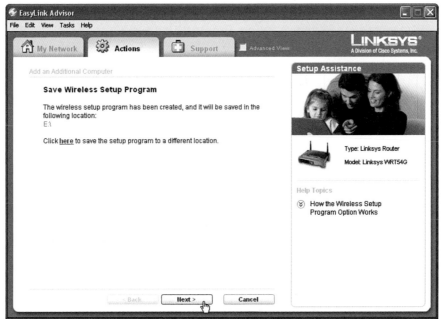

Step 7   EasyLink saves a program file to the USB memory key, as shown in Figure 8-24.

Figure 8-24   Wireless Profile Program Saved on the USB Memory Key

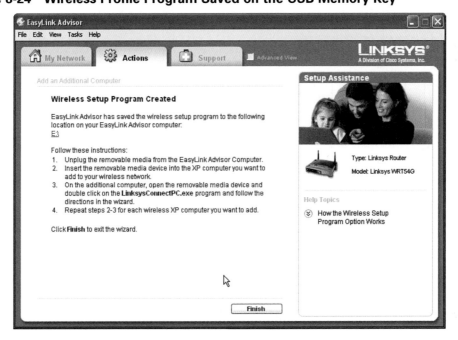

Step 8 Remove the USB memory key and take it to the computer you want to add to your wireless network. Plug in the USB memory key to an open USB port. Double-click **My Computer** and then double-click the USB memory key "drive" (E:/ in this example). You will see a program on the USB memory key named LinksysConnectPC.exe, as shown in Figure 8-25. Double-click the program icon to launch the program.

Figure 8-25 Launch the Wireless Profile Creator Program on the USB Memory Key

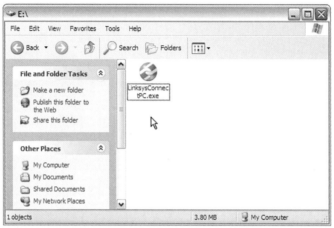

Step 9 A very small version of the Linksys EasyLink Advisor program starts executing on the computer you are adding to the wireless network, as shown in Figure 8-26. Click **Next**.

Figure 8-26 Linksys EasyLink Advisor Wireless Profile Creator Utility Launches

Step 10 As shown in Figure 8-27, the program creates a wireless profile using the wireless network information from the wireless router (that it has stored on the USB memory key). Click **Finish**.

Figure 8-27   Wireless Profile Created

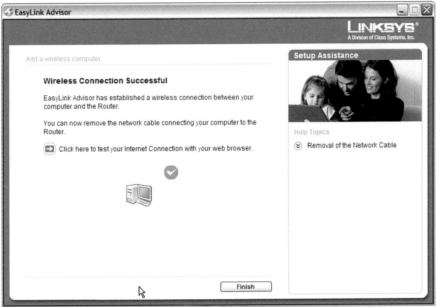

Step 11   Go back to the computer where the (main) EasyLink Advisor program is installed and see if the router now "sees" the computer we just added. Click the **My Network** tab. As shown in Figure 8-28, you can now see graphically that two computers are now connected to the wireless router: Computer1, which is the wired computer we used in Chapter 7 to set up the wireless router, and Computer2, which is the computer we just added to the wireless network.

Figure 8-28   Newly Added Computer Appears in the Network Diagram

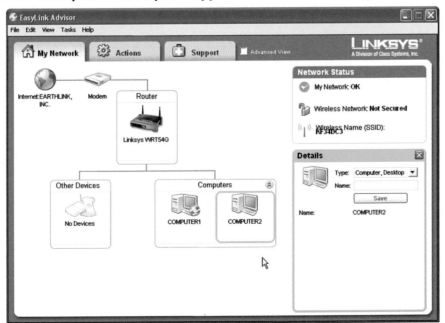

Step 12   If desired we can set the type of computer (Laptop in this example) and even assign a name so we know which computer it is (Susie in this example). As shown in Figure 8-29, set the type and name and then click **Save**. This does not change the computer's own name; it simply gives it an alias that EasyLink Advisor remembers.

Figure 8-29   Assign a Type and Name to the Added Computer

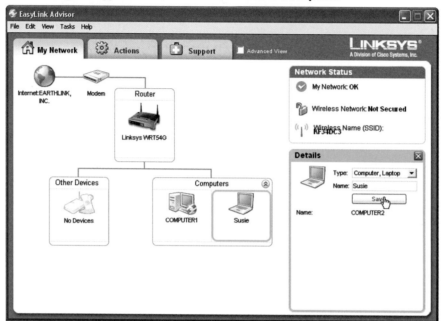

Step 13   Take the same USB memory key to additional computers (running Windows XP) and add them as well. Just repeat Steps 8 through 12 for each computer you want to add. For this example we added a third computer, as shown in Figure 8-30.

 Note: The USB memory key you created is valid until you change any of the settings on your wireless network. We recommend keeping it handy (hang it on the side of your refrigerator or some other easily accessible place). When you have a guest staying at your home who wants to connect to your wireless network, you can hand them the USB memory key and walk them through creating a wireless profile on their Windows laptop.

At this point the wireless profile should be created and your wireless NIC should associate with your wireless router. Just like in the other examples, start your Internet browser and see if you can now browse a web page.

As you can see, EasyLink Advisor provides a fairly easy way to add computers to your home wireless network. In Chapter 9 we will see how to turn on wireless security with EasyLink Advisor.

Figure 8-30   Third Computer Added Now Appears

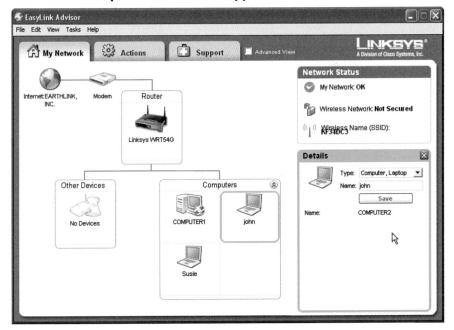

Summary

The two major steps to setting up a wireless NIC in your computers are installing the NIC itself (assuming one is not already built in to your computer or laptop) and creating a wireless profile so that the NIC can associate to your wireless router.

You can manage the wireless connections on your computers in one of a few different ways, including using the Windows Wireless Network Connection utility or using a separate program utility provided by the NIC manufacturer, such as the Linksys WLAN Monitor program. Use the Windows Wireless Network Connection utility unless the NIC requires its own program for some reason (see the installation documentation that comes with the NIC).

Managing wireless connections and adding new wireless profiles with Windows XP is pretty easy.

If you are using the Linksys EasyLink Advisor program to manage your wireless router, there is also a very nice way to set up your wireless profiles by using a USB memory key to propagate the wireless network information to each of your computers. As Linksys evolves this program, it will no doubt provide more extensive capabilities for easy management of your wireless computers.

We intentionally separated out information on troubleshooting into a separate section of this book. If you run into trouble at any point, seek out the troubleshooting chapters in Part IV.

Where to Go for More Information

For more information about the Windows Wireless Network Connection utility, visit the Microsoft website and view the article "Set Up a Wireless Network": www.microsoft.com/windowsxp/using/networking/setup/wireless.mspx.

For more information about Linksys EasyLink Advisor, go to the Linksys main website: www.linksys.com.

Also check out Bradley Mitchell's article on About.com titled "Networking with a Router: Using a Router on Broadband and/or Wireless Home Networks": http://compnetworking.about.com/od/homenetworking/a/routernetworks.htm.

Wireless Security Setup

With the wireless router set up and all the computers now communicating with it, it is time to turn our attention to securing the wireless network.

 Note: The starting assumption is that you have already been successful in setting up the home wireless network without security in Chapters 7, "Wireless Router Setup," and 8, "Wireless NIC Setup." If not, stop and do that first. Turning security on in a wireless network that is already having issues is only going to increase the problem, not solve it.

As discussed in Chapter 5, "Wireless Security: What You Need to Know," wireless networks have no security enabled when you buy the router and NICs. This is necessary because the wireless router and NICs have to be set up with the same security information (that you choose) to communicate with each other. For the reasons discussed in Chapter 5, it's very important to take the few extra steps that are necessary to properly secure your wireless network. The steps are pretty easy:

- Enable encryption (either WEP or WPA) between the wireless router and wireless NICs.
- Disable SSID broadcast on the wireless router.
- Prevent unintentional roaming on all wireless NICs.
- Turn on the firewall on the wireless router (applies to any router, wireless or otherwise).
- Change the wireless router's administration password (applies to any router, wireless or otherwise).

This chapter shows how to set up wireless security.

Setting Up Wireless Encryption

The first (and most important) step to securing your home network is to turn on encryption between the wireless router and the computers in your home network. In order for the computers on your home network to communicate with the wireless router, both sides of the wireless connection (wireless router and wireless NICs) must be using the same type of encryption and the same encryption key.

Figure 9-1 shows what the security options look like before and after.

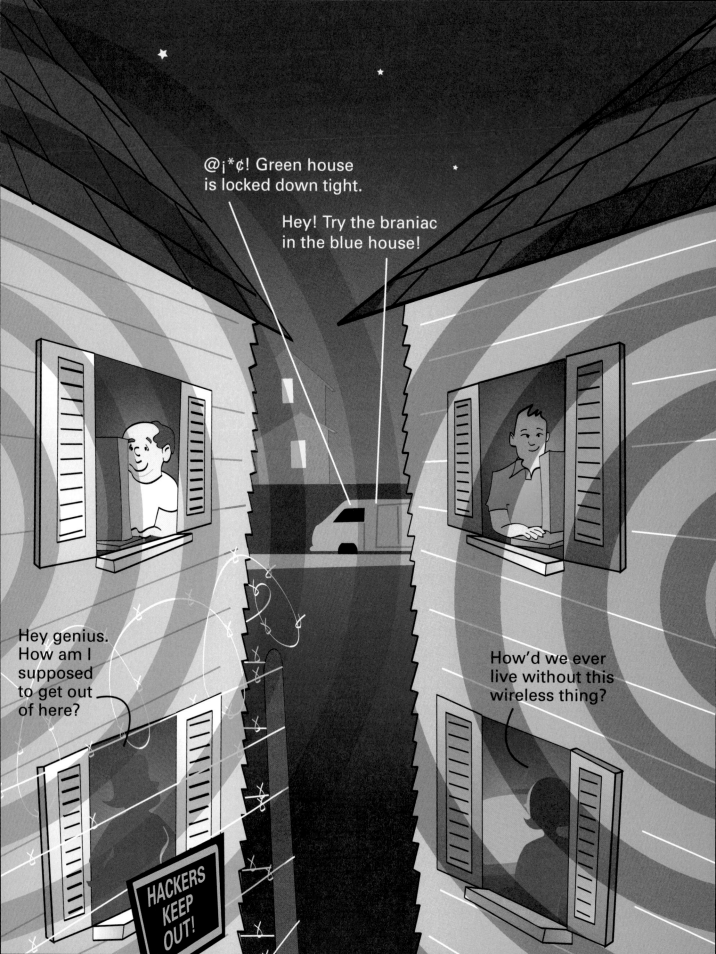

Figure 9-1   Adding Encryption to a Home Wireless Network

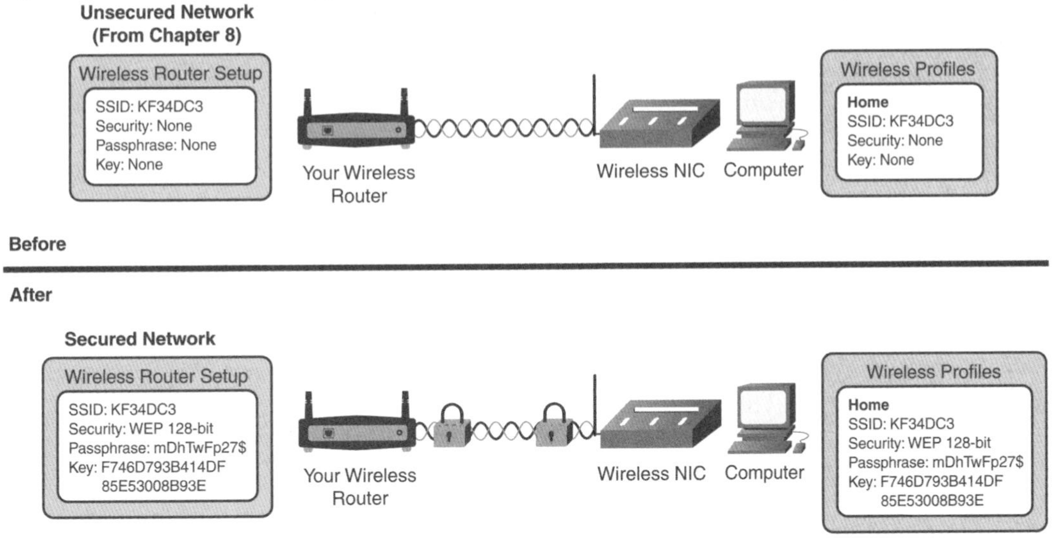

First, we will turn on encryption and assign security key information that is unique to our home wireless network. Then, we will "teach" each wireless NIC in each computer how to "speak" the same security language as the wireless router. The security information will be added to the wireless profile for the home network, including both the type (WEP or WPA) and the unique encryption key.

Tips Before We Start

Before we start turning on wireless encryption, there are a few important things to understand and a couple of tips to follow.

First, understand the difference between some of the terminology that will be used in this chapter:

- **WEP key**—26-character key code (assuming 128-bit WEP) consisting of the characters 0–9 and A–F, which is the actual encryption key. All wireless routers and NICs that support WEP use a WEP key

- **WEP passphrase**—8- to 16-character passphrase, like a password, consisting of upper- and lowercase letters, numbers, and special characters. Linksys wireless routers and NICs can use a passphrase to generate a WEP key for you. The Linksys passphrase is not supported on non-Linksys routers and NICs. If you mix vendor equipment (for example, if you have a NETGEAR router and a Linksys NIC), you need to manually type in the WEP key.

- **WPA preshared key (PSK)**—8- to 63-character key, like a long password, consisting of upper- and lowercase letters, numbers, and special characters. All wireless routers and NICs that support WPA use a WPA PSK.

If you are using WEP as your encryption for security, you can either create your own lengthy 26-digit key (assuming 128-bit WEP) or create a passphrase and ask the Linksys wireless router to generate a WEP key for you. In the latter case, any Linksys NICs can also use the same passphrase to generate the WEP key.

If you are using WPA as your encryption for security, you will create an 8- to 63-character key that you will "share" with both the wireless router and NICs.

 Note: Your network can support only one type of encryption, so make sure the router and all the NICs are using the same type of encryption. If you use WPA and one of your computers has an older NIC (one that only has WEP), that computer will not be able to access your wireless network.

You might find enabling encryption on the wireless NICs a little confusing right now, because it depends on the type of NIC and whether it is being managed with the Windows Wireless Network Connection utility or with its own program such as the Linksys WLAN Monitor. The next few sections walk through different types of setups.

Regardless of the type, there are a several tips that are critical to remember:

Tip 1 Write it down. Keep a notebook and write down the SSID, the type of encryption (WEP, WPA, WPA2), the WEP passphrase and key, or the WPA PSK. Keep the notebook in a locked drawer or cabinet.

Tip 2 Keep your terms straight. Understand whether you are using a WEP key, a WEP passphrase, or a WPA PSK. Write them down that way in the notebook. Avoid labeling them as "wireless security key" or other terms that are too general.

Tip 3 Case can be important. Whether you are using upper- or lowercase letters matters *a lot* for a WEP passphrase and for a WPA PSK. Case does not matter for a WEP key itself.

Tip 4 If you cannot get it working, turn wireless security off on the wireless router and NICs and start over.

If Only It Were That Easy

How you enable wireless encryption on your wireless home network will depend on how you set up your network in Chapters 7 and 8 earlier. If you set up your wireless router using either the Internet browser method or using the Linksys Setup Wizard, you will use your Internet browser to set up wireless security. (See the following section, "Manually Setting Up Wireless Encryption.")

One exception would be if your Linksys wireless router and Linksys wireless NICs support Linksys SecureEasySetup. SecureEasySetup provides a push-button way to enable wireless security (see "Setting Up Wireless Encryption with Linksys SecureEasySetup" later in this chapter).

If you set up your wireless router using Linksys EasyLink Advisor, you will also use EasyLink to set up wireless security (see "Setting up Wireless Encryption with Linksys EasyLink Advisor").

Confused? Yes, there are quite a few different options available. Table 9-1 simplifies the decision about which steps you need to take. Start with the left column and determine which method you are using to manage the wireless security settings on the wireless router: using an Internet browser (in other words, manual), using Linksys SecureEasySetup, or using Linksys EasyLink Advisor.

Table 9-1   Wireless Security Settings Setup Method Summary

	Linksys NICs Managed with Linksys Utility	Linksys NICs Managed with Windows	Other NICs Managed with Windows	Other NICs Managed with Other Utility
Linksys Wireless Router Using Internet Browser (Manual Setup)	Generate a key from WEP passphrase or enter WPA PSK	Enter WEP key or WPA PSK	Enter WEP key or WPA PSK	See the instructions that came with the NIC
Linksys Wireless Router Using SecureEasySetup (SES)	Push the SES button on the router and NIC	Enter WPA PSK generated by SES	Enter WPA PSK generated by SES	See the instructions that came with the NIC
Linksys Wireless Router Using EasyLink Advisor	Generate WEP key from passphrase or enter WPA PSK generated by EasyLink Advisor	Use a USB media key to transfer the EasyLink Advisor settings	Use a USB media key to transfer the EasyLink Advisor settings	See the instructions that came with the NIC

After you determine which method you are using, find the column to the right that matches how the wireless NIC you need to configure is managed. For Linksys NICs, as discussed in Chapter 8, you may be using Windows to manage them or using a Linksys software utility, such as WLAN Monitor. For non-Linksys NICs, such as one already built in to your laptop, see the "Other NICs" columns.

In general, this book will help with those other NICs managed using Windows. For non-Linksys NICs managed with a program that comes with the NIC, we can't give the details here due to space limitations, but the general approach is the same. The same goes for non-Linksys wireless routers: See the instructions that come with the equipment if you purchase non-Linksys routers or NICs.

Each of the cases shown in Table 9-1 in green are covered in the rest of this chapter.

Manually Setting Up Wireless Encryption

If you set up your wireless router in Chapter 7 using either the Internet browser method or the Linksys Setup Wizard, you will use your Internet browser to set up wireless security.

One exception would be if your Linksys wireless router and Linksys wireless NICs support Linksys SecureEasySetup. SecureEasySetup provides a push-button way to enable wireless security (see the section "Setting Up Wireless Encryption with Linksys SecureEasySetup" coming up).

To enable encryption manually, Figure 9-2 shows the steps we will go through.

Figure 9-2   Manually Setting Up Wireless Encryption

First, we will enable encryption on the wireless router. We will do this using an Internet browser to

26 Digit WEP Key

Internet Browser
1. Turn on encryption (such as WEP 128-bit).
2. Generate WEP key from passphrase.
3. Write down/print out WEP key information.

Windows Wireless Network Connection Utility
1. Turn on encryption (such as WEP 128-bit).
2. Manually type in the WEP key.

Wireless NIC   Computer

Your Wireless Router

OR

Wireless NIC   Computer

Linksys WLAN Monitor Utility
1. Turn on encryption (such as WEP 128-bit).
2. Generate WEP key from passphrase.

WEP Passphrase

connect to the router and generate an encryption key from a passphrase. How we enable encryption on the computers depends on what we are using to manage our wireless connections (Windows Wireless Network Connection utility, Linksys WLAN Monitor, and so on), as discussed in Chapter 8.

Note: You will want to do this step using a physical (wired) connection to your router. If you do this over a wireless link, you may be disconnected as soon as you enable the changes you are about to make.

We will show one example with the Linksys WAN Monitor utility, where we can simply enter the same WEP passphrase as the router and generate the encryption key. We will also show an example using Windows XP to manage the connection, in which case we need to enter the WEP encryption key manually, as Windows does not support the ability to generate the key from the passphrase. The first encryption example we show will be done using 128-bit WEP. The second will be shown using WPA.

Enabling WEP Encryption on the Wireless Router

First, let's take an example of implementing 128-bit WEP encryption. We will pick a passphrase of mDhTwFp27$.

Note: When choosing a WEP passphrase or a WPA preshared key, you should use the same process as picking a password. Make it a strong password, not a weak one, using at least eight characters consisting of upper- and lowercase letters, numbers, and special characters. Avoid passphrases that spell something either literally or phonetically. For a more thorough discussion of strong passwords, pick up a copy of *Home Network Security Simplified*.

Now, let's program the wireless router to use this WEP key:

Step 1   Access the wireless router using your Internet browser. Click the **Wireless** tab.

Step 2   Click the **Wireless Security** subtab (see Figure 9-3). From the Security Mode field, choose **WEP**.

Figure 9-3   Select WEP as Your Security Mode

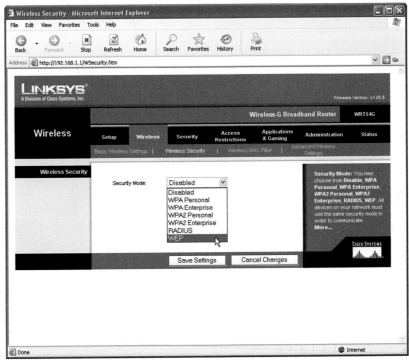

Step 3   On the line labeled WEP Encryption, select **128 bits**. In the Passphrase field, enter the passphrase you made up. In our example, we chose mDhTwFp27$ (see Figure 9-4). Click **Generate**. This translates the passphrase into the actual key to be used (F746D793B414DF85E53008B93E). Do not forget to write down the passphrase and the generated key.

Step 4   Click **Save Settings**.

Immediately after you click Save Settings, any computers that were connected with a wireless card to the wireless router will lose connectivity. This is normal, because you have just changed the way they are supposed to communicate with the wireless router, but you have not told them the super-secret password to use yet.

Figure 9-4   Generate the WEP Key

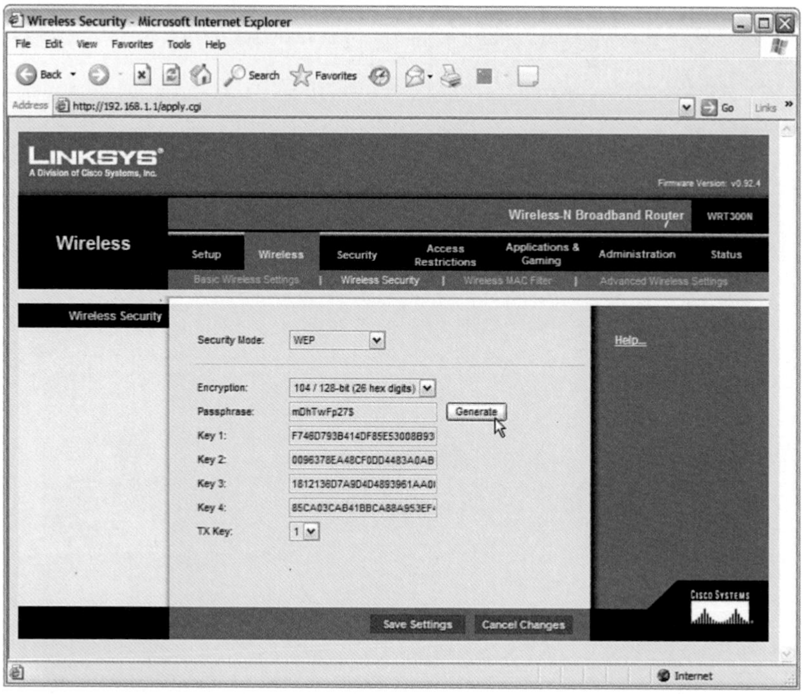

Note: You may notice that four keys are listed after you generate the WEP key. In general, you can choose any of the four keys, but most often you can just pick Key 1. The other three keys are just alternate keys that you can use if you want to keep the same passphrase but change the actual key. Regardless of which key you use, write the chosen key down in the notebook we suggested that you keep. Whenever you have visitors who want to use your network, they will need to enter either the passphrase or the key depending on whether or not they are using gear from the same manufacturer.

Enabling WEP Encryption on the Wireless NIC

As discussed in Chapter 8, there are a couple different ways to manage the wireless connection in each of your computers. Windows offers a built-in function for wireless NIC management. For computers with older versions of Windows (2000, 98SE, and so on), you most likely need to use a wireless management program that comes with the NIC. The same wireless connection manager you use to associate and set up wireless connections is used to also enable wireless security.

The sections that follow show two examples:

■ A Windows XP laptop computer with a PCMCIA wireless card that we set up with the Linksys WLAN utility

■ A Windows XP laptop with a built-in wireless NIC that we set up using the Windows Wireless Network Connection utility

Enabling WEP Encryption Using the Linksys Utility

First, let's walk through an example of setting up WEP encryption on a computer running Windows XP, using a PCMCIA wireless NIC (Linksys WPC54G) and the Linksys WLAN utility:

Step 1   Launch the Linksys WLAN Monitor by double-clicking the icon on the far right of your Windows taskbar (the example shows a computer running Windows XP). If you do not see such an icon, try going through **Start > Programs > Linksys Wireless Card > WLAN Monitor**.

Step 2   Notice that there is no connection to the wireless router (the signal bars are not "lit up"). This is normal since we enabled encryption on the wireless router but have not yet enabled it on the wireless NIC. (See Figure 9-5.)

Step 3   Click the **Profiles** tab.

Figure 9-5   Launch the WLAN Monitor Utility

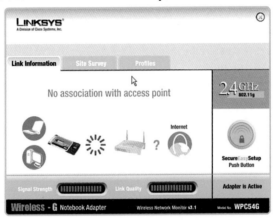

Step 4   Select the profile for your home wireless network and click **Edit** (see Figure 9-6).

Figure 9-6   Select and Edit the Wireless Profile

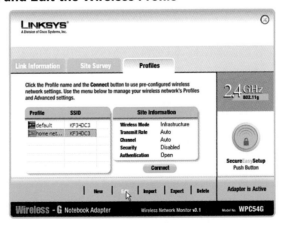

Step 5 Click **Manual Setup** (see Figure 9-7).

Figure 9-7 **Click Manual Setup**

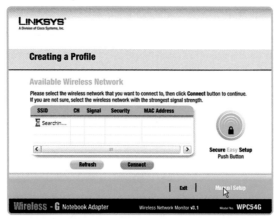

Step 6 No changes are needed to the network settings (see Figure 9-8). Click **Next**.

Figure 9-8 **Network Settings Stay the Same**

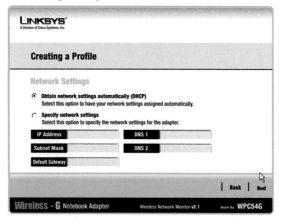

Step 7 No changes are needed to the wireless mode either (see Figure 9-9). It should be set to Infrastructure Mode and have the SSID we set in Chapter 8. Click **Next**.

Step 8 The Wireless Security window appears (see Figure 9-10). Choose **WEP** and click **Next**.

Note: You will see several options in the Security drop-down list, including WPA-Enterprise, RADIUS, and LEAP. These are options for corporate networks, not home networks, so just ignore them.

Figure 9-9   Wireless Mode Stays the Same

Figure 9-10   Choose WEP as the Security Type

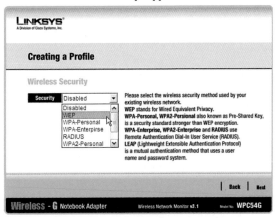

Step 9   A second Wireless Security settings window appears (see Figure 9-11). From the WEP field, choose **128 Bits**.

Figure 9-11   Enter the WEP Key

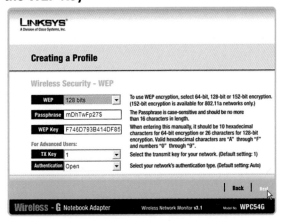

Step 10 In the Passphrase field (also shown in Figure 9-11), enter the passphrase exactly as you entered it earlier when you enabled WEP on the router (mDhTwFp27$ for this example). You will see the WEP key being built as you enter the passphrase. After you enter the complete passphrase, click **Next**.

Note: Make sure to enter the passphrase exactly as you did on the wireless router. Lowercase *a* is different from uppercase *A*. The two keys (on the router and on the wireless card) must be identical. If the passphrases on the router and the NIC do not match, then the computer and the router will not be able to communicate.

Also, remember that when you use a passphrase, the first key (of the four created) is the one that will be used by default.

Step 11 A confirmation window appears (see Figure 9-12). Double-check the new security settings and click **Save**.

Figure 9-12   Confirm the New Settings

Step 12 A Congratulations window appears (see Figure 9-13). Click **Connect to Network**.

Figure 9-13   Activate Your New Settings

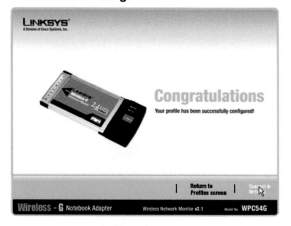

Step 13   Click the **Link Information** tab. If you entered everything correctly, the Signal Strength and Link Quality should reappear as green bars (see Figure 9-14).

Figure 9-14   Successfully Connected

The green bars may or may not be solid the whole way across. It depends on the strength of the wireless signal and how far away you are from the wireless router, much like a cell phone.

If the link information shows no connection, you probably entered something incorrectly. Repeat the steps and double-check the settings, particularly that the passphrase is typed in exactly the same on the router and the wireless NIC. Also see Part IV of this book, "Honey, This Stupid Wireless Thing Is Not Working," particularly Chapter 10, "Troubleshooting: I Can't Connect at All."

You can further test the connection by trying to browse the Internet. Launch your web browser (such as Internet Explorer) and see if you can browse a web page.

Enabling WEP Encryption Using Windows XP

Now let's look at an example of enabling WEP encryption using the Windows Wireless Network Connection utility to configure the USB wireless NIC we installed in Chapter 8 (Linksys WUSB54G). The steps to enable encryption are as follows:

Step 1   Choose **Start > Connect To > Show All Connections**. Select the USB wireless NIC in the right side of the dialog box and then click **Change Settings of This Connection** on the left side (see Figure 9-15).

Step 2   Click the **Wireless Networks** tab (see Figure 9-16). You will see a list of wireless network profiles. Locate your wireless network in the list. The SSID you chose should be displayed (in our example, we used KF34DC3). Select the SSID and click **Properties**.

Figure 9-15   Locate the Wireless NIC

Figure 9-16   Open the Wireless Connection Properties

Step 3   Choose **Open** as the Network Authentication type. From the Data Encryption field, choose **WEP**, as shown in Figure 9-17.

Figure 9-17   Confirm Connection to an Unsecured Wireless Network

Step 4   In the Network Key and Confirm Network Key fields, enter the 26-character WEP key (not the passphrase). Type in the whole key that you wrote down when you enabled WEP on the router (F746D793B414DF85E53008B93E in our example). You cannot generate the key from the passphrase; you need to manually enter the key itself on both lines. Leave the Key Index field set to 1. When you are done, click **OK**, and then click **OK** again.

Step 5   The NIC will reassociate to the wireless router, this time using the WEP key. In the View Available Wireless Networks dialog box, the status will change to Connected, as shown in Figure 9-18.

Figure 9-18   Connected to Wireless Network

You can test the connection by trying to browse the Internet. Launch your web browser (such as Internet Explorer) and see if you can browse a web page.

WPA Encryption Example

To compare enabling WEP encryption to enabling WPA encryption, let's take an example of WPA. Enabling WPA encryption is similar to enabling WEP encryption, with three main differences:

- With WPA you do not choose a passphrase or generate a key. Instead, you choose a preshared key (PSK). A PSK looks a lot like a passphrase: It's a series of random letters and digits that you create that acts as a password for joining into your wireless network. Only wireless NICs that have the PSK can join your network.

- With WPA you must choose whether to use the TKIP or AES mode for WPA encryption. If your wireless router and all wireless NICs support AES, use it, because AES is more secure than TKIP; otherwise, use TKIP. You cannot mix modes. In other words, you can't set some NICs to use TKIP and others to use AES. All NICs must use the same mode.

- With WPA you must decide what length of time an encryption key can be used before a new key is assigned, which is called a *key renewal period*. The shorter the period, the less time a hacker has to try to "crack" the key. For example, if you set the time period to 1800 seconds (which is

30 minutes, for you non-math majors), a key is used for 30 minutes, and then the wireless router and wireless NIC create a new key. If a hacker "cracks" the key within 30 minutes (which is pretty tough to do), the key is valuable only for the remainder of the 30 minutes, after which it is switched to an entirely new key, and the hacker would have to start all over.

■ With WPA, if a longer WPA preshared key (more characters) is used, there is an added security benefit (whereas WEP keys are fixed length and WEP passphrase length does not directly impact the strength of the key). Some security experts recommend choosing a WPA PSK of at least 20 characters.

 Note: So how long should you set the key renewal period? There is no great answer, although if you have the value set too low (1 to 2 minutes, for example), it could cause connectivity issues for some NICs. We recommend following manufacturer recommendations (or defaults).

Again, we must set the security settings to be identical on both the wireless router and the wireless NIC. The next couple sections show an example of how to set up WPA.

Enabling WPA Encryption on the Wireless Router

First, we need to set up WPA on the wireless router:

Step 1   On the Wireless Security subtab (see Figure 9-19), from the Security Mode field, choose **PSK Personal**. (On some Linksys products, the choice is called WPA Pre-Shared Key.)

Figure 9-19   Enabling WPA Encryption on the Wireless Router

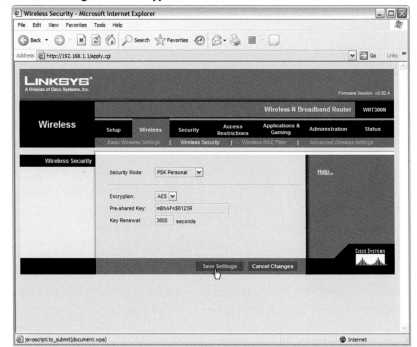

Step 2   From the Encryption field (see Figure 9-19), choose either **TKIP** (for WPA1) or **AES** (for WPA2). If your wireless router and all wireless NICs support AES mode, choose it, because AES is more secure. If any of them does not, choose TKIP. You cannot configure some with TKIP and some with AES.

Step 3   In the Pre-Shared Key field, enter the preshared key you made up (in our example, mBhAFn$6123R).

Step 4   In the Key Renewal field, enter the number of seconds that you want the key to be used before changing it. We chose 3600 (60 minutes) for this example.

Step 5   Click **Save Settings**.

Enabling WPA Encryption on the Wireless NIC

With WPA, we also then need to tell the super-secret password to each of the devices with wireless cards so that they know how to decode the conversations with the wireless router. Here is an example for a PCMCIA laptop NIC (Linksys WPC54G) managed with the Linksys WLAN Monitor utility:

Step 1   Launch the Linksys WLAN Monitor by double-clicking the icon on the far right of your Windows taskbar (the example shows a computer running Windows XP). If you do not see such an icon, try going through **Start > Programs > Linksys Wireless Card > WLAN Monitor**.

Step 2   Notice that there is no connection to the wireless router (the signal bars are not "lit up"). This is normal since we enabled encryption on the wireless router but have not yet enabled it on the wireless NIC. (See Figure 9-20.)

Step 3   Click the **Profiles** tab.

Figure 9-20   Launch the WLAN Monitor Utility

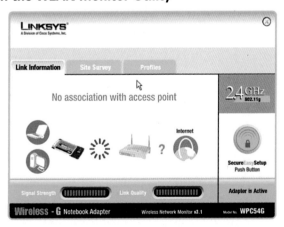

Step 4   Select the profile for your home wireless network and click **Edit** (see Figure 9-21).

Figure 9-21   Select and Edit the Wireless Profile

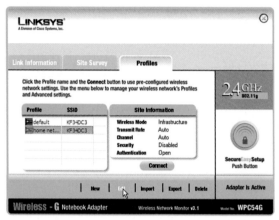

Step 5   No changes are needed to the network settings (see Figure 9-22). Click **Next**.

Figure 9-22   Network Settings Stay the Same

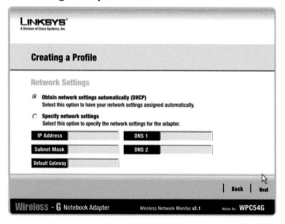

Step 6   The Wireless Security window appears, as shown in Figure 9-23. Choose **WPA-Personal** (on some Linksys wireless NICs, the option may be listed as WPA or WPA Pre-Shared Key). Click **Next**.

Note: As mentioned earlier, you will see several options in the list, including WPA-Enterprise, RADIUS, and LEAP. These are options for corporate networks, not home networks, so just ignore them.

Step 7   A second Wireless Security settings window appears, as shown in Figure 9-24. From the Encryption field, choose **AES** (or **TKIP**, whatever you selected on the wireless router).

Figure 9-23   Choose WPA-Personal as the Security Type

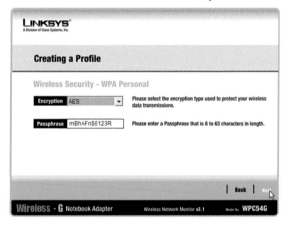

Figure 9-24   Enter the WPA Mode and Preshared Key

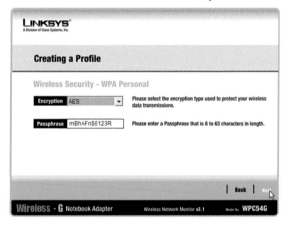

Step 8   In the **Passphrase** field, enter the WPA preshared key exactly as you entered it earlier when you enabled WPA on the router (mBhAFn$6123R for this example). Click **Next**.

Note: Make sure to enter the PSK exactly as you did on the wireless router. Lowercase *a* is different from uppercase *A*. The two keys (on the router and on the wireless card) must be identical.

Step 9   A confirmation window appears (see Figure 9-25). Double-check the new security settings and click **Save**. A Congratulations window appears (which is the same as Figure 9-13). Click **Connect to Network**.

Step 10   Click the **Link Information** tab. If you entered everything correctly, the Signal Strength and Link Quality should reappear as green bars (see Figure 9-26).

Figure 9-25   Confirm the New Settings

Figure 9-26   Successfully Connected

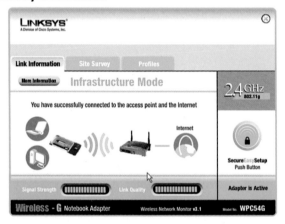

Continue setting up each NIC with the super-secret password, each time checking to see whether the connection is re-established to the wireless router.

Setting Up Wireless Encryption with Linksys SecureEasySetup

To try to simplify the process of setting up a secure wireless network, Linksys released a feature called *SecureEasySetup (SES)*. SES provides a push-button setup process that can automatically set up a secure connection between the wireless router and wireless NICs.

The SES process works as shown in Figure 9-27. When you invoke SES on the wireless router, it automatically creates a WPA PSK. The router then starts accepting new wireless NIC connections.

You then invoke SES on each of the wireless NICs, which automatically receive the WPA PSK directly from the wireless router. There is no need to manually program the WPA key into the wireless NIC yourself.

Figure 9-27   Setting Up Wireless Encryption with Linksys SecureEasySetup

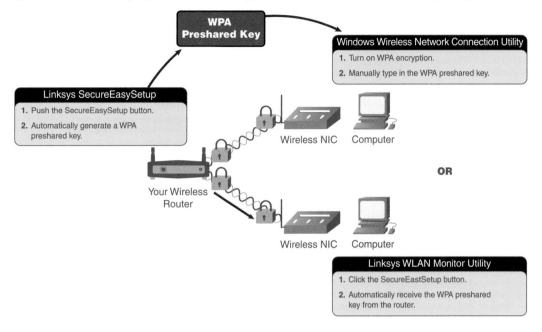

This truly is a push-button approach to wireless security. However, there are some very important limitations to consider:

■ SES is supported on only a subset of Linksys wireless routers and Linksys wireless NICs. Consult the Linksys website at http://www.linksys.com to see which products support SES.

■ Only Linksys wireless NICs can be set up using SES. NICs from manufacturers other than Linksys have to be set up manually or using a utility provided by that manufacturer.

■ If you have a wireless NIC that you manage with the Windows Wireless Network Connection utility, such as one that is built in to a laptop, you have to manually program the NIC to join the wireless network, because SES cannot be used.

■ SES automatically configures wireless security based on WPA and the TKIP mode. If you want to use another security mode, such as WEP, WPA with AES, or WPA2, you cannot use SES.

■ For guests visiting your home or for non-Linksys devices, you need to write down the SSID and WPA key that SES creates, and enter them manually to allow them to join your wireless network.

Limitations aside, if you are setting up a new wireless network and have mainly Linksys products (in other words, a Linksys wireless router and Linksys wireless NICs), and the products all support SES, SES can be an easy and effective way to get your network started quickly, and secured.

The steps to set up a network with SES are shown in the next two sections.

Linksys SecureEasySetup on the Wireless Router

First, we need to set up SES on the wireless router:

Step 1   Access the wireless router using your Internet browser. Click the **Wireless** tab. Click the **Basic Wireless Settings** subtab (see Figure 9-28).

Figure 9-28   Access the Linksys SecureEasySetup Activation

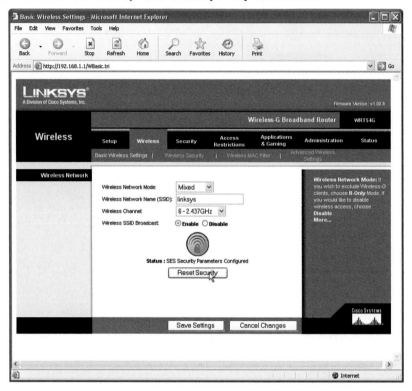

Step 2   You should see a green icon with a padlock on the menu. If you do not, the model of wireless router you have may not support SES. Click **Reset Security**.

 Note: You need to reset the security settings only once for your network, not each time you add new wireless NICs. Resetting the settings assigns a new SSID and WPA preshared key, so wireless NICs that were previously set up and connected to your wireless router will lose their connections.

Step 3   Notice that SES has generated a new SSID (linksys_SES_64409 in this example) for your wireless router (see Figure 9-29). Write it down; you will need it when you have to program wireless NICs that do not support SES.

Figure 9-29   Linksys SecureEasySetup Assigns a New SSID

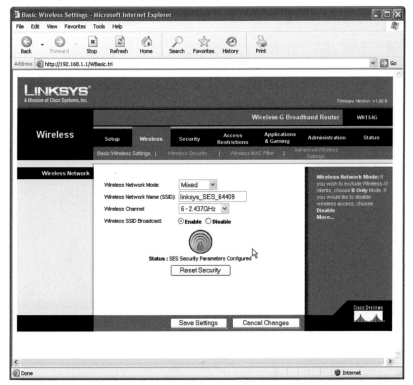

Step 4   Click the **Wireless Security** subtab (see Figure 9-30). You see that SES has set the wireless router to use WPA Personal (on some Linksys routers, this may be WPA or WPA Pre-Shared Key) and TKIP mode. You also see that SES has generated a random WPA preshared key (2iwitleatw9yphq2 in this example). Write it down; you will need it when you have to program wireless NICs that do not support SES.

Step 5   Click the **Basic Wireless Settings** subtab again. You are now ready to trigger the router to accept new wireless NICs using SES. When you are ready (you may want to jump to the section "Linksys SecureEasySetup on the Wireless NIC" before proceeding), click the green padlock icon to begin the SES process. A confirmation dialog box appears, as shown in Figure 9-31, stating that the SES process has been started. Click **OK**.

Figure 9-30   Displaying the WPA PSK Generated by Linksys SecureEasySetup

Figure 9-31   Linksys SecureEasySetup Is Enabled

Step 6 The wireless router will now accept new connections from wireless NICs for about a minute or two. During the acceptance period, the message shown in Figure 9-32 is displayed. When the router returns to the main menu, the SES acceptance period has ended.

Figure 9-32   Wireless Router Is Accepting New Connections

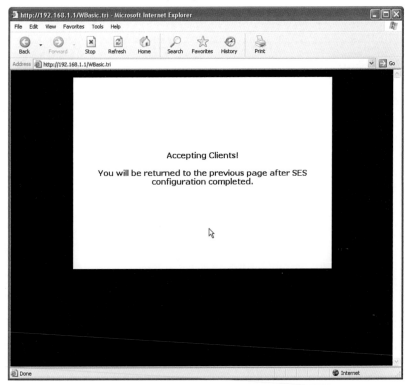

It's important that you synchronize the steps on the wireless router and wireless NIC you are connecting. You need to make sure the wireless router is accepting new clients at the time that you trigger the NIC to associate itself (see the next section).

You can repeat Steps 5 and 6 as many times as necessary to connect a wireless NIC to the wireless router. At a future time, if you need to add a new wireless NIC to your network, you can go straight to Step 5. You should not start with Step 1 in this case, because Steps 1 through 4 are needed for your network only when you initially set it up, not every time you add a new device.

As a caution, though, if you repeat starting from Step 1, you will reset all the security settings for your wireless network and therefore have to repeat Steps 5 and 6 with each computer in your network to obtain the modified settings.

 Note: Alternatively, to enable SecureEasySetup to accept a new wireless device, you can press the Cisco logo or the green circle with a padlock icon on the front of the wireless router instead of following Steps 5 and 6. The logo or icon will start flashing, indicating it is accepting new NIC clients. When it stops flashing, the acceptance period has ended. By the way, you will see the icon flashing if you follow Steps 5 and 6 also.

Linksys SecureEasySetup on the Wireless NIC

With Linksys SES, the wireless NIC obtains the WPA key (and SSID) directly from the wireless router. To use SES, you need to first execute the steps in the preceding section for the wireless router, up through Step 4. When you execute Step 5 in the preceding section, you need to execute the SES process on the wireless NIC. Here is an example for a PCMCIA laptop NIC (Linksys WPC54G):

Step 1   Launch the Linksys WLAN Monitor by double-clicking the icon on the far right of your Windows taskbar (the example shows a computer running Windows XP). If you do not see such an icon, try going through **Start > Programs > Linksys Wireless Card > WLAN Monitor**.

Step 2   Click the **Profiles** tab (see Figure 9-33).

Figure 9-33   Launch the WLAN Monitor Utility

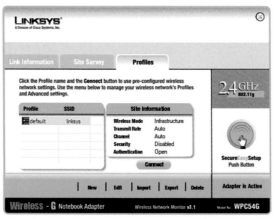

Step 3   Click the green circle with a padlock icon on the right side of the dialog box (refer to Figure 9-33). A dialog box appears telling you it is time to initiate SES on the wireless router, as shown in Figure 9-34. Follow Steps 5 and 6 in the previous section at this point and then return here.

Figure 9-34   Trigger Linksys SecureEasySetup on the Wireless Router

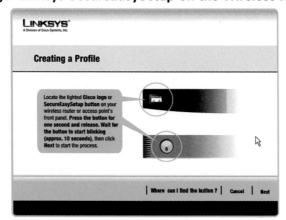

Step 4   Click **Next** on the WLAN Monitor utility. The wireless NIC retrieves the WPA pre-shared key (and SSID) from the wireless router. Figure 9-35 shows a successful result, where you can see that the random WPA key that was created by the router is now programmed into the NIC (2iwitleatw9yphq2 in this example). Also notice that the SSID has been reassigned to the one provided by the router as well (linksys_SES_64409 in this example). Click **Connect to Network**.

Figure 9-35   Wireless Security Settings Are Retrieved

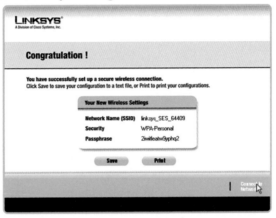

Step 5   A new wireless profile is created automatically by SES for the wireless network just programmed using SES (see Figure 9-36). You can rename the profile to something more recognizable if you want.

Figure 9-36   New Wireless Profile Created

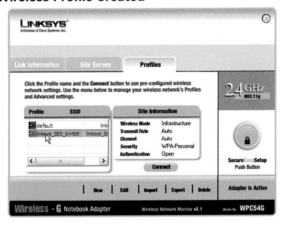

Step 6   Click the **Link Information** tab. The Signal Strength and Link Quality should show green bars, indicating a connection to the wireless router (see Figure 9-37).

Figure 9-37 Successfully Connected

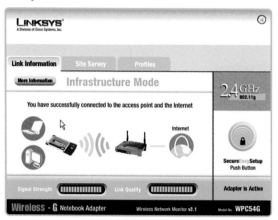

You can repeat this process with each wireless NIC, each time triggering SES to accept clients on the wireless router and then triggering SES on the wireless NIC to retrieve its wireless security settings from the router. In other words, you need to follow this procedure for every NIC that is capable of being set up using SES.

Each time you add a new NIC, check to see whether the connection is established to the wireless router.

Setting Up Wireless Encryption with Linksys EasyLink Advisor

As discussed in Chapters 7 and 8, there is a new software setup utility for Linksys routers (under development at the time of this writing) named EasyLink Advisor. EasyLink provides a simplified way to set up wireless routers and add wireless computers to the network.

You also can use EasyLink to aid in the setup of wireless security. Before starting, you need a USB memory stick. Similar to Chapter 8, if the computer runs Windows XP and higher, we can use EasyLink to create a wireless profile on a USB memory stick, including the wireless security settings (see Figure 9-38), and then simply plug that USB memory stick into the computer we want to join the secure wireless network, automatically updating the wireless profile with the security settings.

Note: In Figure 9-38 you see that 128-bit WEP is being referenced. At the time of this writing, 128-bit WEP is the encryption option that Linksys EasyLink Advisor supports. Newer versions of EasyLink may support additional encryption types.

Also at the time of this writing, using a USB memory key to set up wireless security using EasyLink Advisor works only for computers running Windows and higher, and only when using the Windows Wireless Network Connection utility. It does not work if a separate program utility is required to manage wireless NICs, including the Linksys WLAN Monitor program or other manufacturers' wireless connection manager programs.

Figure 9-38   Setting Up Wireless Encryption with Linksys EasyLink Advisor

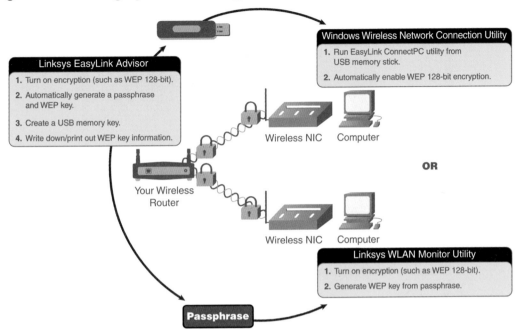

If you are using an older version of Windows (for example, Windows 2000 or 98SE), the EasyLink program helps you print out the wireless profile security settings you need. Then, you have to use the printout to manually configure the wireless security settings on your wireless NIC using a wireless connection manager program, like the example shown earlier in "Enabling WEP Encryption on the Wireless NIC" for the Linksys WLAN Monitor program.

We will continue the example started in Chapters 7 and 8, with a Linksys WRT54G wireless router and two computers with wireless NICs, both running Windows XP.

Linksys EasyLink Advisor on the Wireless Router

When you are using EasyLink Advisor to manage your home network, the first step to setting up encryption is to set up the wireless security parameters on the wireless router. The steps for doing so are as follows:

Step 1   On the computer with Linksys EasyLink Advisor installed, launch the EasyLink Advisor program by double-clicking its icon on the running tasks taskbar or by choosing **Start > Programs > Linksys EasyLink Advisor**. You should see the network. Click the **Actions** tab and then click **Secure My Wireless Network**, as shown in Figure 9-39.

Figure 9-39 Secure Wireless Network with Linksys EasyLink Advisor

Step 2 The Wireless Security Wizard starts up, as shown in Figure 9-40. Click **Next**.

Figure 9-40 Start the Wireless Security Wizard

Step 3 Click the **Override Current Wireless Settings** radio button, as shown in Figure 9-41. Click **Next**.

Step 4 The Wireless Security Wizard turns on 128-bit WEP on the wireless router, creates a random WEP passphrase, and generates a WEP key from the passphrase. When complete, the dialog box shown in Figure 9-42 is displayed. Click the **Yes, I Have Computers or Other Devices That Are Wireless** radio button and then click **Next**.

Figure 9-41   Secure the Wireless Network

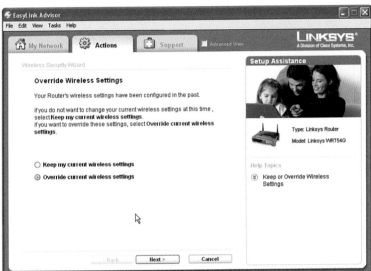

Figure 9-42   Prepare to Propagate Wireless Security Settings to Other Computers

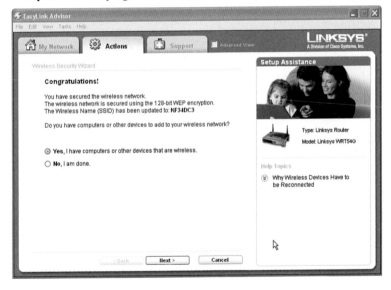

Step 5   The Wireless Security Wizard displays the wireless security settings it created, as shown in Figure 9-43. Write them down in your notebook and print them out. Click **Next**.

Step 6   The Wireless Security Wizard asks if you have an additional computer to add, as shown in Figure 9-44. Click **Yes, I Have an Additional Computer to Add** and then click **Next**. Even though you already said Yes in Step 4 to add computers, you must say Yes again in Step 6.

Figure 9-43   Write Down and Print Out the Wireless Security Settings

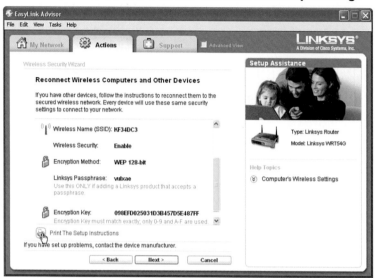

Figure 9-44   Yes, We Want to Add an Additional Computer

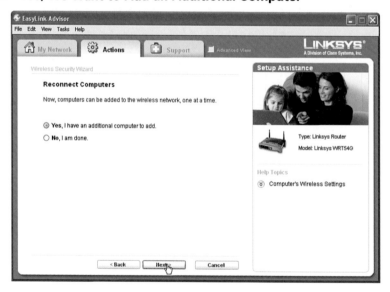

Step 7   The Wireless Security Wizard asks you if the additional computer is wired or wireless, as shown in Figure 9-45. Click **Wireless** and then click **Next**.

Step 8   The Wireless Security Wizard then asks you to plug in a removable media device, as shown in Figure 9-46. Plug a USB memory stick into an open USB port on the computer running EasyLink and click **Next**. The Wireless Security Wizard confirms the location you want to save the wireless profile to (on the USB memory key, in this example E:/). Click **Next**.

Figure 9-45   Yes, It Is a Wireless Computer

Figure 9-46   Wireless Security Wizard Requests to Plug in USB Memory Key

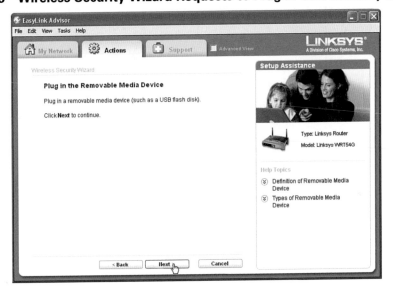

Step 9   The Wireless Security Wizard saves a program file to the USB memory key, as shown in Figure 9-47. You can now remove the USB memory key and take it to the computer you want to add to your wireless network.

Step 10   If you click the My Network tab (as shown in Figure 9-48), you will notice that only the wired computer appears on the network diagram, not the wireless computers. This is normal, because we changed the wireless security settings but have not yet changed the corresponding settings on the computers.

Figure 9-47   Wireless Profile Program Saved on the USB Memory Key

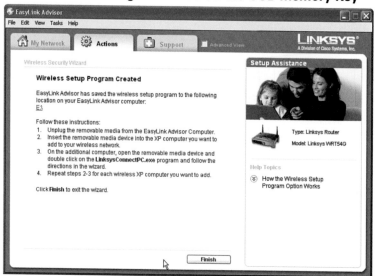

Figure 9-48   Wireless Connected Computers No Longer on the Network Diagram

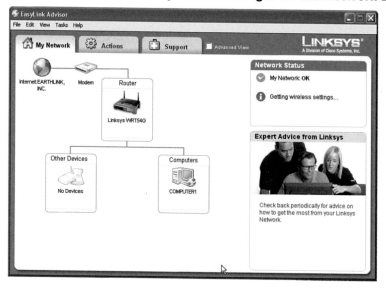

Using EasyLink Advisor to Add Encryption to Wireless NICs

As discussed in Chapter 8, you can manage the wireless connection in each of your computers in a couple of different ways, including with the Windows Wireless Network Connection utility or the Linksys WLAN utility. The same wireless connection manager you use to associate and set up wireless connections is used to also enable wireless security.

The sections that follow show two examples:

■ A Windows XP laptop with a built-in wireless NIC that we set up using the Windows Wireless Network Connection utility

■ A Windows XP laptop computer with a PCMCIA wireless card that we set up with the Linksys WLAN utility

EasyLink Advisor with Windows-Managed NICs

For wireless NICs that are managed with Windows Wireless Network Connection utility, we can easily transfer the wireless security settings from the wireless router to the wireless NIC using a USB memory key. The following steps show how to do so:

Step 1 Plug in the USB memory key to an open USB port. Double-click **My Computer** and then double-click the USB memory key "drive" (E:/ in this example). You will see a program on the USB memory key named LinksysConnectPC.exe. Double-click the program icon to launch the program.

Step 2 A very small version of the Linksys EasyLink Advisor program starts executing on the computer you are adding to the wireless network, as shown in Figure 9-49. Click **Next**.

Figure 9-49 Linksys EasyLink Advisor Wireless Profile Creator Utility Launches

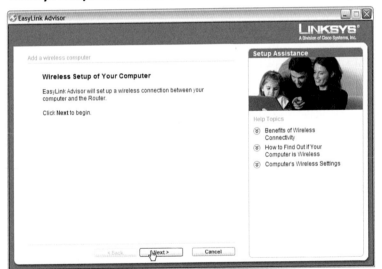

Step 3 The program modifies the wireless profile with the wireless security settings and re-establishes the wireless connection (see Figure 9-50).

Step 4 As shown in Figure 9-51, the program creates a wireless profile using the wireless network information from the wireless router (that it has stored on the USB memory key). Click **Finish**.

Note: The window shown in Figure 9-51 makes a reference to removing the network cable. If you had previously connected the computer to the network with a cable, you can remove it at this point. If this is the first time connecting the computer to the network, ignore the comment.

Figure 9-50 Linksys EasyLink Advisor Re-Establishing the Wireless Connection

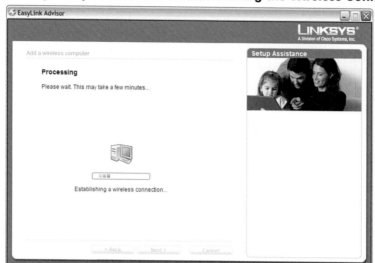

Figure 9-51 Wireless Profile Created

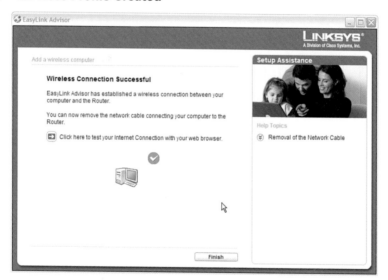

Step 5 Go back to the computer where the (main) EasyLink Advisor program is installed and see if the router now "sees" the computer we just added. Click the **My Network** tab. As shown in Figure 9-52, you can see graphically that there are two computers now connected to the wireless router: Computer1, which is the computer we used in Chapter 7 to set up the wireless router, and now the computer designated as Susie, which is the computer we just re-joined to the wireless network.

At this point the wireless profile should be created, including the wireless security settings, and your wireless NIC should reassociate with your wireless router. Just like in the other examples, start your Internet browser and see if you can browse a web page. You can now remove the USB memory key and take it to the computer you want to add to your wireless network.

Figure 9-52   Computer Reappears in the Network Diagram

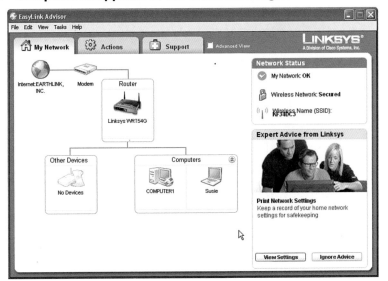

 Note: The USB memory key you created is valid until you change any of the settings on your wireless network. We recommend keeping it handy; hang it on the side of your refrigerator or in some other easily accessible place. When you have guests staying at your home who want to connect to your wireless network, you can hand them the USB memory key and walk them through creating a wireless profile on their Windows XP laptop.

EasyLink Advisor with Linksys Utility–Managed NICs

Now, let's walk through an example of setting up encryption on a computer running Windows XP, using a PCMCIA wireless NIC (Linksys WPC54G) and the Linksys WLAN utility.

In this case, we cannot propagate the wireless security information automatically using a USB media key like we did earlier. We need to take the printout of wireless security settings from EasyLink Advisor and manually enter the key information. The steps to do so follow:

Step 1   Launch the Linksys WLAN Monitor by double-clicking the icon on the far right of your Windows taskbar (the example shows a computer running Windows XP). If you do not see such an icon, try going through **Start > Programs > Linksys Wireless Card > WLAN Monitor**.

Step 2   Click the **Profiles** tab. Select the profile for your home wireless network, and click **Edit** at the bottom of the screen, as shown in Figure 9-53.

Step 3   No changes are needed to the network settings. Click **Next**. The Wireless Security window appears (see Figure 9-54). Choose **WEP** and click **Next**.

Figure 9-53   Select and Edit the Wireless Profile

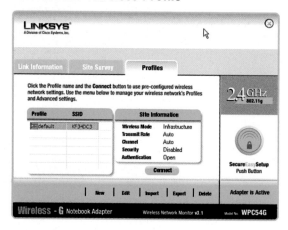

Figure 9-54   Choose WEP as the Security Type

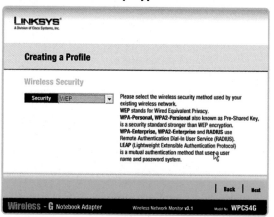

Step 4   A second Wireless Security settings window appears (see Figure 9-55). From the WEP field, choose **128 Bits**.

Figure 9-55   Enter the WEP Key

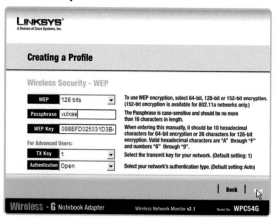

Step 5 Enter in the Passphrase field the passphrase exactly as it appears in the printout from EasyLink Advisor, when you enabled security on the router (vulxae for this example). You will see the WEP key being built as you enter the passphrase. After you enter the complete passphrase, click **Next**.

IMPORTANT NOTE: **Make sure to enter the passphrase exactly as it appears on the printout. Lowercase *a* is different from uppercase *A*. The two keys (on the router and on the wireless card) must be identical.**

Step 6 A confirmation window appears (see Figure 9-56). Double-check the new security settings and click **Save** (with some Linksys wireless NICs, the option may be **Connect to Network**).

Figure 9-56 Confirm and Activate the New Settings

Step 7 Click the **Link Information** tab. If you entered everything correctly, the Signal Strength and Link Quality should reappear as green bars, as shown in Figure 9-57.

Figure 9-57 Successfully Connected

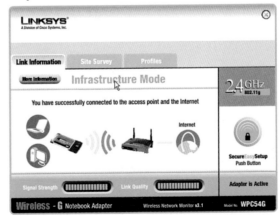

Step 8   Go back to the computer where the (main) EasyLink Advisor program is installed and see if the router now "sees" the computer we just added. Click the **My Network** tab. As shown in Figure 9-58, you can see graphically that there are three computers now connected to the wireless router: Computer1, which is the wired computer we used in Chapter 7 to set up the wireless router, and now Computer2 and Computer3 (which we named Susie and John), which are the computers we just added wireless security to.

Figure 9-58   Computers Reappear in the Network Diagram

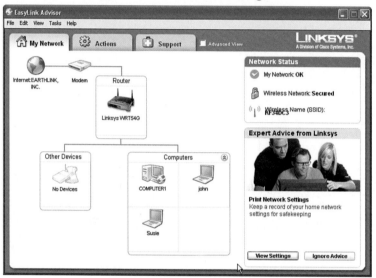

Again, the green bars may or may not be solid the whole way across. It depends on the strength of the wireless signal and how far away you are from the wireless router, much like a cell phone. If the link information shows no connection, you may have entered something incorrectly. Repeat the steps and double-check the settings, particularly that the passphrase is typed in exactly the same on the router and the wireless NIC. Also see the troubleshooting information in Part IV of this book, particularly Chapter 10.

You can further test the connection by trying to browse the Internet. Launch your web browser (such as Internet Explorer) and see if you can browse a web page.

More Wireless Security Steps

Enabling encryption is the most critical step to securing your wireless network. With that completed, there are a couple more simple steps you can take to make your wireless network secure. These steps by themselves will not provide bullet-proof security, but they do add to the security you have just implemented and they only take a few moments each to implement. First, we can stop "advertising" to other wireless NICs. Then, we can make sure the firewall function is enabled on the wireless router. Finally, we can make sure our NICs do not unintentionally roam to other wireless routers. These steps are discussed in the next few sections.

Stop Advertising Your Wireless Network

By default, wireless routers are set up to broadcast their SSID to make it easy for wireless cards to locate the wireless network without having to know information in advance. Nice feature, bad security practice. Broadcasting the SSID of our wireless home network is entirely unnecessary. So, one step to securing our network is to shut it off. To do so, follow these steps:

Step 1   Access the wireless router using your Internet browser. Click the **Wireless** tab.

Step 2   For Wireless SSID Broadcast, click the **Disable** radio button (see Figure 9-59). Click **Save Settings**.

Figure 9-59   Disable SSID Broadcast on the Wireless Router

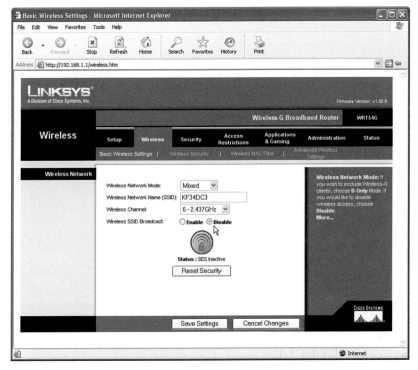

Just by taking these simple steps, you have made your wireless network relatively invisible and fairly anonymous so that people looking for signals will not see a router with your name on it.

 Note: As a reminder, do not use the default SSID that the wireless router is set up with. (For Linksys products, the default SSID is linksys.) If the SSID is not being broadcast but is easily guessed by intruders, your wireless network is still vulnerable. Change the SSID to something else, such as a random series of upper- and lowercase letters and numbers. Write it down.

Turn On the Firewall

Most (Linksys Brand) wireless routers are shipped with a Stateful Packet Inspection (SPI) firewall. An important step to securing the wireless network is to make sure this firewall is enabled. To enable the firewall, follow these steps:

Step 1   Access the wireless router using your Internet browser. Click the **Security** tab.

Step 2   For SPI Firewall Protection, click **Enabled**, as shown in Figure 9-60. Click **Save Settings**.

Figure 9-60   Enable the Firewall on the Wireless Router

By enabling the firewall, you have added another level of protection for your wireless network.

Note: Firewalls are beyond the scope of this book. For more information on the use of firewalls and other security steps you need to take to properly protect your home network, pick up a copy of *Home Network Security Simplified*.

Prevent Unintentional Roaming

Wireless networks are a bit like cell phones. Your cell phone tries to find the closest cell tower so that you can get the most bars of signal strength to have high-quality voice calls. Wireless NICs work in a similar way in that they try to find the wireless router that has the strongest signal. The assumption is that the router the NIC finds is yours because it is the closest and therefore has the strongest signal.

However, that is not always true. If you have poor signal strength in a particular room of your house and your neighbor's router actually has a better signal in that room, your wireless NIC might try to roam onto your neighbor's router, unless you instruct it not to.

You do not want your laptop unintentionally hopping over to your neighbor's wireless router whenever it sees a stronger signal or for whatever reason loses connectivity with your own router. Using the Linksys NIC management utilities (such as WLAN Monitor), avoiding such hopping is pretty easy. Simply do not add your neighbor's wireless SSID as a profile. When using Windows to manage wireless connections, an additional step is required. This is another good reason to change your SSID, because chances are that at least some of your neighbors will leave their SSID at the default of linksys, which may cause confusion later.

Another type of unintentional roaming is to inadvertently permit ad hoc wireless connections. As discussed in Chapter 4, "Planning Your Wireless Network," we recommend for security reasons that you operate your wireless home network in infrastructure mode, meaning a wireless router provides the central point of the network and all wireless computers communicate only with the central point, and not with each other directly (which is called *ad hoc*). This is a relatively low security risk, but there is a small possibility that those sitting next to us in an airport or other public location may try to make an ad hoc connection directly between their laptop and ours.

Because we plan to only ever use our laptop computers connected to a wireless router in infrastructure mode, we should disable ad hoc networking mode so that it is not possible for another laptop computer to attempt to make a connection directly to our laptop at all. Using the Linksys NIC management utilities (such as WLAN Monitor), we do this by selecting infrastructure mode. Again, when using Windows to manage wireless connections, an additional step is required.

The following steps describe how to take care of both issues:

> **Step 1**   Access the properties for the wireless NIC by choosing **Start > Connect To > Show All Connections**, select the wireless NIC, and click **Change Settings for This Connection**. Click the **Wireless Networks** tab, as shown in Figure 9-61.

Figure 9-61   Verify the Preferred Networks List

Step 2   Make sure that only your wireless network profile appears in the Preferred Networks list. If other networks are listed that you do not recognize, delete them.

Step 3   Click the **Advanced** button. Click **Access Point (Infrastructure) Networks Only** and make sure that Automatically Connect to Non-Preferred Networks is *not* checked (see Figure 9-62).

Figure 9-62   Verify Network Access Settings

Step 4   Click **Close** and then click **OK**.

Now, if the wireless NIC sees your neighbor's wireless router, it will not try to connect to it because it is not in the list of preferred networks. Similarly, if we encounter another computer with a wireless NIC that attempts to set up an ad hoc connection, our wireless NIC will not respond to the attempt, keeping our wireless network (and laptop) secure.

MAC Address Locking

One additional wireless security measure that you can take that has not yet been discussed is MAC address locking (often called MAC address filtering). Because each wireless card has a unique identifier called a MAC address, we could instruct the wireless router to accept connections only from the wireless cards that we know. This is called *MAC address locking*.

Turning on MAC address locking is not trivial and can be a bit of trouble. Remember, with every security measure enabled, you typically lose some flexibility. For example, with MAC address locking enabled, you need to change the configuration on the wireless router if you buy a new wireless card or device. Also, if you have visitors who want temporary Internet access, you would have to grant them access by adding their MAC address to the permission table. MAC address locking does provide an additional level of protection. If you want to enable it, see Appendix A, "MAC Address Filtering."

Top Troubleshooting Tips for Wireless Encryption

Chapters 10, 11, and 12 are dedicated to troubleshooting problems with wireless networks, including encryption-related issues. However, here are the top tips to follow if any of the computers do not re-establish communication. Items to check include the following:

❑ Make sure the encryption method chosen on both the wireless router and *all* wireless NICs is the *same*.

❑ Make sure the passphrase for WEP key generation (or WPA) is entered exactly the *same* on both the wireless router and *all* wireless NICs. The passphrase is case sensitive, which means that *p* is different from *P*. Take care to make sure the entered phrase matches *exactly*, including lower- and uppercase letters.

❑ If all else fails, disable encryption on both the wireless router and all wireless network adapters, reverify the connections without encryption turned on, and then start the encryption setup from scratch.

Summary

Wireless networks are extremely beneficial, but you must take some simple steps to protect them. Failing to take the steps in this chapter is the equivalent of locking the front door and leaving all windows and back doors unlocked and standing open. It is pretty easy (and *so* critical) to add appropriate security. Here's a quick checklist to refer to:

❑ Change the password on the wireless router from the default (for example, admin).

❑ Change the SSID from the default (for example, linksys) to a random series of lower- and uppercase letters and numbers.

❑ Enable WEP or WPA encryption on the wireless router and all wireless network adapters. Use the strongest encryption level that all devices support.

❑ Use a WEP or WPA passphrase that is a random series of lower- and uppercase letters and numbers.

❑ Disable SSID broadcast on the wireless router.

❑ Disable ad hoc wireless networking on all network adapters (applies to Windows XP).

❑ Disable autoconnection to nonpreferred networks on all wireless network adapters.

The steps in this chapter are what most people need to take to keep their wireless network secure in all but the most extreme cases. The fact is that your SSID can be guessed or discovered, encryption schemes can be cracked (especially WEP), and MAC addresses can be spoofed (via a method called MAC address cloning); but doing all of this takes a great deal of skill, time, and money. If you want more protection than that described in this chapter, you can get it, but if you are still worried about wireless security, your best solution might be to stick with a wired network. Another good tip that we strongly recommend is to just turn off your wireless router and modem when you leave the house for an extended period or even over night. If it's not turned on, it can't be hacked.

Where to Go for More Information

The following are good sources of information for additional learning about wireless security:

Wikipedia has an entry for wireless security: http://en.wikipedia.org/wiki/wireless_security

Practically Networked is a good source for additional wireless security information: www.practicallynetworked.com/support/wireless_secure.htm

Tony Bradley has a helpful article on about.com titled *Introduction to Wireless Network Security*: http://netsecurity.about.com/od/hackertools/a/aa072004b.htm

You might also want to check out *Home Network Security Simplified*, one of our other books (Cisco Press, 2006)

PART IV

"Honey, This Stupid Wireless Thing Is Not Working"

Problems? We don't need no stinking problems.

Okay, so we would like to be able to say that wireless networks are so darn easy that you won't run into any issues. Unfortunately, we cannot do that. Wireless networks are a relatively new and fast-moving technology, which is the high-tech industry's way of saying stuff changes quite a bit, and stuff does not always work the way it's supposed to.

So invariably if you build a wireless home network of any kind, sooner or later you are going to hear those eight words: "Honey, this stupid wireless thing is not working." What do you do then? Because we cannot promise there won't be any problems, we give you some skills to figure out the most common problems and solve them. If nothing else, you will learn enough to be able to talk intelligently to a professional, should you need to call one in. That's what Part IV is all about.

Chapter 10, "Troubleshooting: I Can't Connect at All," shows you how to troubleshoot basic communications issues. We cover how to figure out why a wireless NIC and wireless router are not talking, and how to figure out who the likely culprit is. Then we show you what to do to get them talking again.

Chapter 11, "Troubleshooting: I Can Connect Sometimes," shows you how to troubleshoot range issues, meaning problems related to signal strength. Wireless networks are a lot like cell phones: no bars, no "workie." We cover how to figure out if you have dead spots in your house and give some tips for improving coverage.

We wrap up Part IV with Chapter 12, "Troubleshooting: I Can Connect, but It's Slow," which shows you how to get the best performance out of your wireless network. It may work, and you may get Internet access from the deck, but are you getting the speed you should be? We cover how to examine the speed you are getting between your computers and wireless router and give some tips for improving performance. We also show you how to figure out if your wireless network or broadband service is creating the slowdown.

The first step to figuring out what is wrong is to determine the type of problem you are having. Then, based on that determination, you can dive into the right troubleshooting steps. Here's a quick reference table to get you started:

Type of Problem	Start Here
My computer will not connect over wireless.	Chapter 10
My computer connects over wireless in certain places in my house but it won't connect in others.	Chapter 11
My computer connects over wireless but drops the connection at times.	Chapter 11
My computer connects over wireless but the connection is slow.	Chapter 12
My computer connects over wireless but cannot reach the Internet.	Chapter 12

Troubleshooting:
I Can't Connect at All

Usually, wireless networks are pretty easy to set up and connect to, but, as we said earlier, due to the fast-moving nature of the technology, sometimes the network does not work as it is supposed to. In this chapter we will cover what to do if you cannot get a computer or laptop to connect over the wireless connection to the wireless router. Start here if you cannot get the computer and router to connect at all. If you can connect sometimes but not others, skip to the next chapter.

Before jumping into troubleshooting, let's first take a look at what happens during the steps when your wireless NIC connects to your wireless router and at what can go wrong during that process.

Gasp! I'm right in the middle of IM-ing Cody and the network goes down. Now, if I don't reply in the next 15 seconds, he'll think I'm mad at him and ask Zoe out!

What up? I'm ready to destroy my nemesis Ray-Dar in *Inter-Planetary Drive-By* and bam! I'm booted.

You are not connected.
Your security is mismatched.

Steps to Connecting

When a wireless NIC and wireless router want to establish a connection, several steps need to occur, as shown in Figure 10-1 and described in the following sections. The example assumes your wireless NICs can see signals from two wireless routers, KF34DC3, which we have been using in previous examples as your router, and a second system named homenet, which is a neighbor's wireless router.

Figure 10-1   How a Wireless NIC Joins a Wireless Network

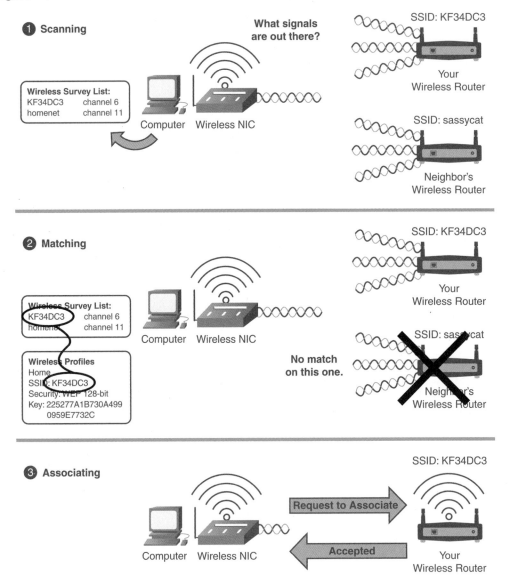

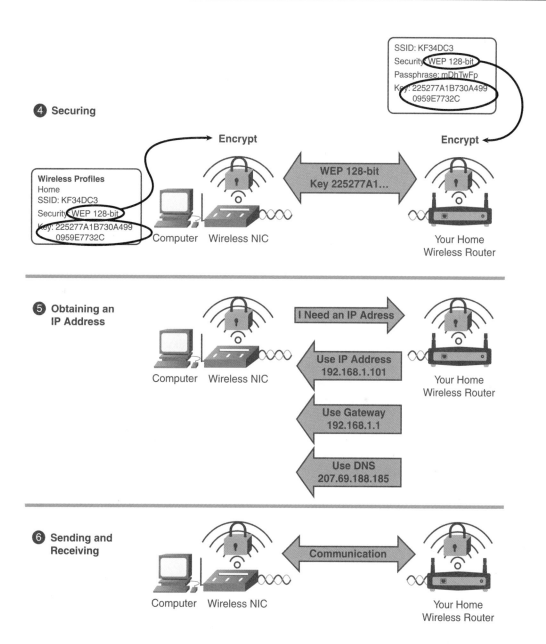

Scanning

First, the wireless NIC must perform a scan for available wireless signals, similar to the way your cell phone searches for a network when you turn it on. The NIC makes a list of the available wireless networks, including their SSID and channel. In this example the systems found were KF34DC3 and homenet.

Matching

Second, the wireless NIC checks the list of available signals to its wireless profiles to see if there is a system it recognizes, again much like your cell phone tries to match the cellular systems it sees with your provider. The NIC matches the SSID, in this example KF34DC3. There is no match on the other system, homenet.

Associating

Third, the wireless NIC selects the system that was matched *and* with the highest signal strength (this will become important in Chapter 11, "Troubleshooting: I Can Connect Sometimes"). In this example, there is only one match, so signal strength is not a factor. The wireless NIC sends an association request to the wireless router, which basically says, "Hey, mind if I join your wireless network?" Assuming it is permitted, the wireless router responds with an acceptance. The wireless NIC is then associated with the wireless network.

Securing the Connection

Next, the wireless NIC and wireless router both use the security information they have been programmed with, such as a WEP key or WPA key, and start sending information between them using encryption. If the security information matches and each side is using the correct key, the conversation is understood and can proceed. Now the wireless NIC and wireless router can freely, and securely, send and receive packets to and from each other.

Note: Technically speaking, with WPA there is an additional step that happens called *authentication*, where the two sides of the communication (the NIC and the router) exchange a WPA key to verify the identity of the NIC. We are combining that step with the securing step, for simplicity.

Obtaining an IP Address

Next, the wireless NIC needs to be assigned an IP address that it can be known by on the home network. We have set up the wireless router to assign IP addresses dynamically (as they are needed) to the home network, from a pool of addresses in the range of 192.168.1.100 to 192.168.1.149. This is the recommended way to set up home networks. In this step, the wireless NIC requests an IP address and is assigned 192.168.1.101.

Typically, a couple other important pieces of information—the gateway and DNS addresses—are passed to the NIC as well. The gateway is the address the NIC will always send traffic to in order to reach the Internet. The DNS is the server that will translate URLs such as http://www.cnn.com into the actual IP address on the Internet. The gateway is typically the wireless router, and the DNS is provided by your Internet service provider (ISP).

Sending and Receiving

With the connection fully established, the computer with the wireless NIC can send and receive information to and from the home network, as well as the Internet.

What Can Go Wrong

Sounds pretty easy, right? In most cases it is, but joining a wireless network is a little like traveling on a trip with a very tight itinerary: If one leg of the journey does not go as planned, you miss a connecting flight, and it can mess up the whole trip.

What can go wrong? Well, during each of the steps discussed in the previous section, something can go wrong. Some of the issues are shown in Figure 10-2 and described in the following sections.

Figure 10-2 Things That Can Go Wrong Joining a Wireless Network

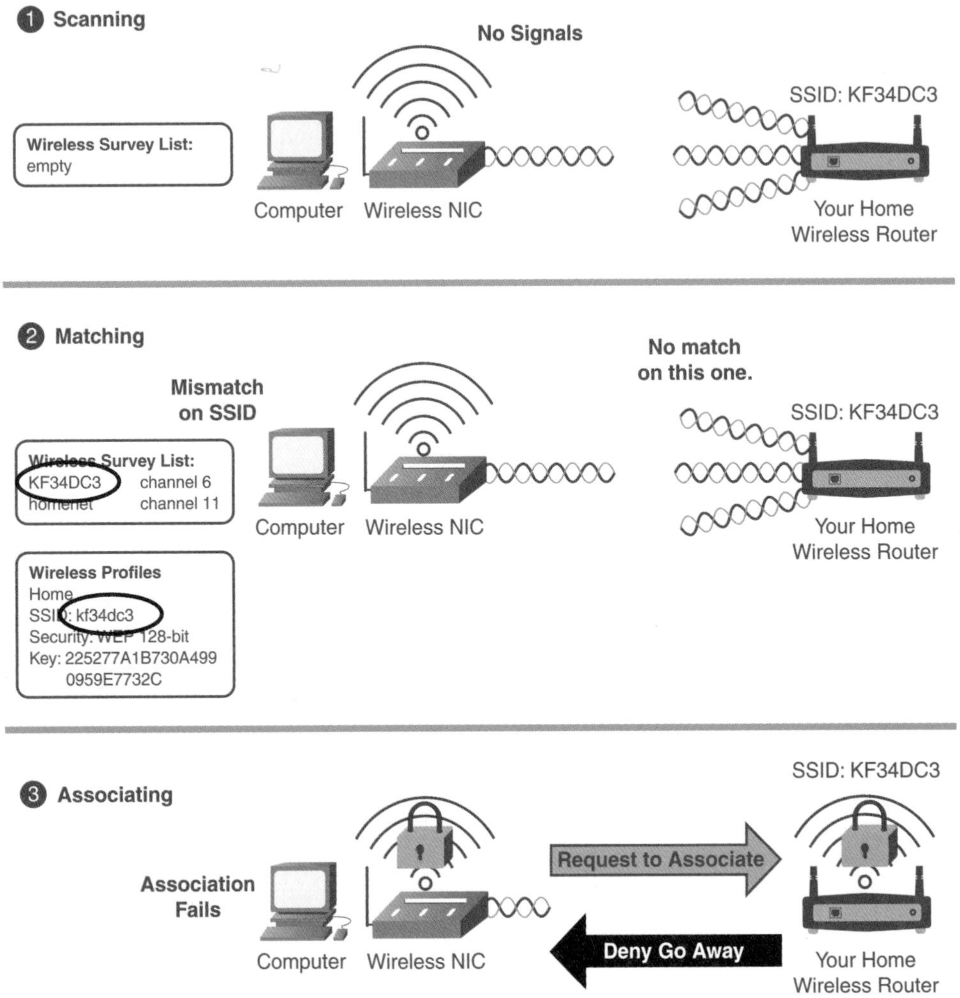

Problems During Scanning

If your wireless NIC does not see any wireless signals from a wireless router, you are pretty much dead in the water. Reasons for this could be that you are using the wireless NIC in a room of your house (or outside) with poor coverage. Another very common reason is that your laptop has a switch that turns the NIC on and off to save power, and you forget to turn it on. Unfortunately, most laptop built-in NICs we have seen do not alert you that you simply forgot to switch it on, but instead just give you an indication that there are no wireless signals in range. Quite maddening.

Don't worry if you have the SSID broadcast turned off on your router. When the NIC scans for a router, it will find it even if the broadcast function is turned off. If this is confusing, think of it this way: When broadcast is on, the router will continuously shout out to every NIC that is in range "I'm here! I'm here! I'm here!" When the broadcast function is turned off, the router will only answer "I'm here!" when the NIC first shouts "Are you there?"

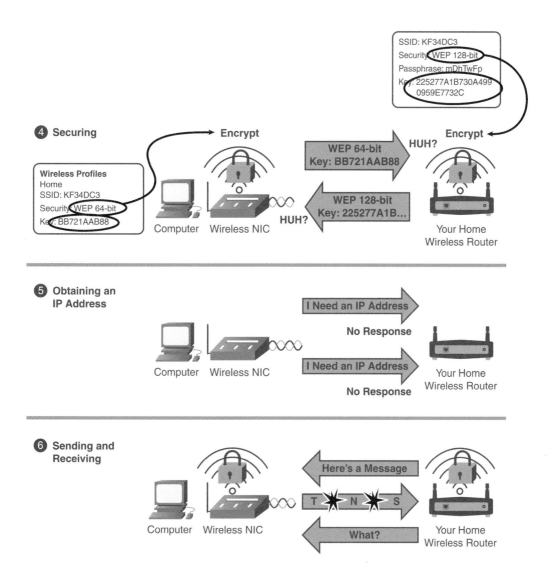

Problems During Matching

During the matching step, it is possible that the wireless networks "in range" do not match those in the wireless profiles. In this example, we made an error setting up the wireless NIC. The wireless router is set up with an SSID of KF34DC3 but the wireless NIC is set up with an SSID of kf34dc3. You may be staring at the page saying, "Huh? These look the same to me." They are similar, but capitalization matters, so from a wireless network point of view, these are two different SSIDs. There are no indications or help in this case from the wireless NIC. It will not attempt to associate with the other SSID (KF34DC3) that is not in its wireless profiles and will keep scanning for one it recognizes.

Problems During Association

During the association step, it is possible the wireless router may not accept our association request. One reason could be that when we enabled MAC filtering/blocking as a security measure on the wireless router, we either configured it incorrectly or perhaps typed in the MAC address of the wireless NIC incorrectly. Again, there will be little indication of a problem by the wireless NIC. If you are lucky you may get a message from the wireless NIC manager utility you are using saying that the association failed. More than likely you will not be told anything, and the wireless NIC will go on about its merry way, scanning for another system.

Problems Securing the Connection

During the securing step, a couple of things can go wrong. The most likely problem has to do with mismatched security settings between the wireless NIC and wireless router. If you set the security type differently—for example, 64-bit WEP on the NIC and 128-bit WEP on the router—that is a problem. Another example is if you made an error typing in the WEP key or WPA key, such as mDhTwFp on the router but MDhTwFp on the NIC. These look the same, but the difference between "m" and "M" is huge from a WEP or WPA key perspective.

Once again, you will not get an indication that there is a security mismatch. The NIC and the router will be unable to communicate, so the association will simply fail, and the NIC will move on to try another system. From a security point of view, giving no indication of the failure is actually what we want it to do. After all, we do not want the wireless router or wireless NIC giving hints to a hacker trying to join our wireless network uninvited. But this has the consequence of not being much help to us in diagnosing our own legitimate wireless joining problem.

Problems Obtaining an IP Address

In most cases, once we make it past the securing step, establishing a connection goes pretty smoothly. However, for whatever reason, the wireless NIC might be unable to obtain an IP address from the wireless router. Fortunately, when this error occurs we can at least see an indication that it has happened, although we do not receive much else in the way of why it happened.

Problems Sending and Receiving

With the connection fully established, we are in the clear, right? Not always. Sometimes you can associate and get connected, but then your data gets garbled during sending and receiving, possibly from interference from other wireless devices, like a cordless phone, microwave, or even a neighbor's wireless network. In this case, usually the result is slower performance. Problems sending and receiving can also occur when you are just on the edge of coverage, so sometimes you get a good enough signal, and the next minute you don't. Sound familiar? Yes, your cell phone has probably given you similar fits. We can see when this is happening with a wireless network, and Chapter 11, "Troubleshooting: I Can Connect Sometimes," and Chapter 12, "Troubleshooting: I Can Connect, but It's Slow," discuss these problems more in depth.

Five Things to Look At First

Before you roll up your sleeves to troubleshoot in depth, you may want to take a look at the five most common things that keep people from getting connected to the Internet on their wireless network:

- **Check whether you have a working Internet connection**—Using a computer that has a wired network connection to the ports on the back of the wireless router, confirm that you can access the Internet by trying to browse a web page. If you cannot access the Internet from the wired computer, you are not going to be able to access it from a computer that is wireless either. See the section "How to Tell if You Do Not Have a Connection" that follows for more information.

- **Make sure the wireless NIC is turned on in your PC**—If you have a laptop, it usually has a way to power off the wireless NIC to save battery life (and for required shut-off on airplanes during flight). Make sure it is turned on. See the section "Wireless Turned Off" later in this chapter for more information.

- **Check for a good wireless signal**—Using the wireless NIC management utility (such as the Windows Wireless Network Connection utility, Linksys WLAN Monitor, Boingo, and so on), confirm that you can get a wireless signal. Sit the laptop next to the wireless router. If you still see no signal or a weak signal, something else is wrong. Make sure you are trying to connect to the right wireless router (SSID) and that the wireless router is functioning. Try rebooting the wireless router and laptop also.

- **Check whether you have disabled SSID broadcast**—Disabling SSID broadcast is a good security measure, but it makes troubleshooting more difficult. Enable SSID broadcast on the wireless router and leave it enabled until you have a well-functioning wireless network with no connection issues.

- **Check whether you can connect with the security disabled**—Turn off the wireless security measures, including WEP or WPA, on both the wireless router and wireless NICs. Can you make a wireless connection without security enabled? If so, that gives you a good indication that security settings are mismatched somewhere. See the section "Security- and Encryption-Related Issues" later in this chapter for more information.

Once you have confirmed that none of these is the issue, it is time to try some more in-depth diagnosing of the problem, which is the topic of the rest of this chapter.

How to Tell if You Do Not Have a Connection

The most common way to determine whether or not you have a wireless connection is to try accessing the Internet with an Internet browser, such as Internet Explorer, on the computer with the wireless connection. If you get the infamous "The page cannot be displayed" message, as shown in Figure 10-3, that is a good indication that you have some kind of problem.

Figure 10-3   Internet Browser Cannot Access the Internet

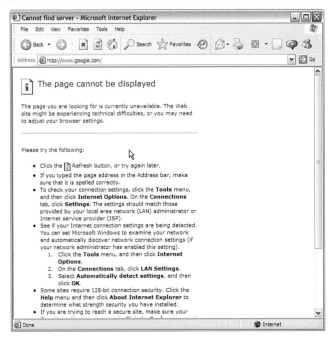

Before you go any further in troubleshooting the computer with the wireless connection, walk over to a computer that has a wired connection to the wireless router and try to access the Internet first from that computer. Many perceived wireless network issues turn out to be just a general problem with the broadband service.

If you cannot access the Internet from a wired computer, troubleshoot getting your wireless router to properly connect to the broadband modem, and so on. Start with Chapter 7, "Wireless Router Setup." If you need more in-depth help getting the wireless router to work with your broadband service, pick up a copy of *Home Networking Simplified*, which contains more information.

Once you have confirmed that your Internet access is working from a wired computer and that it is still not working from your wireless-connected computer, the next thing to check is to see if you have a wireless connection. Depending on which wireless connection manager you are using to manage your wireless NIC, each has a slightly different way to tell if you have a good connection to the wireless router. They generally display a fairly straightforward visual indicator that tells you if you have a connection or not.

If you are using the Windows Wireless Network Connection utility, choose **Start > Connect To > Show All Connections**. Select the wireless NIC and then click **View Wireless Networks**. Figure 10-4 shows that the wireless network with SSID KF34DC3 has a few bars of signal strength, but the status listed is Not Connected.

Figure 10-4   Verifying a Wireless Connection with Windows XP

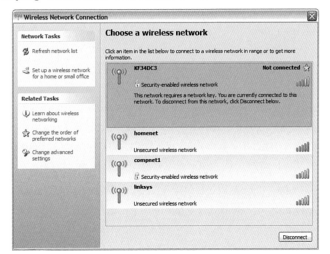

If you are using the Linksys WLAN Monitor utility, double-click the icon on the desktop to launch the utility or choose **Start > Programs > Linksys Wireless Card > WLAN Monitor**. Figure 10-5 shows that there is no connection to the wireless router. Very clearly, the utility tells us there is "No association with access point," meaning the NIC and the router are not communicating.

Figure 10-5   Verifying a Wireless Connection with Linksys WLAN Monitor

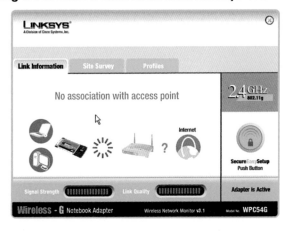

Figuring Out Why It Will Not Connect

Earlier in this chapter we talked about the steps that a wireless NIC and wireless router go through to connect to each other, and also what can go wrong. Here is the secret to figuring out where the trouble is: follow the connection steps and find out which step is not occurring correctly. This seems simple, but we have seen many people trying random remedies. Eventually they may get it, mainly by accident, but sometimes they walk away frustrated. Trust us, and we may save you a lot of time and frustration with the methodical approach we have put together here.

Let's review our six connection steps: scanning, matching, associating, securing, obtaining an IP address, and sending/receiving. This section covers each of these steps, describes how to recognize a problem, and offers some remedies.

Scanning-Related Issues

During the scanning phase, the wireless NIC searches for available wireless networks. The wireless router sends out a "beacon" letting wireless NICs know that it is there (this is what SSID broadcast is, and the beacon only works when the feature is enabled). When the NIC detects and reads the beacon, it makes a record of this network as being available.

If you perform a "survey" using your wireless NIC manager (Windows Wireless Network Connection utility, Linksys WLAN Monitor, or one of the other options such as Boingo; see Chapter 14, "Wireless to Go") and do not see your home network wireless router SSID in the list of available networks, this is a scanning issue.

Why would your wireless NIC not be able to see your wireless router? There are three common issues that can occur, including incompatible wireless standards, a disabled wireless NIC, or poor signal coverage.

Incompatible Wireless Standards

In Chapter 2, "Wireless Standards: What the Letters Mean," and Chapter 3, "Selecting the Right Wireless Standard for Your Network," we covered the different wireless standards, including which standards are compatible and which are not. As an easy rule of thumb, 802.11b, 802.11g, and 802.11n work together, and 802.11a is special. If you have an 802.11a wireless NIC and an 802.11g router, your NIC will never see the router.

Some NICs and routers that support multiple standards offer the ability to limit the modes in operation. For example, an 802.11b/g router may allow you to set it to function as g-only, meaning disable the 802.11b mode and thereby accept only 802.11g wireless NICs. If you then try to connect with an 802.11b NIC, it will not see the router.

Here is another example where a wireless NIC supports 802.11a, b, and g, but the NIC has been inadvertently set to a-only. Under Windows XP, choose **Start > Connect To > Show All Connections**. Select the wireless NIC, click **Change Settings of This Connection**, and then click the **Configure** button. Figure 10-6 shows the result on a laptop with a built-in Intel 802.11a/b/g NIC.

Here we can see that the NIC is set to 802.11a only. If we are connecting to an 802.11g router, this NIC will never see the router. Figure 10-7 shows the corrected setting of 802.11b and 802.11g.

Figure 10-6   Checking the Wireless Mode on a Multi-Standard NIC

Figure 10-7   Correcting the Wireless Mode on a Multi-Standard NIC

By the way, you do not have to check this setting every time you have a wireless connection issue. Just check it the first time you are trying to set up your network and have an issue.

Wireless Turned Off

It seems like a pretty foolish mistake, but not turning on your wireless NIC is probably the single biggest cause of wireless network problems. You may be reading this thinking, "No way! Do they think I'm stupid or something?" Trust us, we have done it ourselves many times, as have those around us. No matter how stupid it may seem, please check it, and check it again.

For good measure, don't forget to check that the wireless router is turned on and wireless is enabled, too. It may seem like a silly thing to do, but it beats troubleshooting for two hours only to find out your router was turned off.

If you are using the Wireless Network Connection utility, choose **Start > Connect To > Show All Connections**. Select the wireless NIC and then click **View Wireless Networks**. Figure 10-8 shows an example.

Figure 10-8   Determining if the Wireless NIC Is Turned On in Windows XP

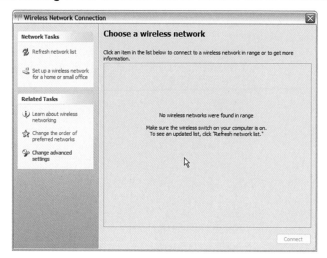

Here we see that the NIC has detected no networks within range, and Windows XP suggests that we make sure the wireless NIC is on. It could mean either that the NIC is off or (unfortunately) that the NIC is on and there are really no signals detected. Windows XP does not have the ability (apparently) of telling us definitively if the NIC is on or off. So, we just have to go check it ourselves.

Many laptops have a hard switch on the outside to turn the NIC on and off (to save battery life or on airplanes where it is required to be turned off). Most laptops also have a "soft" switch, where you press a function key to toggle the NIC on and off. For example, on an IBM ThinkPad, simultaneously pressing the blue Fn key and the F5 key shows the NIC toggle function display, as shown in Figure 10-9. We can see that the wireless NIC is off. Clicking the Turn On button will power the NIC on, where it will immediately begin the scanning step.

Some laptops also have an LED indicator that tells you if the wireless NIC is on or off. Consult the user guide for your laptop.

Figure 10-9   Toggling the Wireless NIC On and Off with an IBM ThinkPad

Figure 10-10 shows the result for a built-in Intel 802.11 a/b/g NIC. Choose **Start > Connect To > Show All Connections**. Select the wireless NIC, click **Change Settings of This Connection**, and then click the **Configure** button. Figure 10-10 shows that the wireless NIC is off, and we can use the selection list to turn it on by choosing **Wireless On**.

Figure 10-10 Toggling the Wireless NIC On and Off with Windows XP

Each laptop manufacturer provides a slightly different method, so check the user manual for your laptop to see how your particular wireless NIC can be turned on and off.

Poor Signal Strength

Another very common issue with wireless networks is signal coverage. Think of it as being similar to your cell phone and the cell tower. As you are driving away from the cell tower, you see the number of bars shrinking on your cell phone display. Sometimes, if you take your cell phone into the interior of a building or into an elevator, you lose the signal altogether. Wireless networks function in the same way. Wireless routers reach only so far, and the more objects, such as floors and walls, between your computer and the router, the more *attenuated* the signal becomes.

Attenuation refers to how much of the wireless signal gets absorbed by natural objects while it is traveling from the transmitter (wireless router) to the receiver (wireless NIC). In general, 802.11a networks have more attenuation than 802.11 b/g/n networks, so the distance away from the router in which you can receive a strong signal is not as far for 802.11a networks.

The ranges printed on the boxes of the routers do not take attenuation into account and are "idealized" ranges.

How do you tell if you have a weak signal? Most NIC utilities have an indicator much like your cell phone that displays a series of bars indicating a weak or strong signal. If you are using the Windows Wireless Network Connection utility, choose **Start > Connect To > Show All Connections**. Select the wireless NIC and then click **View Wireless Networks**. Figure 10-11 shows an example.

In this example we can see that for the wireless network with SSID KF34DC3, we have two out of five bars of signal strength. We do not necessarily need five bars to make a good connection, but if the signal shows only a single bar (or, with some NICs, even two bars) of signal strength, the signal could be too low to make a good connection.

Figure 10-11 Checking Wireless Signal Strength with Windows XP

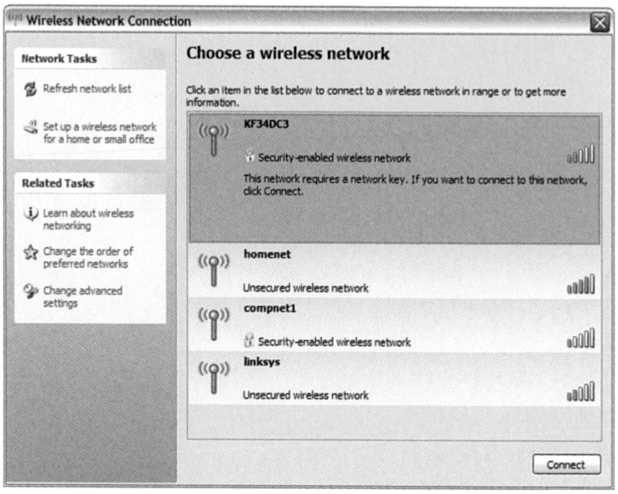

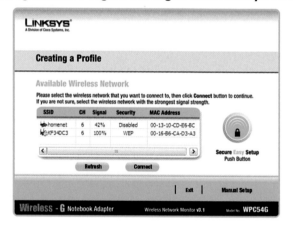

If you are using the Linksys WLAN Monitor utility, double-click the icon on the desktop to launch the utility or choose **Start > Programs > Linksys Wireless Card > WLAN Monitor**. Click the **Site Survey** tab. Figure 10-12 shows an example of a strong signal.

Figure 10-12 Checking Wireless Signal Strength with Linksys WLAN Monitor

In this example we see that the signal strength for the wireless network with SSID KF34DC3 is 100 percent. This is a good, strong signal. You do not need 100 percent to have a good connection, but if you see between 0 percent and about 20 percent, the signal could be too low to make a good connection.

One remedy to try if you see very low signal strength is to move the laptop or computer much closer to the wireless router, preferably in the same room. You should see a much stronger signal strength. If not, you may have some other issue and may want to check if the wireless router is functioning correctly. Make sure the wireless is enabled on the wireless router, and try rebooting it.

If the problem was a very low signal strength in the room you were trying to use the laptop in, before going much further in this chapter, you should probably take a look at Chapter 11, which focuses on signal strength and coverage issues.

You may also want to click the **Refresh** button (or **Refresh Network List** in the case of Windows Wireless Network Connection utility) a few times and note if the signal level changes. If the signal strength fluctuates between good and poor, you may have some form of interference that is causing trouble for your wireless network. In this case you may want to take a look at Chapter 12, which focuses on intermittent problems and performance issues.

If you have a strong, steady signal and the darn thing just will not connect at all, proceed with the rest of this chapter.

Matching-Related Issues

Once you have confirmed that the wireless NIC is scanning properly and detecting the wireless router, move on to the matching step. During matching, the wireless NIC compares the list of wireless SSIDs it has detected during scanning to the list of wireless SSIDs that are set up in the wireless profiles on the laptop or computer. A wireless profile (as you recall from Chapter 8, "Wireless NIC Setup") is a set of the characteristics for a wireless network that you previously connected to, or that you programmed in advance of connecting to.

Why would your wireless NIC not match on your wireless router? Two common issues can occur, including an SSID mismatch and a "bug" related to SSID broadcast.

SSID Mismatch

A common problem in matching on a wireless network is a mismatched SSID. This is especially true if you had to manually type in the SSID to set up the wireless NIC. If you used a more automated setup process, such as the Linksys EasyLink Advisor utility, the SSID can be programmed into the NIC automatically.

The most common error people make is to overlook that the SSID is case sensitive and that the wrong case has been used, or to overlook that a number and letter have been confused, such as the letter *O* being used in place of the number 0.

To verify that the SSIDs match in your wireless network, first double-check that you have written down the exact SSID that is set up in the wireless router. To do so, access the router using an Internet browser. Click the **Wireless** tab, as shown in Figure 10-13.

Figure 10-13 Verifying the SSID on the Wireless Router

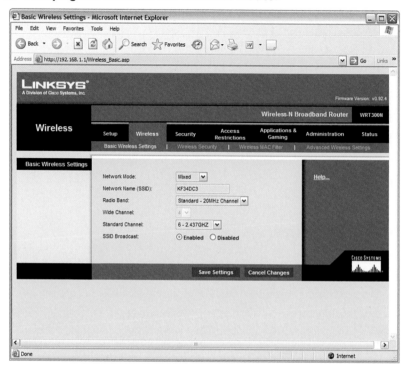

We can see that the router is set up with an SSID of KF34DC3. Write it down *exactly* as it appears, paying attention to upper- and lowercase letters.

Now let's check the wireless NIC to make sure it has that exact SSID programmed into the wireless profile. If you are using the Windows Wireless Network Connection utility, choose **Start > Connect To > Show All Connections**. Select the wireless NIC and then click **Change Settings for This Connection**. Click the **Wireless Networks** tab. Figure 10-14 shows that the SSID is set to kf34dc3. This is not the same SSID entered on the wireless router, because of the difference in case, so the NIC will never match on the wireless network.

Figure 10-14 Verifying the SSID on the Wireless NIC Using Windows XP

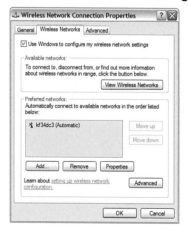

Unfortunately, in Windows XP, there is no way to edit the SSID for an existing wireless profile. Instead, you have to click **Remove** to delete the wireless profile and then click **Add** to create a new one with the right SSID. Figure 10-15 shows an example, with the correct SSID of KF34DC3.

Figure 10-15 Correcting the SSID on the Wireless NIC with Windows XP

If you are using the Linksys WLAN Monitor utility, double-click the icon on the desktop to launch the utility or choose **Start > Programs > Linksys Wireless Card > WLAN Monitor**. Click the **Wireless Profiles** tab. Select the profile for your home wireless network and click the **Edit** button. Click **Next** until you find the SSID, as shown in Figure 10-16 (to save space, all the preceding dialog boxes are not shown here).

Figure 10-16 Verifying the SSID on the Wireless NIC with Linksys WLAN Monitor

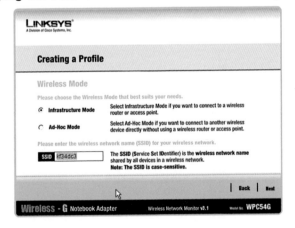

Similar to the Windows XP example earlier, we can see that the SSID is set to kf34dc3, which is a case mismatch with the SSID of the wireless router. In this case, though, we can simply change the setting to the correct value of **KF34DC3**, click **Next** several times until we reach the Confirmation dialog box, and then click **Save** to save the settings in the wireless profile.

With the SSID corrected, and with any luck, the wireless NIC may find the wireless router and connect properly now. If not, unfortunately, there is no conclusive way to verify that the SSID matching is occurring correctly. We can only verify it, double-check it, and move on (or perhaps call someone else into the room, a different pair of eyes, to triple-check it for you).

SSID Broadcast

In Chapter 9, "Wireless Security Setup," we told you that it is a good security practice to disable the SSID broadcast function on your wireless router. This instructs the wireless router not to "beacon" the SSID, effectively to stop advertising your wireless router to anyone in the immediate vicinity.

However, if you are having wireless connection issues, you *definitely* want to enable SSID broadcast on the wireless router. First of all, troubleshooting is more difficult if SSID broadcast is disabled. If you are having connection issues, enable SSID broadcast and leave it enabled until you have no more issues and are confident you can disable it.

Depending on the wireless connection manager you are using, wireless routers with the SSID disabled may not show up in the list. So if you have a mismatch in SSID, knowing that would be difficult because you won't be able to actually see the router.

Secondly, we have seen a few NICs that simply cannot locate a wireless router if the SSID broadcast function is disabled, even if the SSID is programmed perfectly into the wireless profile of the NIC. This is actually a "bug," an error in the product. So again, enabling SSID broadcast will uncover if this is the situation with the wireless NIC you are using.

To enable SSID broadcast on your wireless router, access the router using an Internet browser. Click the **Wireless** tab, as shown in Figure 10-17. On the **SSID Broadcast** line, click **Enabled** and then click **Save Settings**.

Figure 10-17 Enabling SSID Broadcast on the Wireless Router

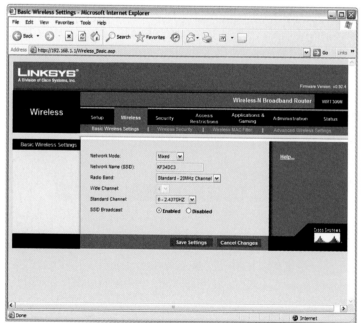

Retry the laptop or computer you were having an issue with and see if it can now connect to the wireless router successfully.

Association-Related Issues

After the wireless NIC locates the wireless router's signal and matches the SSID, it sends an association request to the router to formally join the wireless network. Without this association, a computer or laptop is not permitted to send packets to or receive packets from the wireless network. It can only stand outside looking in the windows at the party.

Why would the wireless router refuse an association request? There are not very many reasons, actually. The most common reason is that MAC filtering (a form of security), which we referred to in Chapter 9 and discuss more in depth in Appendix A, "MAC Address Filtering."

MAC filtering, which you can enable on the wireless router, restricts the computers and laptops that can join the wireless network, by keeping a list of the authorized MAC addresses—the unique identifier of each wireless (and wired) NIC. Each NIC on planet earth has a unique MAC address.

MAC filtering can examine the MAC address of a computer trying to join the wireless network, and refuse entry if it is not on the preauthorized list. It makes for a pretty good additional security measure, but it can cause problems.

The three most common errors people make when enabling MAC filtering are as follows:

- Enabling Prevent instead of Permit, effectively reversing the function of MAC filtering to exclude a list of MAC addresses instead of authorizing them

- Forgetting to add a MAC address for a new device or computer to the authorized list

- Making an error when manually typing the MAC address into the authorization list

To see if MAC filtering is causing an issue, the best thing to do is turn it off and see if the problem goes away. To disable MAC filtering, access the wireless router using an Internet browser. Click the **Wireless** tab and then the **Wireless MAC Filter** subtab, as shown in Figure 10-18. Click **Disabled** and click **Save Settings**.

If it was already disabled, MAC filtering is not the problem; move on to the next troubleshooting step. If it was enabled and turning it off corrects the issue, then something is wrong with the way MAC filtering is set up on your wireless router.

When checking the MAC filtering setup, first see if the Prevent/Permit option is set correctly. On the same Wireless MAC Filter subtab of your wireless router, make sure that the Permit PCs Listed Below to Access the Wireless Network radio button is selected, as shown in Figure 10-19. If **Prevent PCs Listed Below from Accessing the Wireless Network** is selected, it will reverse the operation and keep your computers from accessing the network. Don't forget to click **Save Settings** if you change the setting.

Figure 10-18 Disabling MAC Filtering on the Wireless Router

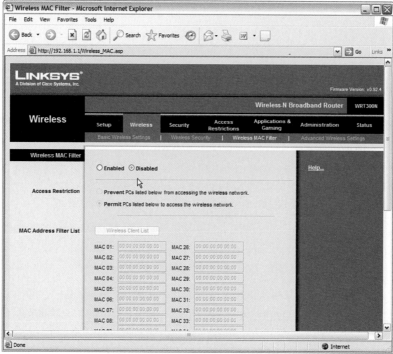

Figure 10-19 Verifying the MAC Filtering Setting on the Wireless Router

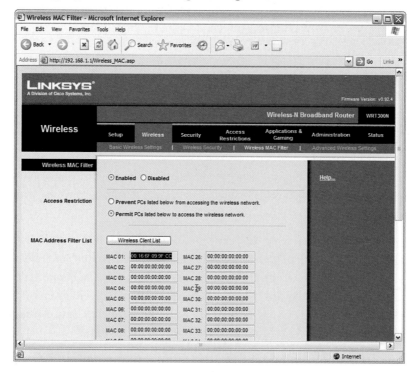

Next, we need to verify that the MAC address is correctly entered. Find the MAC address for the wireless NIC again. It is usually printed on the NIC itself, the packaging, or on a label on the underside of the laptop.

You can also find the MAC address with Windows XP. Choose **Start > Connect To > Show All Connections**. Select the wireless NIC and then click **View Status of This Connection**. Click the **Support** tab and then click the **Details** button. Figure 10-20 shows an example.

Figure 10-20 Finding the MAC Address with Windows XP

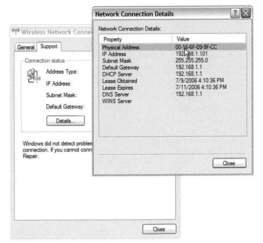

The physical address is the MAC address, in this example 00-16-6F-09-9F-CC. Write it down. MAC addresses are not case sensitive, so 6f is the same as 6F.

On the same screen on the wireless router, double-check that the MAC address in the authorization list is identical, as shown in Figure 10-21.

If it is not correct, then click **Edit MAC List** and correct the entry. Note that ":" is substituted for "-" in this case. If you change anything, remember to click **Save Settings**.

As discussed earlier, if MAC filtering is on, start by turning it off and seeing if the problem is corrected. Then, if you want to turn it back on, check and correct the settings as discussed.

Figure 10-21 Verifying the MAC Address on the Wireless Router

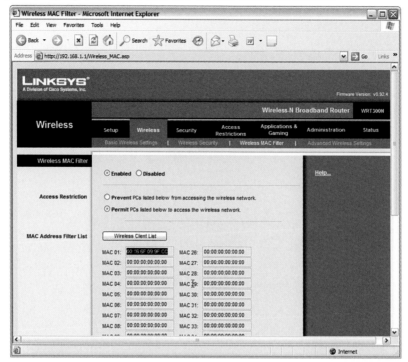

Security- and Encryption-Related Issues

After the wireless NIC successfully locates, matches on, and associates with a wireless router, the next step is to secure the connection with encryption. As we discussed in Chapter 9 and several times earlier, it is essential that you turn encryption on in your wireless network to protect against casual eavesdroppers and others. Turning on encryption is getting easier, but it can still be a little tricky.

If encryption is causing an issue on your wireless network, you will unfortunately not get a very good indication from either the wireless NIC or the wireless router. You may see the wireless NIC associate briefly, but then not "stay on" the wireless network, and start scanning again. You most likely will not receive a message such as "WEP key does not match" or "Wrong WPA key." Whenever you try to connect, the result after attempting will be "Not connected."

What kinds of problems would cause security and encryption not to work properly? There are three primary reasons: a mismatch of encryption type, a mismatch of the encryption key, or a mismatch of Windows XP authentication settings.

Encryption Type Mismatch

The first major step to troubleshooting security is to make sure you are using the same encryption type throughout the wireless network. As discussed in Chapters 5, (Wireless Security: What You Need to Know,) and 9, currently there are two major types of wireless encryption available: WEP and WPA.

You have to run the same encryption on both the wireless router and *all* wireless NICs. You cannot mix and match. So the first step is to verify on the wireless router and all wireless NICs that you are using the same encryption type. WPA is preferred over WEP because it is more secure. Some older NICs may not support WPA.

Note: Wired NICs do not have or need encryption, so just ignore those.

Encryption Key Mismatch

WEP and WPA each have two additional settings that are critical to making encryption work, as described in the following sections.

WEP Key Length Mismatch

If you are using WEP to encrypt your wireless network, there are essentially two types of WEP: 64-bit WEP and 128-bit WEP. The only difference is the length of the key used to encrypt and decrypt the packets being sent and received on the wireless network. The longer the key, the more secure the encryption is. If the wireless router and wireless NIC are using different WEP key lengths, they will not be able to understand each other and the connection will fail.

Note: 64-bit WEP is pretty obsolete and very easily compromised. It's better than nothing, but use it only if no other form of encryption is available.

Let's say we have decided to use 128-bit WEP on our wireless network. To see if WEP key length is causing an issue, start by checking the setting on the wireless router. Access the wireless router using an Internet browser. Click the **Wireless** tab and then the **Wireless Security** subtab, as shown in Figure 10-22.

Figure 10-22 Verifying WEP Key Length on the Wireless Router

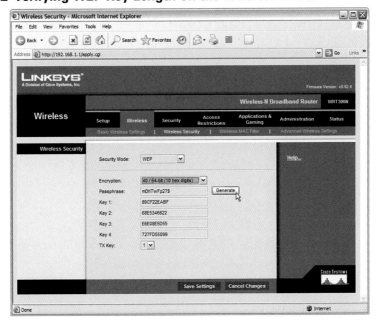

In Figure 10-22, we can see that the WEP key length is set to 64 bits, not 128. If our wireless NICs are set to use 128-bit WEP, this will cause them to be unable to join the wireless network. Click the drop-down arrow of the Encryption field and choose the setting for 128-bit WEP, as shown in Figure 10-23. Click **Save Settings** if you changed the setting.

Figure 10-23 Setting WEP Key Length to 128 Bits on the Wireless Router

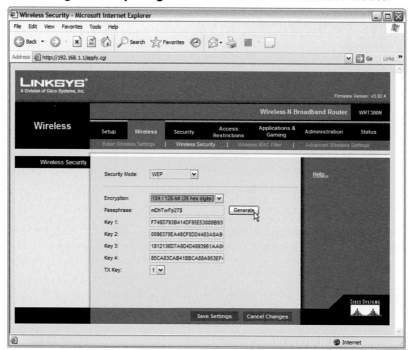

Now let's take a look at the wireless NICs to verify that their WEP key length is set correctly.

If you are using the Windows Wireless Network Connection utility, choose **Start > Connect To > Show All Connections**. Select the wireless NIC and then click **Change Settings for This Connection**. Select the home network profile and then click **Properties**. Figure 10-24 shows an example.

In Figure 10-24, we can see that for the wireless network with SSID KF34DC3, WEP is correctly set as the encryption type. Unfortunately, though, with Windows XP, we cannot actually see an indication of whether we set the key length correctly. The key length is determined based on how long the key is when you type it in. If you type in a key using 10 hexadecimal digits, the key length will be set to 64 bits. If you type in 26 hexadecimal digits, the key length will be set to 128 bits.

So if we want to make sure the key length is correct, we simply would have to type the key again. Fortunately, when you type the key in, Windows XP forces you to enter either 10 digits or 26 digits. If you have any doubt about whether you entered the full 128-bit WEP key, enter it again into both the **Network Key** and **Confirm Network Key** fields and click **OK**.

Figure 10-24 Verifying the WEP Key Length Setting in Windows XP

If you are using the Linksys WLAN Monitor utility, double-click the icon on the desktop to launch the utility or choose **Start > Programs > Linksys Wireless Card > WLAN Monitor**. Click the **Wireless Profiles** tab. Select the profile for your home wireless network and click the **Edit** button. Click **Next** until you find the **Wireless Security** dialog box, shown in Figure 10-25 (to save space, all the preceding dialog boxes are not shown here). Similar to the Windows XP example earlier, we can see that the encryption type is correctly set to WEP. Click **Next**.

Figure 10-25 Verifying WEP on the Wireless NIC with Linksys WLAN Monitor

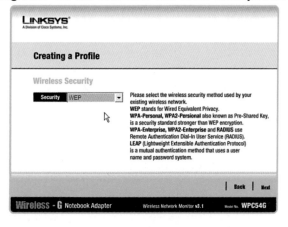

Figure 10-26 shows that the WEP key length is incorrectly set to 64 bits. This will cause a mismatch with the wireless network if the wireless router is set to use 128-bit WEP.

Figure 10-26 Verifying WEP Key Length with Linksys WLAN Monitor

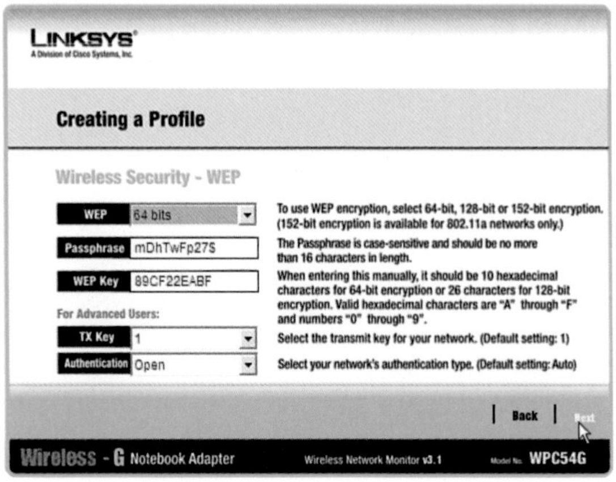

Click the drop-down arrow of the WEP field and set the value to **128 Bit**, as shown in Figure 10-27.

Figure 10-27 Correcting WEP Key Length with Linksys WLAN Monitor

Click **Next** several times until you reach the Confirmation dialog box. Click **Save** to save the settings in the wireless profile.

WEP Key Mismatch

Once you verify the correct encryption type and key length, the other problem that can occur is that the key itself does not match. If the wireless router and wireless NICs are using a different key, they will not be able to understand each other and the connection will fail.

First, double-check the WEP key on the wireless router. Access the wireless router using an Internet browser. Click the **Wireless** tab and then the **Wireless Security** subtab, as shown in Figure 10-28.

Figure 10-28 Verifying the WEP Key on the Wireless Router

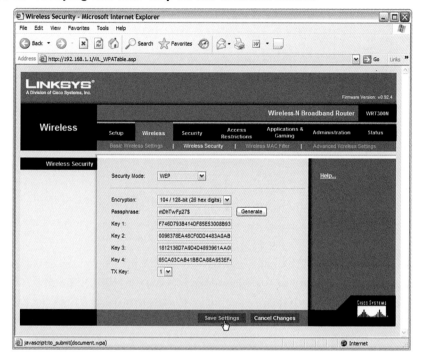

Here we can see that the WEP key passphrase is set to mDhTwFp27$ and the WEP key (Key 1, which is the important one) is set to F746D793B414DF85E53008B93E. These are the values we created in Chapter 9 when we secured the wireless network. Recall that the WEP key was actually generated by the router after we created and entered a passphrase.

Write down both the WEP passphrase and the WEP key. The passphrase is case sensitive, so pay attention to the upper- and lowercase letters.

The WEP key is *not* case sensitive (so 6A is the same as 6a). But, the key is a lot of digits (10 or 26), so make sure to write it down accurately, not missing any digits or getting any out of order.

Now, let's confirm the WEP key on the wireless NICs. If you are using the Windows Wireless Network Connection utility, choose **Start > Connect To > Show All Connections**. Select the wireless NIC and then click **Change Settings for This Connection**. Select the home network profile and then click **Properties**. Figure 10-29 shows that for the wireless network with SSID KF34DC3, WEP is correctly set as the encryption type.

With Windows XP, we cannot see whether we typed in the WEP key correctly, because the display is masked for security purposes (presumably so someone cannot look at it over your shoulder or something). So if we want to make sure the WEP key is correct, we simply have to type the key again. Type the key that you previously wrote down from the router (the key, not the passphrase) into both the **Network Key** and **Confirm Network Key** fields, and click **OK**.

Figure 10-29 Verifying the WEP Key in Windows XP

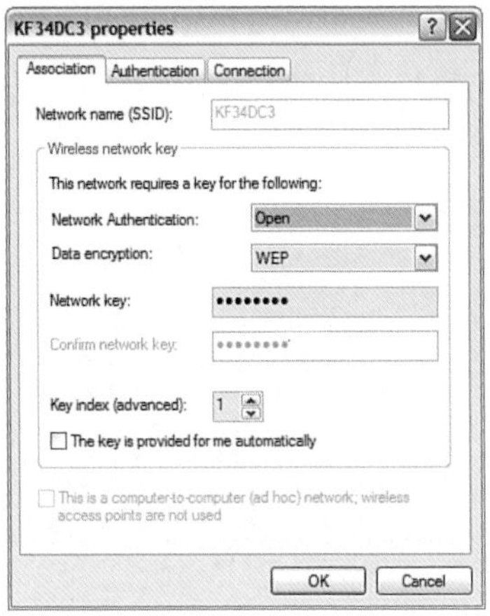

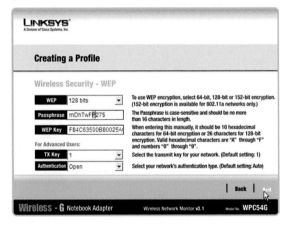

If you are using the Linksys WLAN Monitor utility, double-click the icon on the desktop to launch the utility or choose **Start > Programs > Linksys Wireless Card > WLAN Monitor**. Click the **Wireless Profiles** tab. Select the profile for your home wireless network and click the **Edit** button. Click **Next** until you find the Wireless Security – WEP dialog box, shown in Figure 10-30 (to save space, all the preceding dialog boxes are not shown here).

Figure 10-30 Verifying the WEP Key with Linksys WLAN Monitor

We can see that the WEP passphrase is incorrectly set to mDhTwFP27$, causing a mismatch with the wireless router. The router WEP passphrase has a lowercase *p* as one of the characters, whereas the NIC WEP passphrase has an uppercase *P*. That small difference is enough to render the wireless connection inoperable.

Also notice the WEP key just below the passphrase. That small difference in the passphrase completely changed the WEP key that was generated.

Edit the WEP key passphrase to the correct value, as shown in Figure 10-31. Notice that the WEP key generated now matches what was generated on the wireless router. That is a good way to double-check that you have entered the passphrase correctly.

Figure 10-31 Correcting the WEP Key with Linksys WLAN Monitor

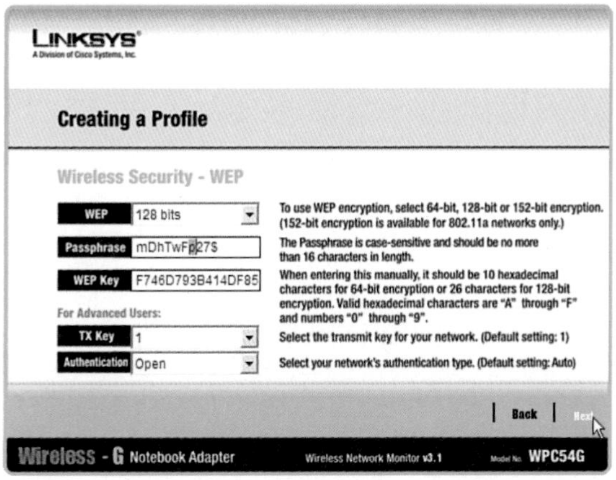

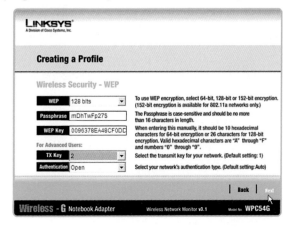

As a final note on WEP keys, make sure the WEP TX Key field is set to **1** on both the wireless router and the wireless NICs. Changing this value will change the WEP key used. For example, Figure 10-32 shows that changing the value to 2 means a completely different WEP key will be used, and again there will be a mismatch with the wireless router.

Figure 10-32 Verifying the WEP Key Number with Linksys WLAN Monitor

Although possible, we do not recommend messing around with the TX key number. It is a feature that is meant to be able to generate multiple WEP keys from a single WEP passphrase. Instead, if you want to use a different WEP key, we recommend that you just create a new WEP passphrase on the wireless router and generate a new key.

Click **Next** several times until you reach the Confirmation dialog box. Click **Save** to save the settings in the wireless profile.

WPA Type Mismatch

If you are using WPA to encrypt your wireless network, there are essentially two types of WPA: TKIP and AES. The difference is the type of encryption used to encrypt and decrypt the packets being sent and received on the wireless network. AES is considered more secure than TKIP, but not all wireless routers and wireless NICs support AES yet. If the wireless router and wireless NIC are using different WPA types, they will not be able to understand each other and the connection will fail.

Let's say we have decided to use WPA with AES on our wireless network. To see if the WPA type is causing an issue, start by checking the setting on the wireless router. Access the wireless router using an Internet browser. Click the **Wireless** tab and then the **Wireless Security** subtab, as shown in Figure 10-33.

Figure 10-33 Verifying the WPA Type on the Wireless Router

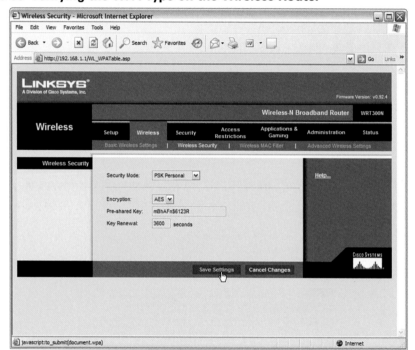

Here we can see that the WPA type is set to AES, as we intended. Now let's take a look at the wireless NICs to verify that their WPA type is set correctly.

If you are using the Windows Wireless Network Connection utility, choose **Start > Connect To > Show All Connections**. Select the wireless NIC and then click **Change Settings for This Connection**. Select the home network profile and then click **Properties**. Figure 10-34 shows an example.

WPA can be a little confusing because there are two ways to provide a key for WPA networks:

- Sharing the key in advance with all NICs

- Providing a key when you join from a central authentication server

In general, home networks use the *preshared key (PSK)* method, while corporate networks use the *key provided* method.

Figure 10-34 Verifying the WPA Type Setting in Windows XP

Figure 10-35 Changing the WPA Type Setting in Windows XP

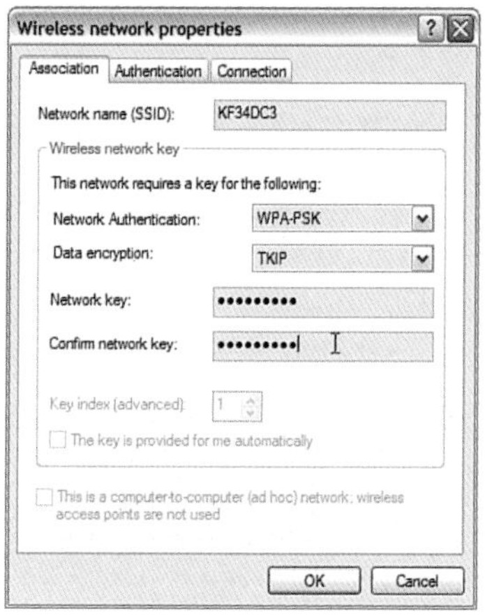

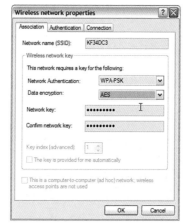

Wireless routers and wireless NICs may refer to these methods slightly differently. With Linksys wireless routers, you want to select WPA-Personal or Personal-PSK. With Linksys wireless NICs managed with Linksys WLAN Monitor, you want to select WPA-Personal. For NICs managed using Windows, the option is WPA-PSK.

In this example we can see that for the wireless network with SSID KF34DC3, WPA-PSK is correctly set as the encryption method. However, we can see that the WPA type is set incorrectly to TKIP.

Click the drop-down arrow for the Data Encryption field and set the encryption type to the correct value of **AES**. Figure 10-35 shows an example. Click **OK** to save the settings.

If you are using the Linksys WLAN Monitor utility, double-click the icon on the desktop to launch the utility or choose **Start > Programs > Linksys Wireless Card > WLAN Monitor**. Click the **Wireless Profiles** tab. Select the profile for your home wireless network and click the **Edit** button. Click **Next** until you find the **Wireless Security** dialog box, shown in Figure 10-36 (to save space, all the preceding dialog boxes are not shown here). We can see that the encryption type is correctly set to WPA-Personal. Click **Next**.

Figure 10-36 Verifying WPA on the Wireless NIC with Linksys WLAN Monitor

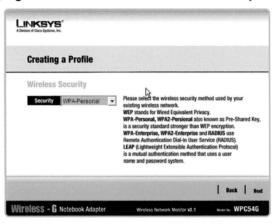

As shown in Figure 10-37, we can see that the WPA type is incorrectly set to TKIP. This will cause a mismatch with the wireless network if the wireless router is set to use AES.

Figure 10-37 Verifying WPA with Linksys WLAN Monitor

Click the drop-down arrow for the Encryption field and set the value to the correct **AES** setting, as shown in Figure 10-38.

Click **Next** several times until you reach the Confirmation dialog box. Click **Save** to save the settings in the wireless profile.

You can use either TKIP or AES as the WPA type. Both are very secure methods for encrypting your wireless network. The critical thing, though, is that you have to choose a single method on both the wireless router and all wireless NICs, because otherwise the wireless router and NIC will not understand each other and the connection will fail.

Figure 10-38 Correcting the WPA Type with Linksys WLAN Monitor

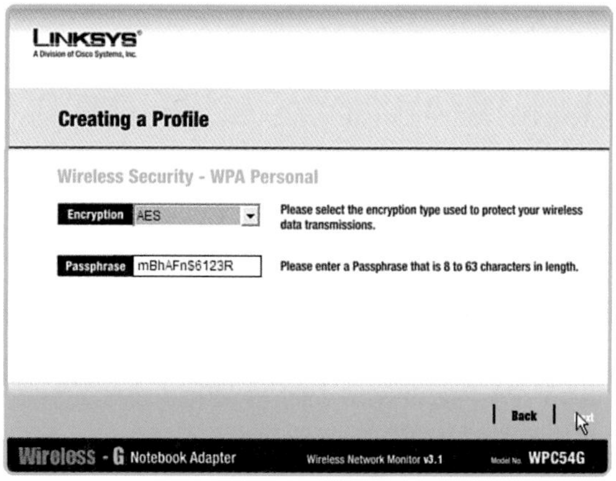

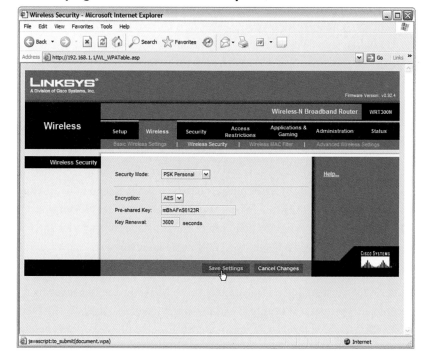

WPA Preshared Key Mismatch

Once you verify the correct WPA type, the other problem that can occur is that the WPA key itself does not match. If the wireless router and wireless NICs are using a different WPA preshared key, they will not be able to understand each other and the connection will fail.

First, double-check the WPA preshared key on the wireless router. Access the wireless router using an Internet browser. Click the **Wireless** tab and then the **Wireless Security** subtab, as shown in Figure 10-39.

Figure 10-39 Verifying the WPA Preshared Key on the Wireless Router

Here we can see that the WPA preshared key is set to mBhAFn$6123R. This is the value we created in Chapter 9 when we secured the wireless network. Recall that, unlike WEP, WPA uses just a passphrase key; there is no additional key that is generated by the router from the passphrase.

Write down the WPA preshared key. Make sure to pay attention to the upper- and lowercase letters.

Now, let's confirm the WPA key on the wireless NICs. If you are using the Windows Wireless Network Connection utility, choose **Start > Connect To > Show All Connections**. Select the wireless NIC and then click **Change Settings for This Connection**. Select the home network profile and then click **Properties**. Figure 10-40 shows an example.

Figure 10-40 Verifying the WPA Preshared Key in Windows XP

In Figure 10-40, we can see that for the wireless network with SSID KF34DC3, WPA-PSK is correctly set as the encryption type. With Windows XP, we cannot see whether we typed in the WPA key correctly, because the display is masked for security purposes (presumably so someone cannot look at it over your shoulder or something).

So if we want to make sure the WPA preshared key is correct, we simply have to type the key again. Type the key that you wrote down earlier from the router into both the **Network Key** and **Confirm Network Key** fields (or cut and paste it from the router dialog to the NIC dialog if you have both up on your screen), and click **OK**.

If you are using the Linksys WLAN Monitor utility, double-click the icon on the desktop to launch the utility or choose **Start > Programs > Linksys Wireless Card > WLAN Monitor**. Click the **Wireless Profiles** tab. Select the profile for your home wireless network and click the **Edit** button. Click **Next** until you find the Wireless Security – WPA Personal dialog box, shown in Figure 10-41 (to save space, all the preceding dialog boxes are not shown here).

We can see that the WPA preshared key is incorrectly set to MBhAFn$6123R, causing a mismatch with the wireless router. The router WPA preshared key has a lowercase *m* as the first character, whereas the NIC WPA preshared key has an uppercase *M*. That small difference is enough to render the wireless connection inoperable.

Edit the WPA key to the correct value, as shown in Figure 10-42.

Figure 10-41 Verifying the WPA Preshared Key with Linksys WLAN Monitor

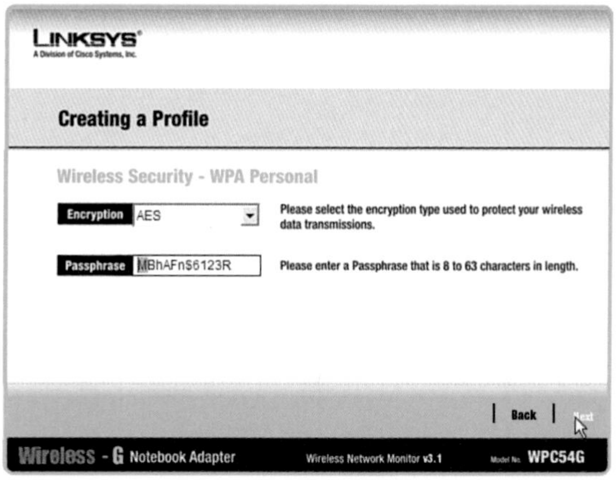

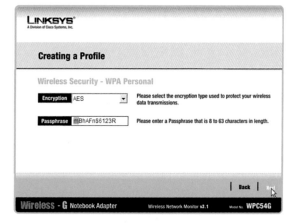

Figure 10-42 Correcting the WPA Key with Linksys WLAN Monitor

Windows XP Authentication Setting Mismatch

Windows XP has an additional setting that can be problematic. For corporate networks, many companies are implementing a security method that requires their employees to provide a user ID and password to log in to the wireless network. This login process uses a technology standard called IEEE 802.1x. How it works is beyond the scope of this book, but suffice it to say that for home networks, 802.1x is not used (at least not yet). Windows XP typically disables or enables this setting automatically based on the encryption method you choose. However, we have seen at least one case where it was incorrectly set and prevented a wireless network connection.

Here is how to confirm that it is disabled on the wireless NIC. Using the Windows Wireless Network Connection utility, choose **Start > Connect To > Show All Connections**. Select the wireless NIC and then click **Change Settings for This Connection**. Select the home network profile and then click **Properties**. Click the **Authentication** tab. Verify that the **Enable IEEE 802.1x Authentication for This Network** setting is *not* checked, as shown in Figure 10-43. If it is, then uncheck it and click **OK** to save the settings.

Figure 10-43 Verifying the Authentication Setting in Windows XP

IP Address Assignment–Related Issues

After you have confirmed that the wireless NIC is now making a connection properly to the wireless router, including encryption, it's time to move on to the last step in the connection process: obtaining an IP address. Joining the wireless network allows the NIC to send and receive packets to and from the router. To be a part of the home network, the NIC also needs an IP address.

Note: IP addressing is a fundamental networking concept that is not covered in detail in this book. The 30-second description is that each device (computer, laptop, and so on) in a home network needs to have an IP address, which is how the device is known on the network. IP addresses have four numbers, separated by a dot (.). Most home networks use IP addresses in the range of 192.168.1.100 to 192.168.1.149, and the router assigns each device an address from this pool when it boots. This is called *dynamic IP addressing*, or Dynamic Host Configuration Protocol (DHCP). To learn more about how IP addressing works, pick up a copy of *Home Networking Simplified*.

With dynamic IP addressing, or DHCP, enabled on the wireless router, when a NIC establishes a new wireless connection, it then requests an address from the router, and the router assigns the next available one from the pool. The wireless NIC can then use the address until the computer is shut down or the laptop leaves the wireless network.

Why would an IP address not be assigned correctly? There is not really a good reason; let's just say that DHCP does not seem to always work properly. Sometimes a wireless NIC gets "stuck," thinking it already has an IP address (maybe from the last network it joined). Also, in very weak signal conditions, the request could get lost, never reaching the router.

On the router side, it's also possible that all the available IP addresses in the pool have been assigned. This is usually not the case, but, depending on how many devices you have on your home network and the size of the address pool, it could be an issue. Occasionally, if one or more devices are having an intermittent connection issue in which they keep losing the signal and then coming back onto the network, they could be requesting a new IP address each time, and the router could exhaust its pool.

Finally, depending on the wireless NIC, sometimes with WPA encryption, if the WPA key does not match, the NIC will appear to connect to the wireless signal just fine but will not be able to properly acquire an IP address from the router. In other words, it looks like a DHCP problem, but it's really a mismatched WPA key.

It's important to be able to recognize when a problem with the IP address assignment is happening, and you may be able to take some actions to remedy the problem. The next few sections give some tips.

Note: Static IP addressing, which is when you turn off DHCP and assign your home network addresses manually, is quite problematic. Problems include duplicate addresses, errors in manually entering IP addresses, and others. We do not recommend using static IP addressing in home networks. If you do, prepare yourself for some frustration.

Determining if an IP Address Is Assigned

You first need to figure out whether you are getting an IP address assigned. Here is how to tell.

If you are using the Windows Wireless Network Connection utility, choose **Start > Connect To > Show All Connections**. Select the wireless NIC and then right-click and select **Status** from the list. Click the **Support** tab. Figure 10-44 shows an example.

Figure 10-44 Verifying IP Address Assignment with Windows XP

In Figure 10-44, we can see that the IP address 192.168.1.101 has been assigned to the wireless NIC. We can also see that a default gateway IP address has been assigned, 192.168.1.1. This is good. We have both an IP address to use for the NIC and a gateway to which to send requests to access the Internet. This should be a complete connection now for us to access the Internet from the laptop or other computer that is connected over the wireless connection.

If you are using the Linksys WLAN Monitor utility, double-click the icon on the desktop to launch the utility or choose **Start > Programs > Linksys Wireless Card > WLAN Monitor**. Click the **More Information** button on the Link Information tab. Figure 10-45 shows the resulting link information.

Figure 10-45 Verifying the SSID on the Wireless NIC with Linksys WLAN Monitor

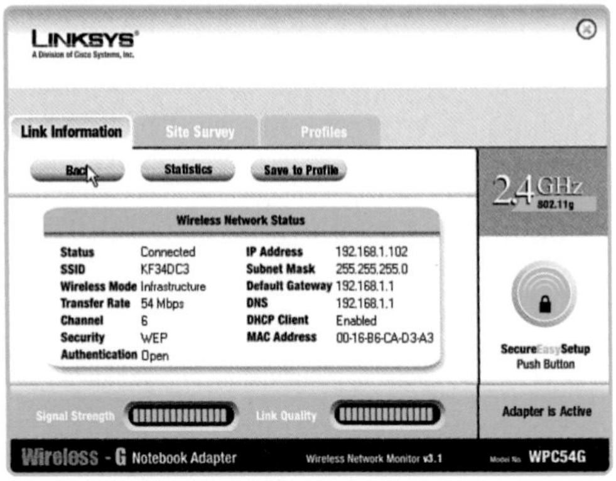

Again, we can see that this wireless NIC has been assigned an IP address of 192.168.1.102 and a default gateway of 192.168.1.1. This should be a completely established connection, and we should be able to access the Internet. If not, then something may be wrong with the broadband Internet connection itself, or the wireless router may not be reaching the Internet for some reason. Try accessing the Internet from a computer with a wired connection. Also try rebooting the wireless router, broadband modem, and computer with the wireless NIC.

Determining if IP Address Assignment Is Failing

There are some indications you can look for to tell if the wireless connection is failing due to an IP address assignment malfunction.

In Windows XP, choose **Start > Connect To > Show All Connections**. Select the wireless NIC and then right-click and select **Status** from the list. Figure 10-46 shows that the wireless NIC is trying to acquire an address from the wireless router. Even though the wireless signal shows five bars, and we see a few packets being sent and received, we can see that the overall status is **Acquiring Network Address**.

If the NIC stays in that status for a relatively long time, say 3 to 5 minutes or more, chances are the address assignment is not going to work. When it ultimately times out and stops trying, you will likely get an indication like that shown in Figure 10-47.

Figure 10-46 Checking the Status of IP Address Assignment in Windows XP

Figure 10-47 Indication of IP Address Assignment Failure in Windows XP

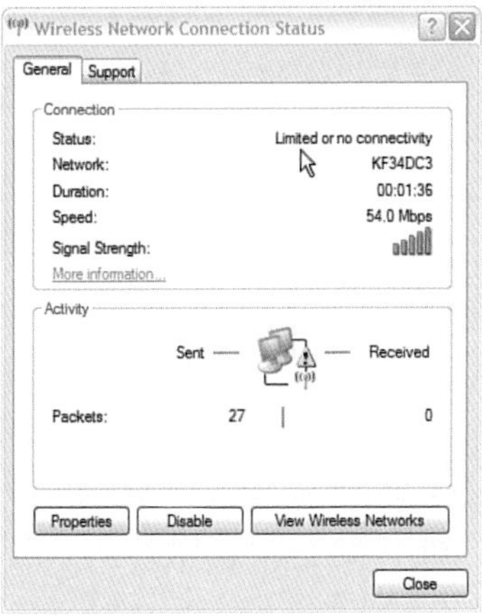

If the status shows **Limited or No connectivity**, that is usually an indication that IP address assignment has timed out and the laptop or computer has no IP address assigned to use. Consequently, the computer is not going to be able to do a whole lot on the home network, including access the Internet.

Clicking the Support tab enables you to get a further indication of what is wrong, similar to the example shown in Figure 10-48. Here you can see that the status is **Invalid IP Address**. This is another indication that something did not work correctly with dynamic IP address assignment.

Figure 10-48 Checking If IP Address Assignment Failed in Windows XP

Clicking the Details button displays a little bit more information, as shown in Figure 10-49.

You can see that it appears that an IP address is assigned, 169.254.236.210. This is not a "real" IP address from the home network; this is the default IP address that occurs when IP address assignment has failed. If you see an address assigned like this, the computer is not going to be able to access the Internet.

Figure 10-49 IP Address Assignment Failure Details in Windows XP

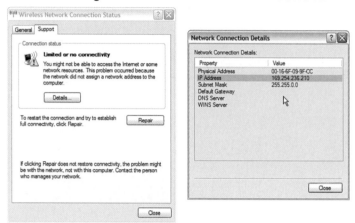

Trying the Windows XP Repair Function

Windows XP has a pretty slick built-in function to attempt to repair a networking connection. The function essentially disables the NIC and then re-enables it, effectively restarting the NIC in a "fresh" state.

Whenever you are having issues with IP address assignment, Windows XP Repair seems to have a pretty good success rate, assuming nothing fundamental is wrong, such as a mismatched WPA key. We have found Windows XP Repair fairly useful to solve DHCP-related problems.

To invoke the Repair function in Windows XP, choose **Start > Connect To > Show All Connections**. Select the wireless NIC and then right-click and select **Status** from the list. Figure 10-50 shows an example.

Figure 10-50 Repairing a Network Connection in Windows XP

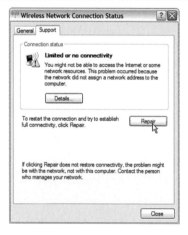

Click the **Repair** button. Windows XP will go through a series of steps and advise you of progress, including disabling the wireless NIC, enabling, connecting to the wireless network, and acquiring an IP address. One of the advisements is shown in Figure 10-51. When it completes, the Repair function will advise you whether it was successful in completing a connection to the wireless network.

Figure 10-51 Repairing a Network Connection in Progress

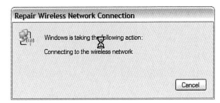

This remedy may correct the issue. If it does not, then chances are something else is wrong, and you should recheck some of the earlier steps. It also does not hurt to try shutting down and rebooting the laptop, and even the wireless router.

Checking the Router's DHCP Client Pool

Once you have pulled enough of your hair out (you be the judge of that), you may want to see what is going on from the wireless router's perspective as well. Access the wireless router using an Internet browser. Click the **Status** tab and then the **Local Network** subtab, as shown in Figure 10-52.

Figure 10-52 Checking the DHCP Status on the Wireless Router

We can see that the DHCP server function is enabled on the wireless router. We can also see the IP address pool that is being used, in this case 50 IP addresses from 192.168.1.100 through 192.168.1.149. That should be plenty for most home networks.

Click the **DHCP Clients Table** button (on some Linksys routers this may be named slightly differently). A table of currently assigned IP addresses will be displayed, like the example shown in Figure 10-53.

We can see two addresses being used: 192.168.1.100 by Computer1 and 192.168.1.101 by Computer2. There does not appear to be anything out of the ordinary.

Figure 10-53 Checking the DHCP Clients on the Wireless Router

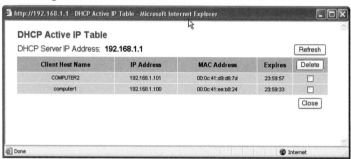

If you see one of the computers listed many times, or a whole list of devices you do not recognize, that could certainly be an issue. In that case, you may want to try rebooting the router and see if the issue clears up.

> **Note:** Checking the DHCP clients table on your wireless router periodically can be a good security practice. If you see computers or other devices listed in the client table that are not yours, it could be a sign that someone is joining your wireless network without your permission. You can then take appropriate measures, such as changing your SSID and WPA key, or turning on MAC filtering. If you see them on again, it's time to take more active measures such as involving the authorities. Many states are starting to pass laws that make it a crime to join wireless networks without an owner's permission. Check the laws in your state (or province, county, parish, planetary body, and so on...).
>
> For more information about security measures for home networks, pick up a copy of *Home Networking Security Simplified*.

Wireless Connection Made

Now that we have made it through all the steps, we need to check if we have a wireless connection yet.

If you are using the Windows Wireless Network Connection utility, choose **Start > Connect To > Show All Connections**. Select the wireless NIC and then click **View Wireless Networks**. Figure 10-54 shows that we are now connected successfully to the network with SSID KF34DC3, having passed all the steps up through obtaining an IP address.

If you are using the Linksys WLAN Monitor utility, double-click the icon on the desktop to launch the utility or choose **Start > Programs > Linksys Wireless Card > WLAN Monitor**. Figure 10-55 shows that we are now connected successfully to the network with SSID KF34DC3, having passed all the steps up through obtaining an IP address.

Figure 10-54 Verifying a Wireless Connection with Windows XP

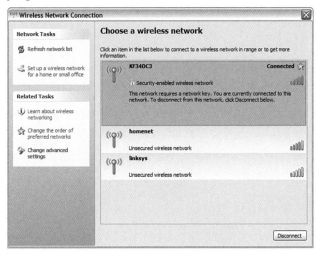

Figure 10-55 Verifying a Wireless Connection with Linksys WLAN Monitor

If you do not have a connection at this point, return to the start of section "Figuring Out Why It Will Not Connect," and try again. You may also want to shut down everything, restart it, and see if that auto-magically fixes the issue.

Oops, How Embarrassing!

Okay, so you have tried everything and nothing seems to be working. Here are a few other things to double-check. Some of them may seem silly, but trust us, we have seen it or we wouldn't list it:

- Is the wireless router actually plugged in and powered on?

- Do you have security turned on in the wireless router but not the wireless NIC?

- Have you tried connecting with a wired connection to see if the computer and the Internet are working?

- Can you connect to the wireless router with any other wireless laptop or computer (in other words, are you sure the wireless router is working at all)?

- Is the wireless NIC actually powered on, plugged in, enabled, and working?

- Can you make a wireless connection without security? Try turning off wireless security (WEP or WPA) on both the wireless router and all NICs and then connecting.

The 10-Minute Miracle

Many professionals who fix computers and networks for a living tell us to always include what they call the "10-minute miracle." Put simply, it means shut everything down, turn everything off, and go have your favorite beverage (they say coffee, we prefer beer, although we have also found that too many 10-minute miracle breaks for beer can be somewhat counterproductive to troubleshooting). Come back in 10 minutes, power things back up, and start looking at it again.

You may be surprised that whatever was not working is now working. Try it, it works sometimes.

Summary

You may read through these steps and say, "No, it can't be that, I am skipping that step." Trust us, do every step no matter how confident you are. Even we have spent 20 minutes trying to figure out why we can't get a connection, only to find out the wireless NIC in our laptop was shut off.

If all else fails, call in help from the kids, a smart neighbor, or a professional service.

Where to Go for More Information

For more home networking and home network security information, refer to our other books, *Home Networking Simplified* (Cisco Press, 2005) and *Home Network Security Simplified* (Cisco Press, 2006).

Microsoft provides an article titled "How to Troubleshoot Wireless Network Connections in Windows XP Service Pack 2" on its website: http://support.microsoft.com/kb/870702.

Bradley Mitchell has an article titled "Troubleshooting, Tips and Tweaks" at About.com: http://wireless.about.com/cs/wirelessproducts/a/howtobuildwlan_5.htm.

Troubleshooting:
I Can Connect Sometimes

Sometimes, your wireless network works well when you set it up, but then when you try to use your laptop over a wireless connection, say in the living room, it does not always connect. You might be experiencing a wireless signal coverage issue. Before assuming so, make sure you have successfully connected your computer to the router via a wireless connection at least once, even if your computer is right beside the router.

If you have never connected to the wireless router successfully, start with Chapter 10, "Troubleshooting: I Can't Connect at All." If you have connected before but are not able to use the wireless network in locations inside your house where you want to, take a look at the rest of this chapter.

How Wireless Coverage Works

Wireless networks are similar to cell phone networks:

- The more bars of service you have, the better the call sounds.

- When you have very few bars of service, you may be able to place a call, but it probably does not sound very good.

- When you have zero bars of service, you cannot make or receive calls.

Wireless networks operate the same way, as shown in Figure 11-1. When you are within the coverage area of your wireless network and have good signal strength (shown in the green area), you will have a good wireless connection and also have at or near the maximum data rate your wireless router supports (54 Mbps for 802.11g, 108 Mbps or higher for 802.11n, and so on).

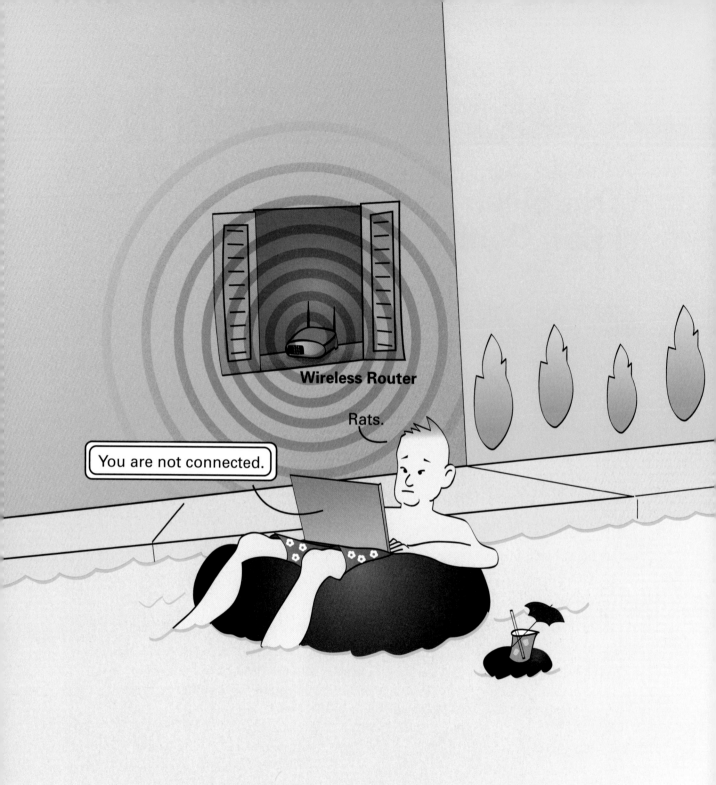

Figure 11-1   How Wireless Network Coverage Affects Usage

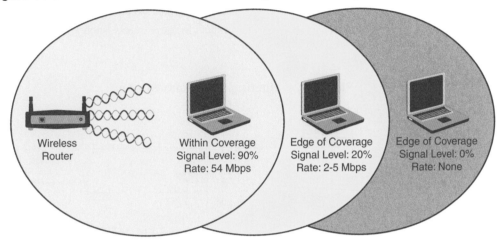

When you are at the edges of your wireless network coverage, you will have relatively low signal strength, say between 5 and 20 percent of signal or 1 to 2 bars, depending on how your wireless NIC displays signal strength. At the edges, you will typically see a lower data rate than your wireless router supports, such as 5 Mbps or 2 Mbps, and you may also see that sometimes the signal strength goes to zero. You may also periodically see the signal disconnecting and then reconnecting. Keep in mind, though, that this is only at the edge of the usable range, and that if you are in the usable range, your performance should be fine.

When you are outside your wireless network coverage, you will have zero signal strength, and the wireless NIC will show a status of disconnected from the wireless network.

Tuning Your Wireless Coverage

Most wireless routers being sold today that are based on the 802.11g or 802.11n standard have pretty good range to cover the average house.

As discussed in Chapters 2, "Wireless Standards: What the Letters Mean," and 3, "Selecting the Right Wireless Standard for Your Network," 802.11a typically provides somewhat less coverage because it operates at the 5-GHz band, where wireless signals inherently just do not travel as far as they do on the 2.4-GHz band (where 802.11g and 802.11n operate).

Quite often when you have coverage issues, you might have done something that is causing the range of the wireless network to suffer unnecessarily. Often, by following a few basic tuning rules, you can get the most out of your wireless router. The rest of this chapter tells you how.

Performing a Wireless Survey

After setting up the wireless router in the preferred location, the next step is to perform a survey of the wireless coverage in your house. Start by thinking about in which locations in your house you want to use a laptop to connect over wireless, and which desktop computers are connected with wireless as well. It may be helpful to make a rough floor plan drawing like we did in Chapter 4, "Planning Your Wireless Network," marking where you expect to use wireless, such as that shown in Figure 11-2.

Figure 11-2   Sample Floor Plan for Conducting a Wireless Survey

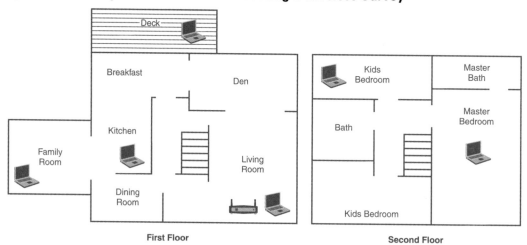

Also make a quick chart, such as that shown in Table 11-1, with the different locations within your house listed in the first column and then a column for current signal strength and one or two columns for modified signal strength. In the sections that follow, we will fill in the chart while taking some readings.

Table 11-1   Wireless Survey Chart—Empty

	Current	**Change 1**	**Change 2**
Living Room			
Kitchen			
Back Deck			
Master Bedroom			
Kid's Bedroom			
Family Room			

Next, we are going to take a laptop from room to room, check the signal strength we see from the wireless router, and record it in the table. Two surveys are shown in the sections that follow: one performed with the Windows Wireless Network Connection utility, and one performed using the Linksys WLAN Monitor utility.

Wireless Survey Using Windows XP

If you are using Windows Wireless Network Connection utility, choose **Start > Connect To > Show All Connections**. Select the wireless NIC and then click **Change Settings for This Connection**. Select the home network profile and then click **Properties**.

For each room in the house, take the laptop to the room, put it in the location in which you plan to use it, and wait a few seconds for the display to update. Figure 11-3 shows an example for the living room. Write down in Table 11-1 that we have five out of five possible bars of service, which is a very good signal level.

Figure 11-3   Living Room Wireless Survey Using Windows XP

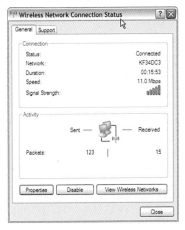

Move to each room in your house, each time waiting a few seconds for the reading to update, and write the figure down. Figure 11-4 shows the reading on the back deck: three out of five bars.

Figure 11-4   Back Deck Wireless Survey Using Windows XP

Figure 11-5 shows the reading upstairs in the family room: no bars, which indicates a very weak signal. Using wireless in this room is going to be a problem.

Figure 11-5   Family Room Wireless Survey Using Windows XP

Keep going through the rest of the house, each time recording the reading in your table. The completed example table is shown in Table 11-2.

Table 11-2   Wireless Survey Chart—After First Survey

	Current	Change 1	Change 2
Living Room	5		
Kitchen	4		
Back Deck	3		
Master Bedroom	4		
Kid's Bedroom	2		
Family Room	0		

We can see from the Table 11-2 that for most of the rooms in the house, we should have a fairly good wireless signal. Any room with a single bar of service or less is a likely problem area. In our example survey, the family room, which is the farthest room away from the wireless router, looks like it will be a problem.

Wireless Survey Using Linksys WLAN Monitor

If you are using the Linksys WLAN Monitor utility, double-click the icon on the desktop to launch the utility or choose **Start > Programs > Linksys Wireless Card > WLAN Monitor**. Click the **Link Information** tab and then the **More Information** subtab.

Again, for each room in the house, take the laptop to the room, put it in the location in which you plan to use it, and wait a few seconds for the display to update. Figure 11-6 shows an example for the living room. Write down in Table 11-1 that we have 15 out of 15 possible bars of service, which is a very good signal level.

Figure 11-6   Living Room Wireless Survey Using Linksys WLAN Monitor

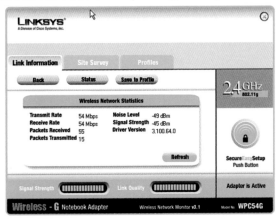

Move to each room in your house, each time waiting a few seconds for the reading to update, and write the figure down. Figure 11-7 shows the reading on the back deck: 5 out of 15 bars.

Figure 11-7   Back Deck Wireless Survey Using Linksys WLAN Monitor

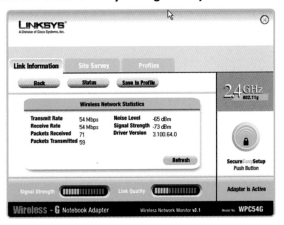

 Note: You may notice that the Linksys WLAN Monitor displays two indicators: Signal Strength and Link Quality. Signal Strength is a measure of how well the wireless NIC can "see" the wireless router's wireless signal. Link Quality measures how well the wireless router signal can be understood. The vast majority of the time, the two go hand-in-hand, so don't get too bogged down worrying about which one to look at. Just record signal strength.

Figure 11-8 shows the reading upstairs in the family room: no bars, which indicates a very weak signal. Using wireless in this room is going to be a problem.

Figure 11-8   Family Room Wireless Survey Using Linksys WLAN Monitor

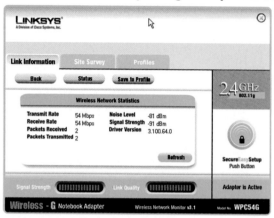

Keep going through the rest of the house, each time recording the reading in your table. The completed example table is shown in Table 11-3.

Table 11-3   Wireless Survey Chart—After First Survey

	Current	Change 1	Change 2
Living Room	15		
Kitchen	6		
Back Deck	5		
Master Bedroom	7		
Kid's Bedroom	3		
Family Room	0		

Again, we can see from the table that for most of the rooms in the house, we should have a fairly good wireless signal. Any room with about two bars of service or less is a likely problem area. In our example survey, the family room, which is the farthest room away from the wireless router, looks like it will be a problem.

What to Conclude from Your Wireless Survey

Looking at the wireless survey, you want to make a couple of decisions. First, verify that your survey shows you have the strongest signal in the room closest to the wireless router. The farther away you get from the router, the weaker the signal becomes. Second, determine whether you have adequate signal coverage in the areas of your house where you want to use a wireless connection. If not, then you may want to take some actions to improve the coverage.

Based on where you plan to use wireless the most within your house, you next need to determine if you've placed the wireless router in the optimal location in your house. (See the "Improving the Location of the Wireless Router" section later in this chapter.)

To some extent you are limited to locations in your house that have the possibility to connect to the broadband Internet service you have (DSL or cable), but you may have some flexibility. DSL can generally be placed anywhere inside your home where there is a phone jack. Cable is a little more restrictive, but can usually be placed anywhere there is a cable jack. In some situations, you may need to have the DSL or cable provider install a more centralized phone or cable jack for the broadband service.

Do keep in mind, though, that you do not need to have the maximum signal strength in every room where you want to use your wireless. We do not recommend installing new DSL or cable jacks unless the room where you want to use wireless gets very bad coverage or no coverage at all.

You can try several remedies to improve your signal coverage. These are described in the rest of the chapter.

What You Can Do to Improve Coverage

Here are the three primary reasons why coverage might not be as good as it can be:

- The wireless router setup or location is not optimal.

- Other devices in your house are interfering with the wireless network.

- The wireless router equipment you have is not adequate for the coverage you need.

If you determine that your coverage is not what you need, what can you do? There are a few things to try. The next few sections give some possible remedies for these limitations. Each time you try one of these remedies, repeat the wireless survey process described in the previous section to see if the change improved the network. Be aware that one change may improve a room that has zero coverage, but then cause another room to suddenly have coverage problems. You may need to attempt a couple of remedies to get the best overall coverage for all the locations in the house in which you want to use wireless.

Improving the Location of the Wireless Router

One of the most important determining factors of how your wireless network will perform is where you locate the wireless router itself. Table 11-4 gives you five simple do's and don'ts for wireless router location in your house.

Table 11-4   Five Simple Guidelines for Wireless Router Location

Do	Don't
Choose a site for the router in a central location in your house, considering all three dimensions (see Figure 11-9). Note the bigger the house, the more important this becomes.	Put the router in the basement, attic, garage, closet, or other isolated part of your house.
Place the router on a wooden table or desk where the router (and especially the antenna) is not obscured.	Place the router on the floor, in a metal bookcase, in a metal enclosure, or in a drawer.
Keep away from potential interfering devices like microwave ovens, cordless phones, and baby monitors.	Keep a cordless phone base or handset next to the router.
Plug into a power strip with a surge protector, and plug the power strip into an empty outlet.	Plug into an outlet along with other electrically "noisy" devices, such as hair dryers, blenders, toasters, and so on.
Keep the antennas free from obstructions, including wires and cables.	Drape electrical cords or cables over the router or antennas, or wrap extra wires around the antennas.

Note: We omitted some pretty obvious guidelines from Table 11-4, but we have heard of these happening, so they are worth mentioning. The funny part is, you will probably read this and think we are kidding:

- You have to actually remove the router from the store packaging and plug it in somewhere in your house for it to work. It's not so much the shrink wrap that causes the problem, but the lack of electricity is hugely limiting.

- Don't put the router in a wet or damp area. This includes an area where pets are likely to urinate on it. By the way, urination on electrically powered devices, such as routers, can be just as detrimental to your pet as it is to the wireless network.

- Aluminum foil generally does not make a good antenna booster, although there is something to be said for empty Pringles cans, and a lot of "research" seems to have been done in this area.

- Unless specifically designed for use outdoors, the vast majority of wireless routers are for use indoors only, and bad things happen if they get rained on. This is true of most things with an electrical plug, by the way.

- A dark, cool, corner room of the basement or root cellar is a great place to store wine. Great places to store wine are not good places for wireless routers.

- You need to be at *home*, or close by, to use your wireless *home* network. If you are out of state on vacation, it is extremely unlikely you will get a signal from your *home* network.

- You may be tempted to mount your router on the ceiling (like they do in the office), but keep in mind that your office has a false ceiling to allow cable runs and, more importantly, your company has people who do this type of installation for a living. We're not saying it wouldn't be cool to do, but you are signing up for a lot of work (and a mess) if you try this at home.

Figure 11-9 Choose a Central Location for the Wireless Router

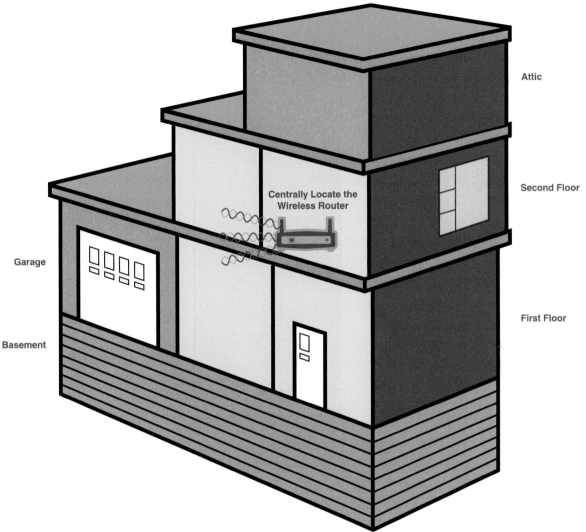

If you follow the guidelines described in this section, you will get the most coverage from your wireless router. If you do not follow them, and do something like putting the wireless router in a metal bookcase or computer desk cubby hole, no amount of tuning is going to help.

Next, let's move on to some other tips to help you get the most from the wireless network coverage.

Trying Different Channels

Wireless networks operate today in what are called *unlicensed frequencies*. The U.S. Federal Communications Commission (FCC), or the equivalent in your country, manages who uses which radio frequencies for what purposes. For example, television broadcasters, FM radio stations, police and fire radios, and cellular phone companies all must be licensed by the FCC to use a particular set of radio frequencies. If the FCC did not regulate this, no one would be able to rely on such services because everyone would be transmitting all over each other, and none of the services would work very well.

However, the FCC designates certain sets of radio frequencies as unlicensed, and as long as a certain set of general guidelines is followed, anyone can build devices that operate at these frequencies. The common public unlicensed frequency bands (in the United States) are 900 MHz, 2.4 GHz, and 5.1 GHz.

Approximately 5 to 10 years ago, cordless phones, baby monitors, and many other home wireless devices commonly used the 900-MHz band. More recently, most home wireless devices are built to operate in the 2.4-GHz band, somewhat because of overcrowding of the 900-MHz band. Finally, many new devices are being built to operate in the higher 5.1-GHz band.

There are not a lot of differences or advantages to frequency bands, except the number of other devices that share the band. Most home wireless networks use the 2.4-GHz band, with a few built for the 5.1-GHz band.

Each band is broken up into a number of usable channels. Table 11-5 shows the band and possible channels for each of the wireless standards.

Table 11-5   Possible Wireless Channels

Standard	Band	Channels	Default
802.11b	2.4 GHz	1–11	6
802.11g	2.4 GHz	1–11	6
802.11a	5.1 GHz	36, 40, 44, 48, 52, 56, 60, 64, 149, 153, 157, 161	52
802.11n	2.4 GHz	3–9	5

802.11b, 802.11g, and 802.11n networks all operate in the 2.4-GHz band. There are 11 channels (in the United States), as shown in Figure 11-10 (Channels 12, 13, and 14 are valid in a few countries outside of the United States.)

Figure 11-10 Channels for 802.11b, 802.11g, and 802.11n Standards

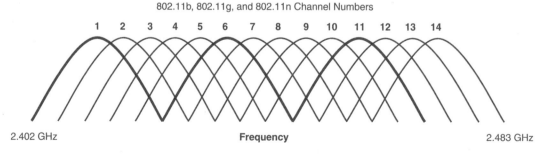

These channels are "overlapping," which means that part of the signal for one channel spills over a bit into the channels above and below it. This means there are three unique channels: 1, 6, and 11. If you have one wireless router using channel 1 and another nearby wireless router on channel 2, these channels partially overlap, so they could cause each other interference.

802.11a networks operate in the 5.1-GHz band (which ranges from 5.150 GHz to 5.825 GHz). There are 12 channels (in the United States), as shown in Figure 11-11.

Figure 11-11 Channels for 802.11a Standard

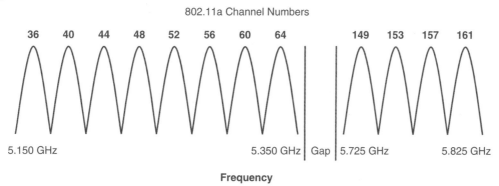

These channels are "nonoverlapping," which means that one channel does *not* spill into channels above and below it. This means that all 12 channels are unique channels for a wireless network. Nearby routers may use channels 44 and 48, for example, without interfering with each other.

Whenever you purchase a wireless router, the manufacturer has preconfigured it to use a particular default wireless channel. For Linksys wireless routers that are built for the 802.11b and 802.11g standards, the default channel is 6. The other defaults are shown in Table 11-5.

Many times, the default channel works very well and you do not need to think about it any further. Sometimes, though, there can be interference from other devices or something in your home that makes the default channel not work as well as possibly another one of the channels.

The types of devices in your home that can interfere with the wireless network include

- Microwave ovens (2.4 GHz)

- Cordless phones (2.4 GHz or 5.1 GHz) depending on which band they are built for

- Bluetooth devices, like wireless cell phone headsets (2.4 GHz)

- Room-to-room wireless audio/video extender (2.4 GHz)

- Wireless USB (2.4 GHz)

- Home automation sensors and controls (2.4 GHz)

- Your neighbor's wireless router (2.4 GHz or 5.1 GHz)

The most common two are microwave ovens, particularly older ones with less than adequate shielding, and cordless phones. As we discussed earlier in this book, we highly recommend that if you have an 802.11b, 802.11g, or 802.11n wireless home network, purchase 5-GHz cordless phones. This way the phones and wireless network will not interfere with each other.

Other than eliminating the source of the interference (preferred, but sometimes you just cannot), another possibility is to try changing the wireless channel that the router uses. It is very easy to do, here's how:

Step 1   Access the wireless router using an Internet browser.

Step 2   Click the **Wireless** tab, as shown in Figure 11-12.

Step 3   From the **Channel** field, change the channel to an alternative channel. If the router is set to the default channel 6, try channel 1 or 11. For this example, we set it to channel 11.

Step 4   Click **Save Settings**.

Figure 11-12 Changing the Channel on the Wireless Router

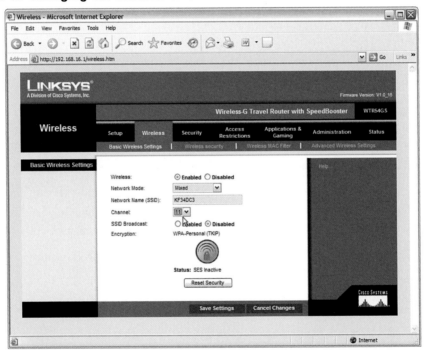

Once you click Save Settings, all wireless NICs on the network will lose connection with the wireless router and start scanning for a wireless network. They should simply re-establish a connection to your wireless network on the modified channel.

After changing the channel, you should conduct another wireless survey, as described earlier in this chapter, to see if the change had a positive or negative impact on your wireless network coverage.

If you are using Windows Wireless Network Connection utility, choose **Start > Connect To > Show All Connections**. Select the wireless NIC and then click **Change Settings for This Connection**. Select the home network profile and then click **Properties**. Figure 11-13 shows an example.

Figure 11-13 Surveying the Channel Change with Windows XP

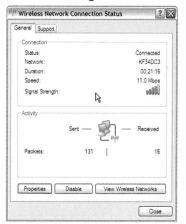

We cannot see the actual wireless channel number in Windows XP. We can just look at the wireless signal level (in terms of bars of service) and visually inspect whether it is improved or not. Here we can see that changing the wireless channel had a positive effect on the wireless signal in the family room, where we were having trouble before.

If you are using the Linksys WLAN Monitor utility, double-click the icon on the desktop to launch the utility or choose **Start > Programs > Linksys Wireless Card > WLAN Monitor**. Click the **Link Information** tab and the **More Information** subtab. Figure 11-14 shows an example.

Figure 11-14 Surveying the Channel Change with the Linksys WLAN Monitor

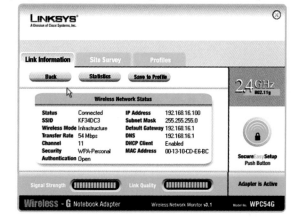

With the Linksys WLAN Monitor, we can see the actual wireless channel, now channel 11. Once again, the wireless coverage in the family room improved in this example.

Update the table we made earlier with the new wireless survey data you collected after the channel change. Sample data for our example is shown in Table 11-6.

Note: When you change the channel on the router, you do not need to make any changes on the wireless NIC, because it automatically searches for and finds the new channel. This is one of the only times you need to change something on the router only and not on the NIC.

Table 11-6   Wireless Survey Chart—Channel Change

	Current	Channel Changed to Channel 11	Change 2
Living Room	15	15	
Kitchen	6	11	
Back Deck	5	10	
Master Bedroom	7	1	
Kid's Bedroom	3	1	
Family Room	0	15	

We can see from the new wireless survey after the change that we improved the coverage in the family room, kitchen, and back deck (very important for surfing by the pool). However, coverage in the master bedroom and kid's bedroom now may be a problem.

This is one of the challenges with wireless networks. They are a bit like squeezing a balloon: You squeeze on one side and the bubble pops out another side.

Assess from your wireless survey whether the channel change addressed the problems adequately. If not, you could try another channel or move on to some other possible remedies.

Trying Different Antenna Positions

Sometimes, simply changing the direction of the antennas on the wireless router can make a big difference in wireless coverage. There is no simple rule for which antenna positions will be best for your network, but there are some general guidelines.

As discussed earlier, first make sure that the location of the wireless router leaves the antennas with open air around them. Putting the router inside a bookcase or enclosure, or where antennas are near a bunch of electric wires or cables, will likely cause the network range to suffer.

Figure 11-15 shows some possible positions that work pretty well. In general, keep the antennas pointed in a direction where they are not folded onto each other or obstructed by other objects (including the router itself). You may have to experiment a bit to see if changing the antenna position has an effect on your wireless coverage, and if it is a positive or negative effect.

Figure 11-15 Possible Wireless Router Antenna Positions

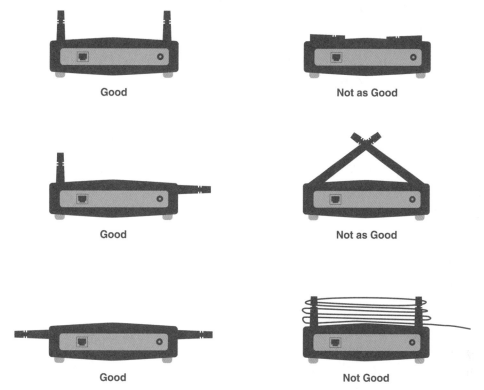

Conduct a wireless survey as before to see what the overall effect on the network was. Table 11-7 shows some sample results for our example.

Table 11-7   Wireless Survey Chart—Channel Change

	Current	Channel Changed to Channel 11	Antennas Moved Upward
Living Room	15	15	12
Kitchen	6	11	9
Back Deck	5	10	9
Master Bedroom	7	1	7
Kid's Bedroom	3	1	8
Family Room	0	15	5

Suppose that the antenna changes had the effects shown in Table 11-7. Now the wireless network is a fairly healthy balance of signal strength in all the locations in which we want to use wireless. This would be a pretty good result. Note the change you made in your notebook in case you need to remember later what tuning steps you performed.

Upgrading the Antenna

Depending on the type of wireless router you have, it may be possible to improve the antennas it uses to expand your wireless home network coverage. Antennas are a bit like ears for your wireless router: You get a default set of ears like everyone, but you can buy a hearing aid if you want.

Most wireless routers are shipped with a default set of antennas that have the type of performance most typically needed by the majority of customers. Sometimes it is possible to purchase a higher-performance antenna for your wireless router.

Before investing in this option, we recommend you exhaust the other options at your disposal. Make sure you have gone through Chapters 10, 11, and 12 to ensure that you do not have some other issue that is much cheaper to correct.

If you decide ultimately that you want to try upgrading the antennas, check with the manufacturer to see what the options are. For example, if you have a Linksys WRT54G wireless router, you can purchase a supplemental antenna set, model HGA7T, that provides two high-gain antennas to replace the default antennas that come with the router. Figure 11-16 shows that upgrading is pretty easy.

Figure 11-16 Upgrading the Wireless Router Antennas

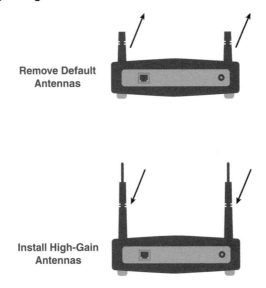

High-gain antennas can certainly give your home wireless network an added boost in terms of range and coverage. However, this option is a bit expensive. High-performance antennas can cost as much as the router itself.

Using Wireless Range Extenders and Additional Access Points

Other options for improving coverage include installing a range extender or additional access point. Range extenders connect to the wireless router with an Ethernet cable, and they act like a wireless bridge, extending the wireless signal out farther.

Access points are wireless routers, without the router part. They provide an additional point of access for wireless NICs in another room and can extend your wireless coverage.

Both of these options are beyond the scope of this book. If you need to go this route, talk to someone who knows what they are doing and has experience with wireless networks, such as the folks at your neighborhood electronics store. The most common cause for needing a range extender is when you have a huge house. In general, you should try all the other options we mention here first. If you have a very large house and have tried all the other options presented here with no success, then a range extender may be called for.

Upgrading the Wireless Router

In general, 802.11b and 802.11g wireless networks have similar coverage ranges, which adequately cover the average house. 802.11a tends to provide a bit less coverage due to its operation at a higher frequency (5.1-GHz band) that causes the radio waves not to travel as far.

802.11n is a whole new ballgame. The wireless N standard was designed with specific range-improvement technologies that can provide up to four times farther range and reduce what are called "dead spots," areas where coverage suddenly dips to near zero in your house.

Upgrading to a wireless N router, such as the Linksys WRT300N product, could certainly be an effective option to extend your wireless network coverage. We evaluated one of the Linksys WRT300N routers, and in an average house size, we had nearly 100 percent signal strength in all rooms of the house.

Summary

When your wireless coverage is intermittent and causing issues with connecting, there are a number of steps you can take to remedy the problem and improve coverage throughout your house. When the remedies do not work, it may be time to take more serious measures, such as upgrading your network to an 802.11n wireless system.

If the remedies here improve your wireless coverage and you now have good performance, enjoy your wireless network and start surfing from poolside.

If you improve the coverage so that you now have pretty good signal strength in all rooms but still have issues with slow or intermittent connection problems, read the next chapter.

Where to Go for More Information

Check out Bradley Mitchell's article "Top 7 Tips for Improving a Wireless Home Network" on About.com: http://compnetworking.about.com/od/wifihomenetworking/tp/improvehomewifi.htm.

You also might find Microsoft's article "10 tips for improving your wireless network" (by Tony Northrup) helpful: www.microsoft.com/athome/moredone/wirelesstips.mspx.

Troubleshooting: I Can Connect, but It's Slow

What if you can connect to your wireless network, it stays connected just fine, but it seems like it is slow? To answer that, we first need to understand what to expect from a wireless network. Is it living up to its potential, or is some problem keeping the network from being as fast as it could be?

A wireless network can be slower than expected for a few different reasons:

- Broadband speed limits Internet access speed

- Operating at a slower wireless standard than expected

- Signal degradation due to interference

We explore each of these possibilities in this chapter.

Is the Broadband Internet Connection the Bottleneck?

There is a lot of competition between wireless home networking equipment makers. As a result, faster and faster wireless routers are all the rage. 802.11b started out with 11 Mbps and then 802.11g (and 802.11a) increased the speed to 54 Mbps. Extensions to 802.11g as well as the newest 802.11n standard are increasing the speed even more to 100 Mbps and beyond.

 Note: Incidentally, 100 Mbps is the speed of most wired networks today. Some are still 10 Mbps. So wireless networking has caught up to, and in some cases surpassed, wired networking in terms of speed. Wired networking is already starting to move toward 1 Gbps, which equals 1000 Mbps.

So, using a faster router means faster Internet access, right? Well, maybe. The Internet access speed really depends on more factors than just the wireless router speed. Figure 12-1 shows why. We have an 802.11g home wireless network, which provides up to 54 Mbps of speed. This means that within the home network, computers and devices can communicate with each other pretty fast. But when accessing the Internet, the speed is limited by the broadband connection to your house in most cases rather than by your router. The speed between the wireless device and wireless router stays the same, 54 Mbps, but the broadband services today typically only offer in the neighborhood of 384-kbps to 2-Mbps uplink speed (toward the Internet) and between 2-Mbps and 6-Mbps downlink speed (from the Internet).

Figure 12-1   Networking Speeds Inside and Outside the Home Network

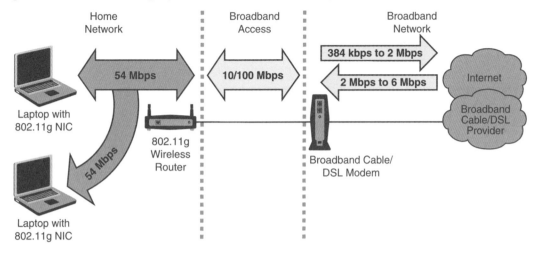

The point is that buying a wireless router capable of 54-Mbps or 100-Mbps speeds does not mean that you get that speed when accessing the Internet. You are limited by the broadband speed.

Checking the Broadband Connection

Sometimes, you can experience issues with your broadband connection that cause your service speed to be slower than you are paying for. This can be caused by an intermittent connection or wiring problem, as well as just general congestion on the broadband service.

We can check whether the router seems to have a good connection to the broadband service. Linksys routers have a built-in utility called *ping* (Windows XP also has this utility) that you can use to perform a rudimentary connection test.

Access the wireless router using an Internet browser. Click the **Administration** tab and then click the **Diagnostics** subtab, as shown in Figure 12-2. Click the **Start to Ping** button.

The wireless router creates and sends a number of test packets to the address in the IP or URL Address field, measuring the success rate and time it takes to receive a response. The results displayed appear similar to the example shown in Figure 12-3.

Figure 12-2   Linksys Router Built-In ping Utility

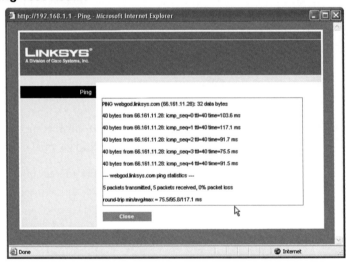

Figure 12-3   ping Test Result

We can see from the results displayed that five test packets were sent and all of them were successful (5 packets transmitted, 5 packets received, 0% packet loss).

We can also see that the time it took for the test packets to travel from our wireless router, across the broadband network, across the Internet to the destination, and back to the wireless router ranged from 75.5 milliseconds (ms) to 117.1 ms. This is pretty good. If you see time delays of 500 ms or 1000 ms (1 second), that could point to a problem in either the broadband network or your broadband connection.

From the Diagnostics screen shown in Figure 12-2, try increasing the Times to Ping field to 20 or 100 and see how the test works. If you see packets being lost, or excessive delays (say, greater than about 500 ms), this could be causing slowdowns on your network. In this case, you may want to talk with your broadband provider about fixing the problem.

 Note: You can ping any website you regularly use, although some website administrators disable responding to ping, so do not be alarmed if you do not get any response. Instead, try a few different websites. Also, if the website being pinged (or some Internet router on the path to the site) is having issues, you may see some ping failures that are not related to your provider. If you do see failures, try a few different ping sites to narrow down the issue. If you get the same issues with multiple sites, then you probably have an issue with your provider network.

Testing Your Broadband Speed

If the connection looks good (no packets being lost and short delay times), next check whether your broadband service is operating at the speed you have subscribed to. There are a few good online broadband speed tests you can do. We like the one at Broadbandreports.com: www.broadbandreports.com/speedtests/.

After you execute a speed test, results are displayed such as the example shown in Figure 12-4.

Figure 12-4   Broadband Speed Test Example

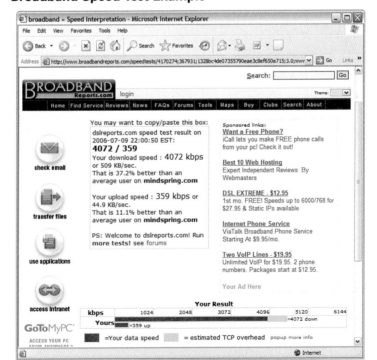

Here we can see that the uplink speed measured was 359 kbps, and the downlink speed measured was 4072 kbps (or 4 Mbps). This matches the broadband subscription in this case of 384 kbps/4 Mbps broadband cable service.

If you see speeds much slower than your subscription speed, you may want to talk to your broadband provider about fixing a problem, or possibly upgrading to a faster service. Make sure someone else in the house is not downloading a big file. You may also want to check your system for spyware, which could also slow down your system or connection.

Is the Wireless Network Too Slow?

After you verify that your broadband service is not creating a bottleneck, you are ready to take a look at the wireless network. As mentioned in the previous section, faster wireless networks do not always mean faster Internet access. But there are times when the wireless network can be an unexpected bottleneck.

Understanding Wireless Standards and Speeds

In Chapter 2, "Wireless Standards: What the Letters Mean," we talked about the wireless standards and the different speeds that they can provide. In Chapter 3, "Selecting the Right Wireless Standard for Your Network," we discussed how mixing different wireless NICs and wireless routers affects the overall network speed. Just to recap:

- 802.11b provides up to 11 Mbps

- 802.11g and 802.11a provide up to 54 Mbps

- 802.11n provides 100 Mbps and higher

One of the most common mistakes people make is that they upgrade their wireless router from 802.11b to 802.11g, increasing the network speed from 11 Mbps to 54 Mbps, but they do not upgrade the wireless NICs in the PCs and laptops. Because the NICs are still 802.11b, the network will continue to operate at 11 Mbps, and of course no noticeable increase in performance will be seen.

Note: The good news here is that, unlike encryption, which forces the whole network down to the lowest standard, the various network standards can work on the same network (assuming they are compatible). This means that if you buy a G-based router and you have one computer with a G NIC and one with a B NIC, both computers will work at the standard of their respective NIC. In other words, the computer with the G NIC will get G performance and the computer with the B NIC will get B performance.

In general, 802.11b wireless networks typically achieve around 5–6 Mbps of throughput speed. This is right on the edge of what is required to fully utilize the typical broadband connection (typically between 2 and 6 Mbps). Upgrading to 802.11g could very well provide a noticeable difference.

Upgrading to 802.11n may or may not provide a speed benefit. Speeds within the home network will certainly be accelerated to 100 Mbps and above, assuming that you upgraded both the wireless router and wireless NICs to 802.11n. However, the broadband service is still between 2 and 6 Mbps, so it is unlikely you will see any performance improvement for accessing the Internet.

The key point to understand is what you should expect from your wireless network. Do not fall into the trap of thinking that faster routers and faster wireless standards automatically mean faster Internet access.

Verifying Wireless Network Speed

One condition that can occur which dramatically slows down the speed of a wireless network is called *automatic speed negotiation.* An example of speed negotiation is shown in Figure 12-5.

Figure 12-5   Automatic Speed Negotiation

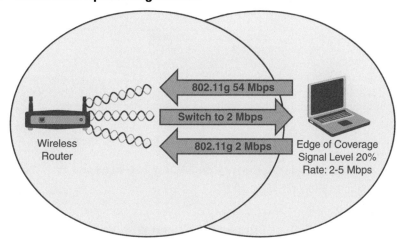

When the wireless router detects that a signal from a wireless NIC is weak or degraded, it "determines" that it is not possible to continue sending and receiving at the maximum speed supported by the standard. So the wireless router reduces the speed of the data between it and the wireless NIC. This automatic behavior is built in to all 802.11 wireless standards and cannot be disabled. But this is preferable to the alternative, which is for the wireless connection to simply drop or work intermittently.

As depicted in the example shown in Figure 12-5, suppose that we have an 802.11g wireless router and NIC. The NIC is on the edge of the coverage area and has a fairly weak signal. First, the NIC tries to transmit to the router at the maximum speed of 54 Mbps. The wireless router determines that there are many errors in the transmission, so it instructs the NIC to "back off" the speed, lowering it in this example to 2 Mbps. It determines that at this rate, transmissions have far fewer errors.

Automatic speed negotiation is a very nice feature that self-corrects many wireless network issues. However, if your wireless laptop is only getting 2 Mbps when you thought it was getting 54 Mbps, that's a problem.

How can you tell if this is occurring? Pretty easily, actually. Here is how. Suppose we have an 802.11g wireless router. Now suppose we have an 802.11b wireless NIC and we are using Windows Wireless Network Connection utility. Choose **Start > Connect To > Show All Connections**. Right-click the wireless NIC and choose **Status**. Figure 12-6 shows an example.

Figure 12-6   Checking Wireless Connection Speed with Windows XP–Good Signal

We can see from Figure 12-6 that we have pretty good signal strength, and we are getting the full rate that the wireless NIC is capable of. Note that even though the router supports up to 54 Mbps, the NIC shows it is connected at 11 Mbps, the maximum rate for an 802.11b NIC.

Suppose now that we take the same laptop with the 802.11b NIC to a room of the house with much weaker signal strength, as shown in Figure 12-7.

Figure 12-7   Checking Wireless Connection Speed with Windows XP–Poor Signal

We can see from Figure 12-7 that we have poor signal strength. As a consequence, the wireless router and NIC have auto-negotiated the data rate down to 5.5 Mbps, essentially 50 percent of the maximum NIC speed.

Next let's look at an 802.11g NIC where we are using the Linksys WLAN Monitor utility. Double-click the icon on the desktop to launch the utility or choose **Start > Programs > Linksys Wireless Card > WLAN Monitor**. Click the **Link Information** tab and then the **More Information** subtab. Figure 12-8 shows an example.

Figure 12-8   Checking Wireless Connection Speed with Linksys WLAN Monitor–Good Signal

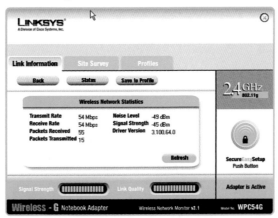

We can see from Figure 12-8 that we have good signal strength, and we are getting the full rate that the wireless NIC is capable of. Note that in this case both the router and NIC support up to 54 Mbps. The NIC shows it is connected at 54 Mbps, the maximum rate for an 802.11g NIC.

Suppose now we take the same laptop with the 802.11g NIC to a room of the house with much weaker signal strength, as shown in Figure 12-9.

Figure 12-9   Checking Wireless Connection Speed with Linksys WLAN Monitor–Poor Signal

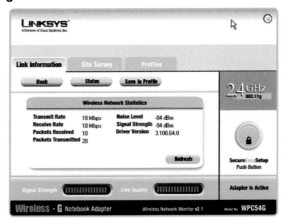

We can see from Figure 12-9 that we have poor signal strength. As a consequence, the wireless router and NIC have auto-negotiated the data rate down to 18 Mbps, essentially only 33 percent of the maximum NIC speed.

Is the Wireless Network Signal Getting Degraded?

One of the reasons that you can experience either poor signal coverage or slower speeds even in good signal coverage is that the wireless signal is being degraded. This means that although the wireless router is sending out a clear and strong signal, something is causing the signal quality to diminish by the time it reaches your wireless NIC (and vice versa).

How can you have a strong signal but the connection is still poor quality? Think about being in a drive-through restaurant and placing your order at the speaker. Often the person taking your order is loud, but you cannot understand what they are saying because they sound muffled or are so close to the microphone that the sound is distorted.

The same is true of wireless networks. You may be able to see a very strong signal, but something may be causing the signal to be garbled, creating errors in the connection. Possible sources of signal degradation include

- Interference from nearby wireless routers

- Interference from other devices, including cordless phones, microwave ovens, Bluetooth head-sets, and so on

- A malfunctioning wireless router or wireless NIC

Let's look at a couple of these issues, how you can recognize if one is occurring, and what you can do about it.

Interference from Other Wireless Routers

Every wireless router manufactured is set up to use a default wireless channel when you take it out of the box and plug it in. For Linksys routers designed for the 802.11b and 802.11g standards, it is channel 6. For Linksys routers designed for the newer 802.11n standard, the default channels are 5 and 7. (802.11n uses two channels in wideband mode. See Appendix B, "802.11n Wireless Channels," for more information.)

Every Linksys wireless router manufactured is set up to use these channels, unless you change them. This means that if you and your neighbor both buy a Linksys router (or any other router), there is a good chance you will be running your wireless networks on the same channel. If your houses are far enough apart, using the same channel is not necessarily a problem. However, if your houses or apartments are near each other, it can cause issues.

Checking for Conflicting Wireless Routers

So how can we see if other routers are using the same channel as ours? With Linksys WLAN Monitor it is pretty easy. Double-click the icon on the desktop to launch the utility or choose **Start > Programs > Linksys Wireless Card > WLAN Monitor**. Click the **Site Survey** tab. Figure 12-10 shows an example.

Figure 12-10 Checking for Conflicting Wireless Routers with Linksys WLAN Monitor

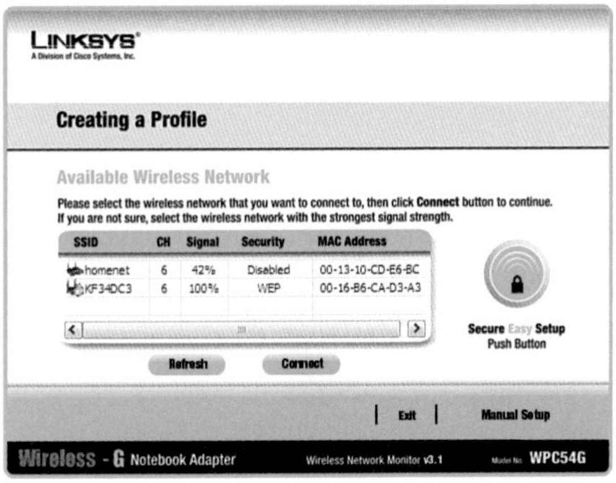

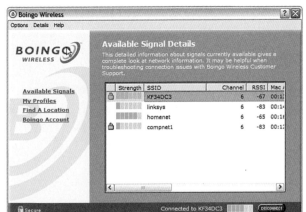

We can see from this example that there are two wireless network signals within range of the wireless NIC, with SSIDs KF34DC3 and homenet. KF34DC3 is our wireless network, so homenet must be the neighbor's. Both are operating on channel 6, the default channel.

If you are using Windows Wireless Network Connection utility to manage your wireless connections, checking for conflicts is not easy, because XP does not display the channel currently connected or the channel of other wireless networks. In this case, you need to add another wireless connection manager, such as Boingo, that can provide the information.

Boingo Wireless offers a free downloadable wireless connection manager that you can use as an alternative to the Windows Wireless Network Connection utility or Linksys WLAN Monitor to manage your wireless profiles. The free program is available here: www.boingo.com/download.html.

After you download and install the program, double-click the icon on the desktop to start it or choose **Start > Programs > Boingo > Boingo** to launch the application. Choose **Details > Available Signal Details**. An example is shown in Figure 12-11.

Figure 12-11 Checking for Conflicting Wireless Routers with Boingo

We can see from this example that there are four wireless signals with SSIDs: KF34DC3, homenet, linksys, and compnet1. The linksys and compnet1 signals are weak, so they should not be an issue. However, you can see that the homenet signal is strong, even stronger than our own wireless network (KF34DC3). All four are using channel 6, the default wireless channel.

Determining Whether the Conflicting Wireless Router Is Causing an Issue

Seeing that there is another wireless router using the same channel is one thing, but is it causing a problem? It's a little tough to answer. There are some telltale signs you can look for, though.

If you are using Linksys WLAN Monitor, double-click the icon on the desktop to launch the utility or choose **Start > Programs > Linksys Wireless Card > WLAN Monitor**. Click the **Link Information** tab and then click the **More Information** subtab. Figure 12-12 shows an example.

Figure 12-12 Detecting Signal Degradation with Linksys WLAN Monitor

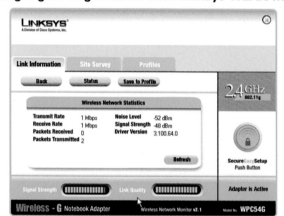

Here, we see strong signal strength, but the data rate is only 1 Mbps. In this situation (with an 802.11g wireless router and NIC), we should be able to have a data rate of 54 Mbps. The reduced rate in spite of a strong signal strength could indicate that the other wireless router operating on the same channel is causing signal degradation.

If you are using Windows XP, you may need to use Boingo again. Double-click the Boingo icon on the desktop or choose **Start > Programs > Boingo > Boingo** to launch the application. Choose **Details > Signal Performance**.

Wait a few minutes and let Boingo monitor the wireless signal for a bit. Boingo will produce a nice graph of the wireless signal level. What we would like to see is a consistent wireless signal like that shown in Figure 12-13.

Now look at the example shown in Figure 12-14.

Figure 12-13 Determining a Steady Wireless Signal with Boingo

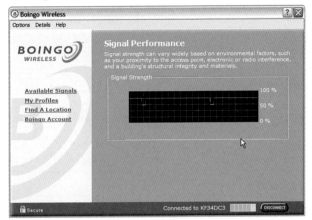

Figure 12-14 Detecting Signal Degradation with Boingo

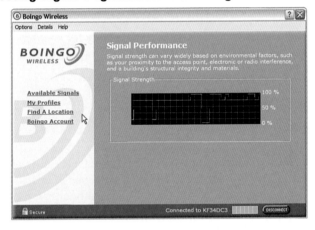

Here you can see that the wireless signal is all over the place, sometimes high and sometimes low, not very consistent. This could be an indication that the other wireless network operating on the same channel is causing a problem.

Correcting a Conflicting Wireless Router Situation

If you detect a potential conflicting wireless router and suspect it may be causing your network to suffer, the best fix is to try changing your wireless network to operate on a different channel.

Follow the procedure described in Chapter 11, "Troubleshooting: I Can Connect Sometimes," to change the wireless channel and then conduct a follow-up wireless survey in your house to confirm that it had a positive effect.

Choose a wireless channel that you do not see another wireless router using. Also see Chapter 11 for more discussion on available wireless channels you can choose from.

Interference from Cordless Phones and Other Devices

As we have mentioned a few times now, cordless phones can be another source of problems for your wireless network. How do you know if your cordless phone system may be incompatible with your home wireless network? The first step is to understand which wireless radio frequency bands each device uses. Table 12-1 shows a very easy rule of thumb.

Table 12-1   Wireless Network and Cordless Phone System Compatibility

	900-MHz Cordless Phones	2.4-GHz Cordless Phones	5-GHz Cordless Phones
802.11b	No problem	Potential problem	No problem
802.11g	No problem	Potential problem	No problem
802.11a	No problem	No problem	Potential problem
802.11n	No problem	Potential problem	No problem

The green areas of the table indicate that there is not a possibility for interference between the type of wireless network and cordless phone system you have. Areas in yellow indicate that there could be an issue—not always, but possibly.

In general, if you have an 802.11b, 802.11g, or 802.11n wireless network, try to buy 5-GHz cordless phones.

 Note: We mention cordless phones through this section, but baby monitors, garage door openers, walkie-talkies, and other wireless types of devices can cause the same problem. The actions you take will be the same, although you have a little less control when it comes to testing the devices for interference (especially if it's your neighbor's garage door opener).

Determining Whether the Conflicting Cordless Phone Is Causing an Issue

If you do think you have the possibility for a conflict between the wireless network and your cordless phone, how can you tell if it's causing an issue? One simple way is to unplug the cordless phone for a while and see if the issue goes away.

Another way is to try detecting the issue using Boingo. Suppose in this example that we have an 802.11g network and a 2.4-GHz cordless phone system.

Double-click the Boingo icon on the desktop or choose **Start > Programs > Boingo > Boingo** to launch the application. Choose **Details > Signal Performance**.

Wait a few minutes and let Boingo monitor the wireless signal for a bit. Boingo will produce a nice graph of the wireless signal level, like the example shown in Figure 12-15.

Figure 12-15 Detecting Signal Degradation with Boingo–During a Call

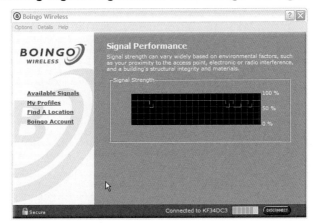

You can see that the wireless signal is quite consistent. Now place a call with your cordless phone. If you look on the right side of the signal chart, you can see that while we made a call, the signal was degraded a bit. The degradation is not terrible, but it is there. It may or may not be causing an issue; it is difficult to say.

To further investigate the issue, we can check whether we see a slowdown in the data rate of the connection. Place a call again using the cordless phone.

If you are using the Linksys WLAN Monitor, double-click the icon on the desktop to launch the utility or choose **Start > Programs > Linksys Wireless Card > WLAN Monitor**. Click the **Link Information** tab. Figure 12-16 shows an example.

Figure 12-16 Checking the Wireless Data Rate with Linksys WLAN Monitor–Phone On

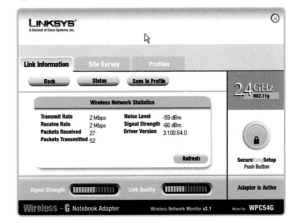

We can see that despite having a pretty good signal level, the data rate has dropped to 2 Mbps during the duration of the call.

Now hang up the phone. As shown in Figure 12-17, the wireless data signal has gone up significantly, and the wireless data rate is also increased back up to 54 Mbps.

Figure 12-17 Checking the Wireless Data Rate with Linksys WLAN Monitor–Phone Off

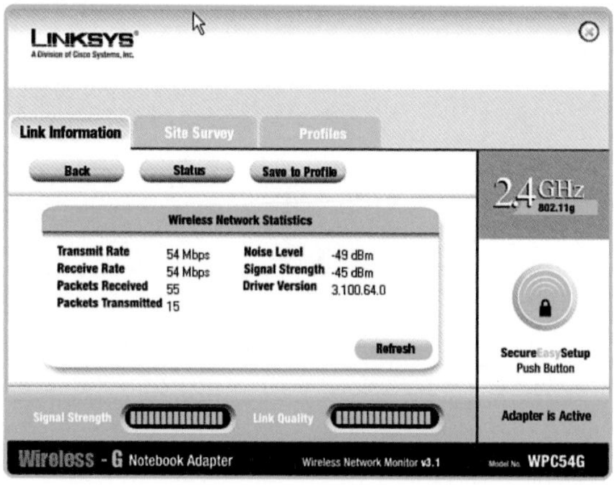

If you see a degradation of either the signal level or wireless data rate, or both, when you place a test call with the cordless phone, you probably have a conflict. Also keep in mind that interference works both ways, so your router can degrade the sound quality of your cordless phone.

Correcting a Conflicting Cordless Phone Issue

If you detect a potential conflict between your wireless network and your cordless phone system, you have several options:

■ Move the base and handset of the cordless phone system well away from the wireless router and where you will use the wireless computers.

■ Change the channel of the wireless router (see Chapter 11).

■ Upgrade your cordless phone system to a type that does not conflict with your wireless network (see Table 12-1).

■ Upgrade your wireless network to a type that does not conflict with your cordless phone system (see Table 12-1).

Whichever change you make, follow the procedures described in Chapter 11 and then conduct a follow-up wireless survey in your house to confirm that it had a positive effect.

You can try the same experiment outlined in this section with your microwave, Bluetooth headset, and other devices that may conflict with your wireless network. Just check the signal level and wireless data rate with the device off and then check it again with the device in use.

Summary

Signal degradation can occur with your wireless network, causing slowdowns or difficulty making connections at all. The most common causes are a nearby conflicting wireless router or another device in your home, such as a cordless phone, that causes interference.

Before assuming the wireless network is causing a slowdown, make sure your broadband service is performing the way your subscription says it should. Also make sure your perceptions are accurate— are you making a bad assumption that upgrading to a faster router will give you faster Internet access?

If you determine that your wireless network is experiencing some issues due to interference, take some steps to correct the problem, using the wireless survey procedure from Chapter 11.

Where to Go for More Information

Read Bradley Mitchell's article titled "Top 6 Reasons Why WiFi Network Connections Drop" at About.com: http://wireless.about.com/od/wifihomenetworking/tp/connectiondrop.htm.

Bradley Mitchell has also written an article titled "Change the WiFi Channel Number to Avoid Interference," also available at About.com: http://compnetworking.about.com/od/wifihomenetworking/qt/wifichannel.htm.

Joseph Moran has a tutorial at Wi-Fi Planet titled "Wireless Home Networking, Part V— Interference and Range Extension": www.wi-fiplanet.com/tutorials/article.php/1497111.

PART V

Bells and Whistles

Whew. Now that we've designed, built, and debugged our wireless network, it's time to do some cool stuff with it. Let the good times roll.

Chapter 13, "Wireless Video and Entertainment," shows you how to use your home wireless network for entertainment. We cover how to add a wireless video camera to the network. Then we show you how to network your video game console (like an XBox) and a Digital Video Recorder (DVR).

Chapter 14, "Wireless to Go," shows you how to take wireless networking with you when you travel. Wireless networks are becoming about as common as electric lights. We cover how to use wireless hotspots when you travel, how to set up your own portable hotspot, and how to give your guests access to your wireless home network.

We wrap up Part V with Chapter 15, "The Future of Wireless Networking," which gives a glimpse into what we think is the future of wireless home networking. We don't have a crystal ball or anything, we just give our best guesses. The technology is moving quickly, so we will probably look foolish in five years, but what the heck. We love to give these little glimpses into the future. It at least gives the appearance that we know what we are talking about.

Wireless Video and Entertainment

Now that we have a well-functioning, secure wireless network, what do you do with it? Well, lots. You can of course use it to surf the Internet and read your e-mail from the back deck. But there is a lot more you can do.

One general category is wireless video and entertainment, including wireless video cameras, media gateways that can display pictures and send music to your TV entertainment system, online gaming, networking your digital video recorder (DVR), and wireless digital jukeboxes.

We cannot begin to cover all the things you can do with your wireless network here, but let's take three pretty cool things to do and see how you would set up and use them:

- Wireless video cameras

- Online gaming

- Networking a DVR, like a TiVo

The network capacity (or bandwidth) within your home network is much greater (three times or more) than the fastest upload/download speeds you will get from your high-speed connection to the Internet. All this excess capacity exists on your home wireless network because many in-home applications—including the three described in this chapter—typically require more bandwidth than is required for Internet browsing or e-mail. This chapter shows you how to set up these three options in your network.

Wireless Video Cameras

Once limited to very expensive closed-circuit television (CCTV) systems, video cameras for fun or for surveillance are now pretty affordable. If you already have a wireless network in your home, a decent wireless video surveillance system costs you only $100 or so. (We say "only" because a basic CCTV system costs more than $1000.)

Wireless video cameras have all sorts of practical uses, including home surveillance for security and nanny cams.

Finding Uses for Wireless Video Cameras

Video cameras that attach to computers are very common, usually used for communicating with other people that have similar video cameras. Also popular recently have been very inexpensive wireless cameras that can be placed anywhere in your house.

The ability to use either of these video cameras for live surveillance while you are not at home is limited. However, newer products like the Linksys wireless Internet video cameras have several distinct advantages:

- No computer is required for them to operate, so they can be located anywhere in your house (or outside, for that matter) where there is an electrical outlet.

- Images from the camera are viewable with any computer from inside your house, or from anywhere outside your house where there is Internet service.

In Figure 13-1, we placed a wireless Internet video camera in a house with a view of the front door.

Figure 13-1 Home Surveillance Using a Wireless Internet Video Camera

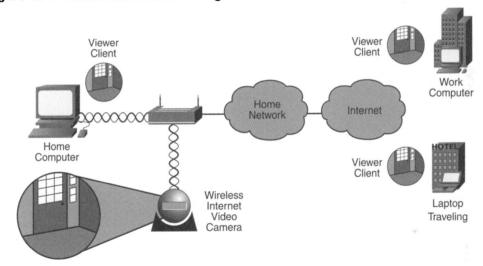

Now, we can use a viewer client to view the real-time video feed. So from upstairs, we could check who is at the front door. We could also use the viewer client on a computer at work to periodically check the residence or to see that the kids got home at the expected time from school. In a similar way, you could even use your laptop to check on the house while traveling on business.

To avoid the need for constant surveillance, you can set up the camera to act as an automated sentry, and notify you only when there is something worth seeing.

You can program the camera to send a signal to a pager, cell phone, or e-mail account to notify you if motion has been detected. You can even have the camera send you a video clip that it captures of the event.

In Figure 13-2, when little Susie arrives home, the camera detects the motion of her entering the front door. It then can send a notification e-mail (including a video clip) so you can verify that it is her. Or the camera could send a text message to your cell phone (via Short Message Service [SMS]) or to your pager (alphanumeric) with a message such as "Susie is home."

Figure 13-2   Automatic Notification of a Child Arriving Home

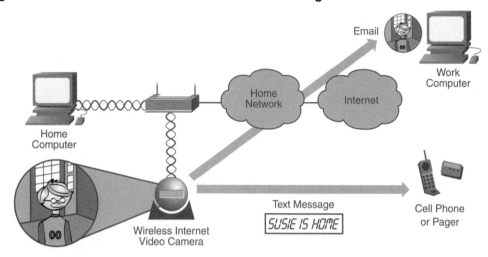

We will walk through how to set up your camera for viewing and as a motion detector later in the chapter. First, we need to pick a camera. Linksys offers a few different camera products. Table 13-1 shows the wireless video camera products from Linksys that we recommend.

Table 13-1   Linksys Wireless Internet Video Cameras

Model	Capability	Wireless Standard	Wireless Encryption Supported
WVC54G	Audio, video, and motion detection	802.11g Also works with 802.11b, 802.11n	64-bit WEP 128-bit WEP WPA-PSK
WVC54GC	Audio, video, and motion detection Compact size	802.11g Also works with 802.11b, 802.11n	64-bit WEP 128-bit WEP
WVC11B	Video and motion detection	802.11b Also works with 802.11g, 802.11n	64-bit WEP 128-bit WEP

The next few sections go through the steps to install a wireless Internet video camera on your home network. Here's an overview of the steps we will go through:

- Connecting the video camera to your wireless network
- Determining who can access the video camera

- Viewing video from within your house

- Viewing video over the Internet

- Using the video camera as a motion detector

Connecting the Video Camera to Your Wireless Network

The first step is to set up the wireless Internet video camera so that it can communicate with the wireless home network. Similar to the wireless NICs we added in Chapters 8, "Wireless NIC Setup," and 9, "Wireless Security Setup," you must tell the video camera how to join your wireless network.

For almost every device or computer we add to the network, it's advantageous to let the wireless router choose and manage the IP addresses for the devices on your network. IP addresses can be assigned as needed, and the actual addresses assigned are not important to us. However, for the wireless Internet video camera, it will be necessary for us to assign a fixed IP address, so that we may access the camera images via the Internet.

The steps to install the wireless Internet video camera are as follows (the example shown is for the Linksys WVC11B Wireless-B Internet Video Camera):

Step 1 Connect the Linksys wireless Internet video camera to the wireless router using an Ethernet cable (ordinary, not crossover), and plug in the power adapter. The LAN LED light on the front should light up.

Step 2 Put the CD that came with the Linksys video camera into a computer on the network (one that is wired is preferred). The Setup Wizard should start automatically. If not, use My Computer to browse the CD and double-click **Setup.exe**. Click the **Setup** button.

Step 3 The Setup Wizard instructs you to connect the video camera to the wireless router. Click **Next**.

Step 4 The Setup Wizard searches for the new video camera on the network (see Figure 13-3). Click **Next**. If it does not locate the camera, try clicking **Search Again**. If it still does not show up, check your cabling. Make sure the LAN LED light is lit on the video camera.

Figure 13-3   Setup Wizard Searches for and Finds the New Video Camera

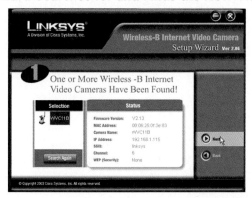

Step 5 You are prompted for the camera administrator name and password. Enter **admin** for both the Administrator Name and Administrator Password fields and click **OK**.

Step 6 Enter a device name (this is something you can just make up) for the video camera (we used Camera_1 in Figure 13-4). Enter the time zone, date, and time. Click **Next**.

Figure 13-4   Enter the Basic Camera Setup Settings

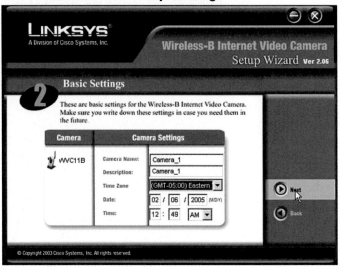

Step 7 Click **Static IP Address** and then click **Next**.

Note: The Setup Wizard recommends choosing **Automatic Configuration—DHCP** if you are connecting the camera to a router. However, if you want to access the camera over the Internet, you need a fixed (static) IP address.

Step 8 Enter an IP address that is unlikely to be assigned on your network by the wireless router (for example, 192.168.1.140). (See Figure 13-5.)

The subnet mask will be 255.255.255.0. The gateway will be 192.168.1.1. For the primary DNS and secondary DNS, enter the addresses listed on the sheet of paper or e-mail you received from your ISP when you subscribed. If you can't find them, access the wireless router using an Internet browser and click the **Status** tab.

After entering all the settings, click **Next**.

Figure 13-5   Configure the IP Address Settings

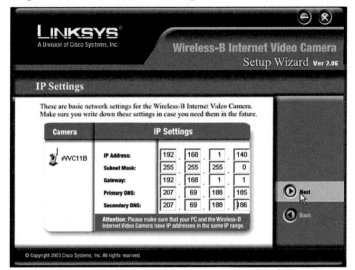

Note: The IP address you choose needs to be in the range of IP addresses for your home network. In Chapter 7, "Wireless Router Setup," we set up the router to use the address range 192.168.1.2 through 192.168.1.254 for our home network (.0, .1, and .255 are reserved). In addition, we set up the router to dynamically assign IP addresses in the range 192.168.1.100 through 192.168.1.149 to computers and devices requesting an address.

The IP address just needs to be unique on the network and within one of these ranges. We chose 192.168.1.140 for this example. Whatever address you choose, write it down, because this will be the address needed when accessing the camera. If you forget the address, you probably have to do a factory reset and start over.

Step 9   The next wizard page asks if your network is ad hoc or infrastructure (meaning based on a wireless router). Select **Infrastructure** and click **Next**.

Step 10   Enter the SSID for your wireless network (see Figure 13-6). For this particular example, the home network is using an SSID of J59wgh21MX. Click **Next**.

Step 11   Set the wireless security setting to **WEP 128 Bit Keys** (or the encryption you are using), as shown in Figure 13-7. Enter the WEP passphrase for your wireless network. In this example, the WEP passphrase is 64Gx3prY19fk2. Click **Next**.

Figure 13-6   Enter the SSID for Your Wireless Network

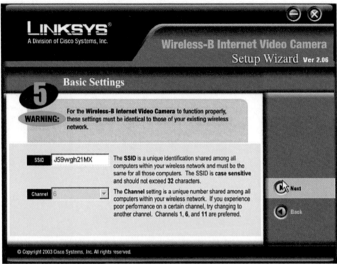

Figure 13-7   Enter the Wireless Security Settings

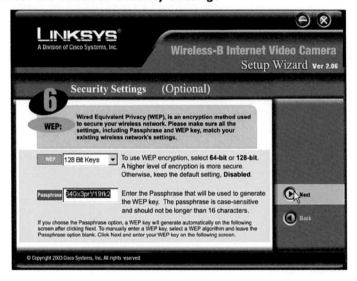

Step 12   The camera generates a WEP key from the WEP passphrase you entered (if it is a Linksys product, that is). Check the WEP key to ensure it matches the key being used on the wireless router (see Figure 13-8). Do not modify the key! Click **Next**.

Note: If the two keys do not match, modify the key value to match what is being used on the wireless router. Normally, the keys will match as long as the wireless video camera and wireless router are both Linksys products.

Figure 13-8   Confirm the Generated WEP Key

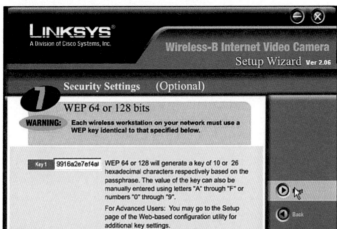

Step 13   The Setup Wizard then displays a summary of the new settings. (See Figure 13-9.) Click **Save**. Click **OK** on the double-confirmation dialog box that appears next.

Figure 13-9   Settings Confirmation

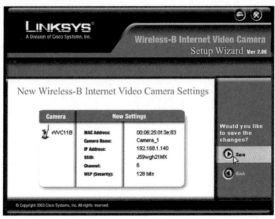

Step 14   You're all done. Leave the Setup Wizard for now. We have to come back to it later.

Unplug the Ethernet cable from the video camera, power it off, and then power it back on. After you complete these steps, the WLAN LED indicator light on the front of the wireless Internet video camera should be lit. You can now unplug the video camera and move it to the location of your choice.

Note: By the way, if you have MAC address filtering turned on in your wireless network as a security feature, you will need to add the wireless video camera MAC address to the list of devices permitted to join your wireless network. This is true of any device you add to the wireless network. Most people remember to add laptops and computers, but they often forget to add other devices.

Determining Who Can Access the Video Camera

Now that the wireless Internet video camera is communicating properly with the wireless network, you need to perform a few steps to finish setting up the security for the camera. You want to change the administrator password for sure. You also may want to restrict who can access the camera, essentially who can view the image. Here is how:

Step 1   Open your Internet browser and type in the IP address that you selected for the video camera (for example, 192.168.1.140, as shown in Figure 13-10). Press **Enter**.

Figure 13-10 Access the Video Camera with Your Internet Browser

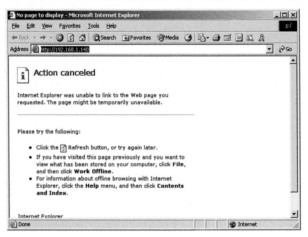

Step 2   The main menu for the video camera should appear (see Figure 13-11). If it does not appear, go back to the installation steps in the previous section.

Figure 13-11 Video Camera Main Menu

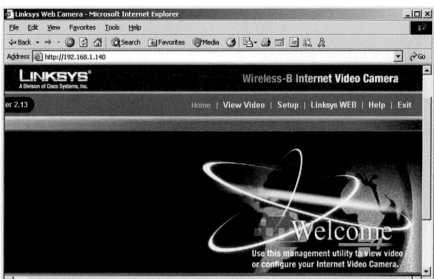

Step 3 Click the **Setup** option and then click **Password**. Enter a new password on both the **Password** and **Verify Password** lines. Write it down in the notebook you have been keeping for your network. Click **Apply**.

Step 4 Immediately, the video camera will reauthenticate (you will be logged out and will have to log back in again). Enter **admin** for the user ID and the new password you created. Click **OK**.

Step 5 Click **Users**. It is possible to set up video camera users who have only viewing privileges and not the authority to modify the video camera itself (see Figure 13-12). Never give out the master administration password. Click **Add**.

Step 6 Enter a username and corresponding password (see Figure 13-13). Do *not* use the same password as the administrator. Click **Apply**. Repeat this step for as many user accounts as you want to add. Click **Close** when you're finished.

Note: The usernames and passwords here are different from your Windows usernames. This is a list of users who are going to have access to your video camera and will have to log in to the camera itself. This prevents people from viewing your camera without your permission.

Figure 13-12 List of Authorized Camera Users

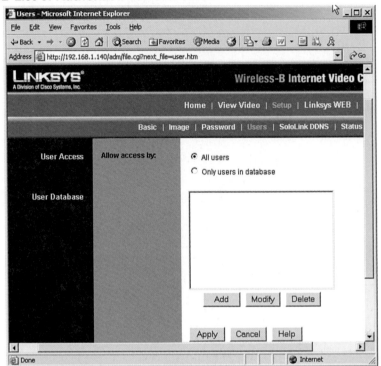

Figure 13-13 Add New Users with Viewing Privileges

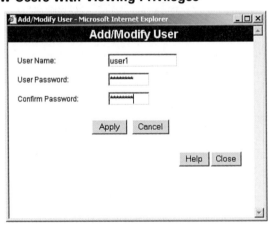

Step 7   THIS STEP IS CRITICAL! If you do not complete it, anyone who tries to access your video camera over the Internet will be granted access. Click **Only Users in Database** (see Figure 13-14). Click **Apply**.

Figure 13-14 Restrict the Video Camera to Authorized Users Only

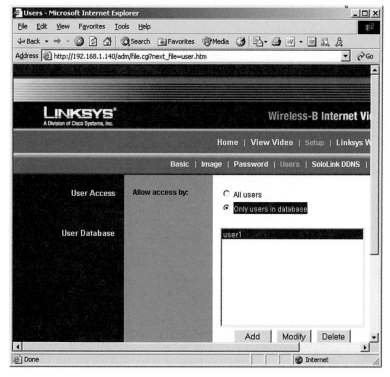

Now the wireless Internet video camera is installed, set up, and ready for use.

Viewing Video from Within Your House

Now that the wireless Internet video camera is set up completely, we can start using it to view video images. There are two ways to view video:

- **Internet browser**—This method is more involved than using the Viewer Client, but you can view video using any computer with an Internet browser, which is useful when trying to check your camera from a friend's house or from a public computer. (Extra steps are required for viewing the camera from outside your home network. See the section "Viewing Video over the Internet," later in the chapter.) With the Internet browser, you can access the other administrative features of the camera, such as setting up motion detection.

- **Viewer Client**—The Viewer Client is software provided on the CD that came with the camera. It is easier to use than the Internet browser and offers a recording feature. However, the Client must be installed on every computer you wish to view the video feed from. The Linksys Viewer Client software works only on computers running Windows XP or 2000, not Windows 98.

Let's look at an example of viewing the video image using an Internet browser:

Step 1 Point an Internet browser to the video camera by entering the IP address (for example, http://192.168.1.140) in the Address field of the browser, as shown in Figure 13-15, and press **Enter**. The main camera dialog box appears. Click **View Video**.

Note: For this example, Microsoft Internet Explorer is assumed to be the Internet browser. Other browsers such as Netscape or Firefox may require additional plug-ins to use them.

Figure 13-15 Access the Camera Using an Internet Browser

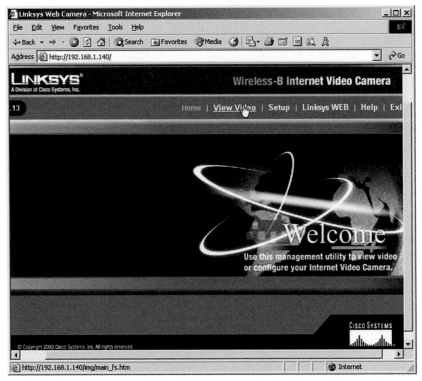

Step 2 Enter a username and password that you created with viewing privileges (see Figure 13-16).

Figure 13-16 Enter the Username and Password of the Viewer Account

Step 3 The first time you want to view video with your browser, a special "plug-in" is downloaded automatically and installed into the Internet browser. You'll see the dialog box shown in Figure 13-17. Click **Yes**.

Figure 13-17 Plug-In Is Automatically Downloaded the First Time

Step 4   It works! (See Figure 13-18.) Isn't she beautiful? Now, you're all done.

Figure 13-18 Viewing a Video Image

At this point, you can do a couple of things to save yourself some time in the future. Add the Video Viewer to your Favorites list by bookmarking the URL in your Internet browser. The next time you use the Internet browser, you can then simply go to the Video Viewer in the Favorites list instead of remembering the IP address.

You also may want to create a shortcut on the Windows Desktop. While still in the Viewer mode, click **File > Send To > Desktop Shortcut** in the Internet browser menu. This puts an icon on the desktop of your computer that you can simply double-click to jump into the Video Viewer mode.

Viewing Video over the Internet

Viewing video from within your home network (which we did in the previous section) is fairly straightforward. Viewing video over the Internet is a bit trickier. First, your home network is set up for access from inside-out, not from outside-in. Second, the actual IP address of your broadband service most likely changes over time (which is normal). It's a little like trying to deliver mail to someone whose address changes each week. Fortunately, there are a couple slick solutions to these potential problems.

First, let's tackle the inside-out/outside-in problem. How do you provide outside-in access to the video camera without compromising the security of your home network? Further, how do you reach the video camera, whose IP address on the home network is unknown to you? From the Internet's perspective, the video camera's IP address of 192.168.1.140 is not accessible. Remember, this is by design from a security perspective.

Setting Up the Wireless Router for Internet Camera Viewing

The trick to being able to access the video camera over the Internet is to use a feature on the Linksys wireless router called *port forwarding*. Using this feature, the wireless router can recognize incoming attempts to access the video camera, and can forward those requests directly to the video camera. Here's how to set up port forwarding on the wireless router:

Step 1 Point an Internet browser to the video camera by entering the IP address (for example, http://192.168.1.140). When prompted, enter **admin** for the user ID and the administrator password. Click **Setup** and then **Advanced**. Check the **Enable Alternate Port for HTTP Connections** check box (see Figure 13-19). Choose an IP port number that you want the camera to use (for example, 63333). Write it down. Click **Apply**.

Figure 13-19 Assign the Video Camera an IP Port Number

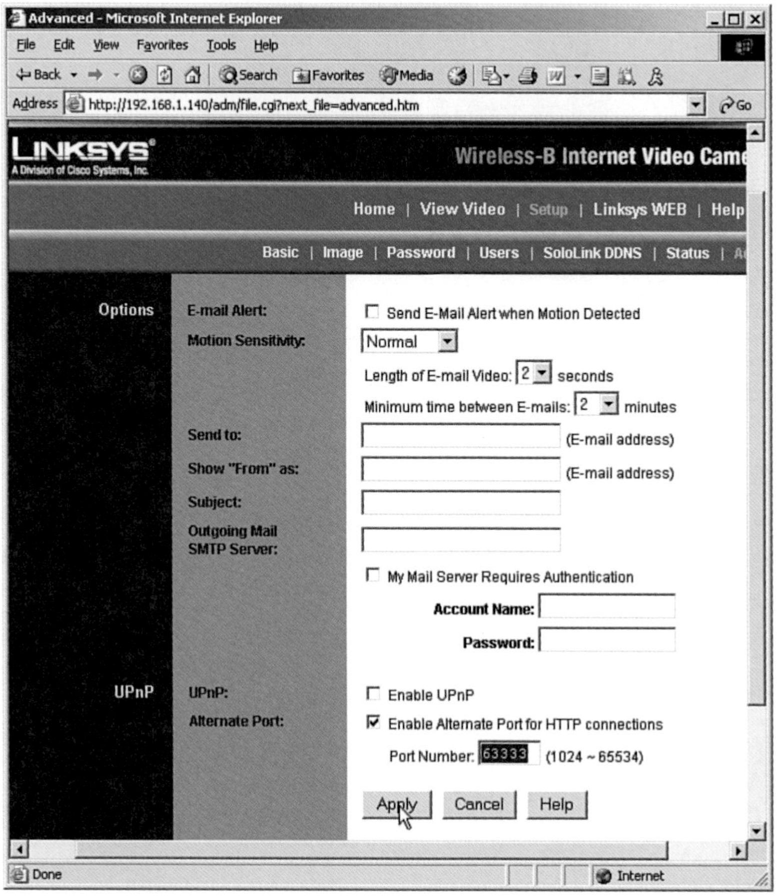

Note: We have not discussed IP port numbers very much. An IP port number is a number from 1 through 65535 that is used by applications (such as an Internet browser) to access the network. If an IP address is like your home address, think of an IP port number as being like a room of your house; it's adding another level of detail to the address.

Applications such as Internet browsers and e-mail programs use particular IP port numbers. We want to assign the camera to an uncommon number, such as between 60000 and 65535.

Step 2 Point an Internet browser to the wireless router by entering the IP address (for example, http://192.168.1.1). When prompted, enter the router's administrator password. Click the **Applications & Gaming** tab and then the **Port Range Forward** subtab (see Figure 13-20). Enter the chosen port number (from Step 1) in both the Start and End fields. Select **TCP** and then enter the IP address of the camera, for example, 192.168.1.140. Check the check box in the **Enable** column. Click **Save Settings**.

Figure 13-20 Set IP Port Forwarding on the Router

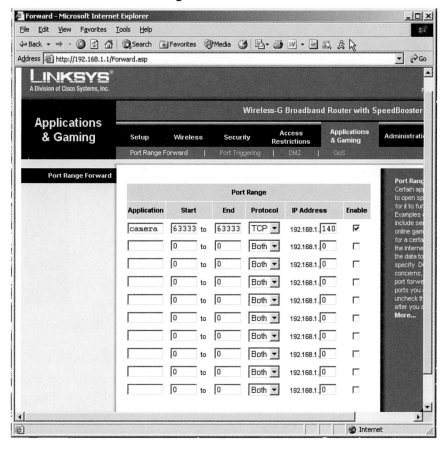

Now when packets are received from the Internet side of the wireless router with port number 63333 (assuming that is what you selected), they will be routed directly to the camera.

How to View the Camera over the Internet

Now we are ready to try to view the camera over the Internet. By the way, you will need to actually be outside your home network, at work or a wireless hotspot, to try this.

Step 1   While still on the wireless router, click **Status**. Find the Internet IP address (in Figure 13-21, it's 24.225.91.164). This is the IP address on the Internet to reach your wireless router (and your home network), so write it down.

Figure 13-21 Finding Your Internet IP Address

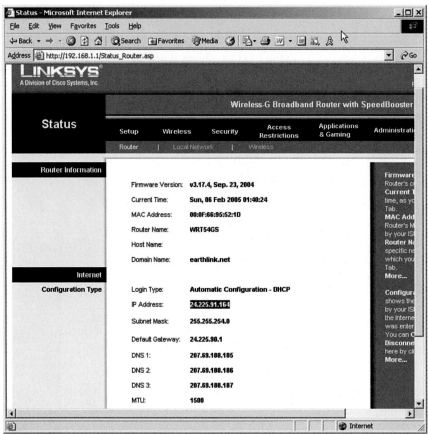

Step 2   Now, when you want to view the video images from a computer outside of your house, you access it in a similar way. Point the Internet browser to the Internet IP address plus the port number we chose, for example, http://24.225.91.164:63333. When prompted, enter the viewing username and password, and click **View Video**.

After completing these steps, you can reach the video camera from outside the home network.

Note: You can also use the Linksys Viewer Client to view video images over the Internet. The details of this process have been omitted here to save space. The procedure is very similar to using the Viewer Client from within your home network, as previously described. The major differences are

- Click **Internet** instead of **LAN**.
- Specify the Internet IP address.
- Specify the port number (for example, 63333).

Problems with Viewing Video over the Internet

There is one other potential issue with viewing your video over the Internet. The broadband networks typically assign a dynamic IP address to your broadband service. *Dynamic* means the IP address can change, typically only if you power off and on your broadband modem. This is usually not an issue because, typically, you will be assigned the same IP address for a long period of time.

If the IP address of your broadband modem does get reassigned, the new address may not match the address you wrote down for the camera. Then, when you try to access the camera, you will get an error message from the Internet browser saying "The page cannot be displayed." In this case, you need to access your wireless router, click the **Status** function, and write down the new Internet IP address.

If you rely on accessing your camera over the Internet, and the IP address changes too often, here are a couple of solutions:

- Subscribe to a dynamic DNS service that automatically tracks your home network's IP address. Linksys offers a pay service called SoloLink. This service automatically tracks the address used to reach your video camera. (See http://www.linksys.com/sololink/. Further detail on dynamic DNS services is beyond the scope of this book.)

- Inquire with your ISP about upgrading your broadband subscription to a static IP address, which means that you pay a little extra per month, but your address never changes.

Using the Video Camera as a Motion Detector

Another very useful feature of the Linksys wireless Internet video camera products is the ability to act as a motion detector for active surveillance. Watching a video feed for hours waiting for something to happen is tedious. Depending on the reason for the video camera, it can be more effective to trigger on motion detected and then perform a notification action. Setting up the motion detector is pretty easy:

Step 1   Access the video camera using the administrator account. Click **Setup** and then click **Advanced**. Check the **Send E-Mail Alert when Motion Detected** check box (see Figure 13-22). Select a length in seconds for a video capture (2–5 seconds). Select the minimum time between e-mail alerts (2–30 minutes).

Figure 13-22 Enabling Motion Detection

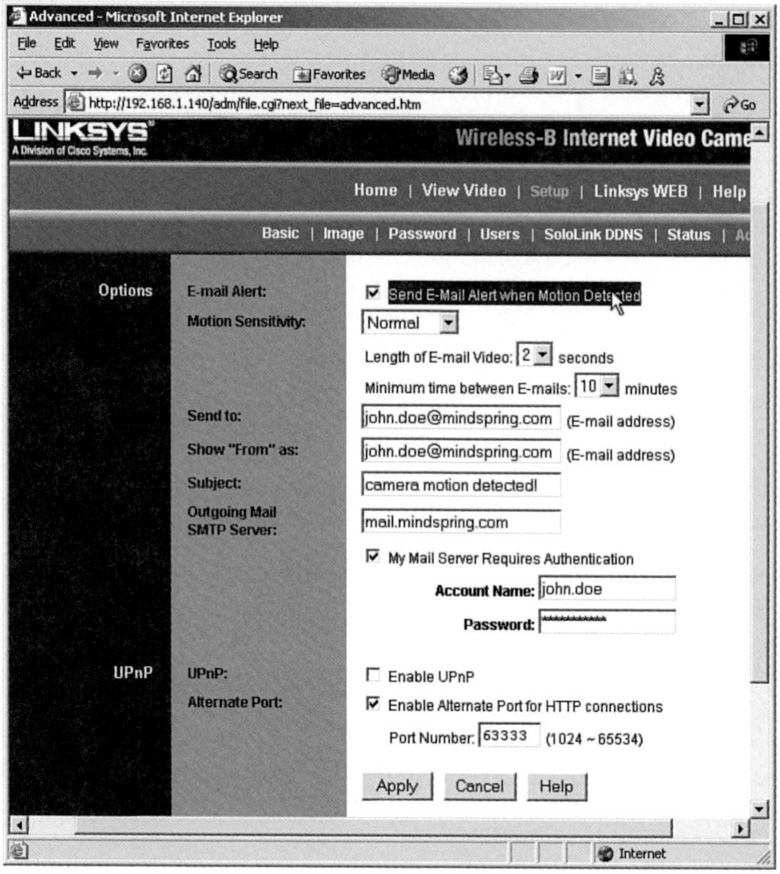

Step 2   In the same dialog box, enter the e-mail account information, including

- Send-to e-mail address

- Show "from" e-mail address

- Subject

- Outgoing mail SMTP server (this is from your e-mail provider)

- E-mail login name and password

Step 3   Click **Apply**.

That's all there is to it. A word of caution, though: As soon as you enable the motion detector func-tion (and until you shut it off), you will receive a video capture attached to an e-mail as often as you have specified. So take care not to leave it enabled for lengthy periods of time, because your e-mail account will promptly fill up.

Note: The Linksys WVC11B model provides video only, but the WVC54G and WVC54GC models provide audio and video.

You also can set up your motion detector to send alerts to a pager or cell phone. Most cell phones and pagers have an equivalent e-mail address that can be used to send a text message to. Simply supply that e-mail address as the alert address. If the camera product supports it, you may want to disable the audio/video clip attachment to cell phone and pager alerts. (The WVC11B camera does not support disabling, but the WVC54G camera does.)

When used properly, alerts based on motion detection can be very effective for verifying that latchkey kids have gotten home from school safely or that a spouse is home, or perhaps even as a security alarm if motion is detected while on vacation due to a home intruder.

Here are a few side notes on video cameras and the Internet:

- Take care where you point your wireless Internet video camera. It may not be a good idea to have an ongoing video feed of the inside of your home being offered up to the Internet. At a minimum, make sure you enable security, including passwords, to protect access to the camera.

- Be advised that Internet video cameras normally do not work well in low-light conditions. This may limit the camera's usefulness as a baby monitor, for example. Conversely, too much light or glare from nearby windows can also spoil images from these cameras.

- Review the laws in your state with respect to video taping of people without their knowledge. Your kids are most likely yours to tape whenever you deem necessary. However, using the video surveillance functions in this chapter to perform surveillance on the activities of an adult (such as a spouse or a babysitter) may be subject to local laws.

- Be careful about letting kids get into the web-cam game. You don't necessarily know who is on the other end watching.

Wireless Online Gaming

When we were 11 years old or so, we each got an Atari gaming system. We spent the entire summer indoors playing Pitfall Harry, and our mothers were constantly screaming at us to go outside and play like normal kids. In the years since, much has changed. The game systems are out of this world. You can play against people from all over the world, so after you whip everyone in your neighborhood, you can find some dude in Vancouver (or wherever) to play against. Our wives have stepped in for our moms and now they scream at us to turn that darn thing off. Good times.

This section walks you through the setup of an online gaming system. Our weapon of choice here is the Microsoft Xbox, which is easy to set up and use online. The online service from Microsoft is called Xbox Live. This system allows you to play one on one against a specific person or join an "open" game to play with or against other people. Some games also allow team play so that several people can cooperatively play the same game. Another feature of this system is audio chat, which allows you to speak live (via voice chat) with the other players during the game to strategize or talk smack (whatever the situation calls for). This feature uses VoIP chat technology. For a further discussion on VoIP, pick up a copy of *Internet Phone Services Simplified* (Cisco Press, 2006).

Gaming Servers

To play video games with other people online, gaming servers are required to provide the connections and communications between people playing the games.

Gaming servers work much like a videoconference bridge in that each individual inputs their own data, and all parties receive the combined stream of all the individuals. In a gaming server, each person on the server is assigned an entity in the program. This entity could be a car, a fighter, or a really mean duck. Within the game, you control the actions of this entity, which could affect other entities or the environment, as do all the other players in the game.

All the information from all the players is compiled in the server and then sent out to all the players in the game. A system like this requires a great deal of computing power and speed (both processing speed and connection speed if the players are remote). Fortunately, with dedicated game systems such as Xbox and broadband download speeds, high-end games lose nothing when you play online. Part of the reason for this is that the gaming server sends as little information as possible, just basic instructions to update the game.

It's important to understand the need for gaming servers, because different video game manufacturers offer varying degrees of online playing services. If you want to participate in online gaming, research the available options before you buy.

Options for Online Gaming

You have a few different options for online game playing, including using a computer or an actual video game console (such as Microsoft Xbox). Table 13-2 compares the options.

Table 13-2   Video Game Options for Online Play

Video Game Platform	Built-In NIC	Number of Online Games	Online Services	Online Play Costs	Voice Chat
Computer	Probable	Many	GameSpy (and others)	Free to $12.95 monthly	Yes
Microsoft Xbox	Built-in wired	Many	Xbox Live	$49.99 annual	Yes
Microsoft Xbox 360	Built-in wired	Many	Xbox Live	Free Silver Membership $49 annual for Gold Membership	Yes
Sony PlayStation 2	Built-in wired (starting Nov. 2004)	Many	Various game publishers	Free to $12.95 monthly	Handful
Sony PlayStation 3	Built-in wired One model has built-in 802.11g Wi-Fi	Many	Various game publishers	Free to $12.95 monthly	Handful

Table 13-2   Video Game Options for Online Play

Video Game Platform	Built-In NIC	Number of Online Games	Online Services	Online Play Costs	Voice Chat
Sony PlayStation Portable (PSP)	Built-in 802.11b Wi-Fi	Many	Various game publishers	Free to $12.95 monthly	No
Nintendo GameCube	Add-on wired NIC for $30-$40	Very few	Sega		No
Nintendo Wii (pronounced "we")	Promises built-in 802.11g Wi-Fi	Promises many	Promises Nintendo Wi-Fi Connection service	Promises Free	TBD

A computer with video game software installed is certainly an option. There are already hundreds of online games available, some for free and some requiring a fee. A good resource to find out what is available is GameSpy (http://www.gamespy.com). However, this type of online gaming device is not the focus of this chapter. This chapter focuses on dedicated video game consoles, because getting these connected takes a bit more work, and there appears to be much less information out there about how to do so.

 Note: If you are truly interested in online gaming, Xbox and PlayStation are the leaders in the field. It does not appear that Nintendo is a serious player here yet, in our opinion. However, Nintendo is promising a major re-entry with the Wii platform (pronounced "we").

How to Connect Video Game Consoles to Your Wireless Network

In this section, we look at how to take video game playing to the next level: online.

The first step to online gaming is to have a network-capable video game console. You then can connect the console to the home network with an Ethernet cable, just as you can with any other computer or device. Because it is probable the video game console and television may be in an entirely different room of the house from the Internet connection, a wireless game adapter may also be incredibly useful. This device will allow a video game console to be connected to the wireless network.

So, let's get online. It is assumed that you have already installed your home wireless network and have high-speed broadband Internet service. The rest of this section goes through the steps to connect a video game over your home wireless network to an online gaming service.

Here's an overview of the steps to set up an online gaming system:

- Setting up the wireless game adapter for your wireless network

- Connecting a video game console

- Setting up an account and connecting to an online game provider

Setting Up the Wireless Game Adapter

After you have chosen your gaming console, you will want to connect it to your home network. If the console happens to be in close proximity to the wireless router, you could use an Ethernet cable and just connect it directly. Often, this is not the case, so in this section, we show how to use a wireless game adapter to connect the console from anywhere in your house.

Table 13-3 shows the Linksys wireless game adapter products that we can choose from.

Table 13-3   Linksys Wireless Game Adapters

Model	Wireless Standard	Wireless Encryption Supported
WGA54G	802.11g Also works with 802.11b and 802.11n	64-bit WEP 128-bit WEP
WGA11B	802.11b Also works with 802.11g and 802.11n	64-bit WEP 128-bit WEP

 Note: The Linksys wireless game adapters will generally work with Microsoft Xbox and other game consoles. Another option is to purchase the wireless module made by the game console manufacturer. Check the instructions for your game console to make sure you can use any game adapter or if you need a specific one.

The steps to connect are as follows (in this example, we use the WGA11B product):

Step 1   Connect the Linksys wireless game adapter to the Linksys wireless router using an Ethernet cable, and plug in the power adapter. Set the X -ǁ switch to ǁ. The LAN LED light on the front should light up.

Step 2   Put the CD that came with the Linksys wireless game adapter into a computer on the network (a wired computer is preferred). The Setup Wizard should start automatically. If not, use My Computer to browse the CD and double-click **Setup.exe**. Click **Setup**.

Step 3   The Setup Wizard searches for the new game adapter on the network. If it is not detected, check the cabling and try powering the game adapter off and back on. Then, return to Steps 1 and 2. If the game adapter is located successfully, the current default settings for it are displayed (see Figure 13-23). Click **Next**.

Figure 13-23 Setup Wizard Searches for and Finds the Game Adapter

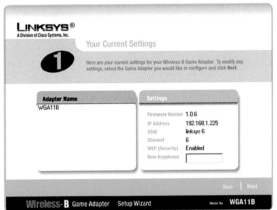

Step 4   Enter the default password, **admin**, and press **Enter**.

Step 5   Click **Obtain IP Address Automatically**. Change the password from the default (admin) to a random series of upper- and lowercase letters and numbers (see Figure 13-24). Write it down somewhere safe for keeping. Click **Next**.

Note: Note that this is the administration password for the wireless game adapter itself, not the wireless router. Wireless NICs generally do not have an administration password, but most other devices, including wireless routers, game adapters, print servers, and so on, have an administration password. You want to change it from the default, and make sure to write it down somewhere.

Step 6   Enter the SSID for your wireless network. (In Figure 13-25, we use J59wgh21MX.) Set the wireless security setting to **WEP 128 Bit** (or the encryption you are using). Enter the passphrase you have been using for your wireless network (in this example, 64Gx3prY19fk2). Click **No** to save the settings.

Figure 13-24 Change the Basic Settings

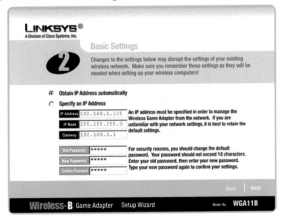

Figure 13-25 Set the Wireless SSID and Security Settings

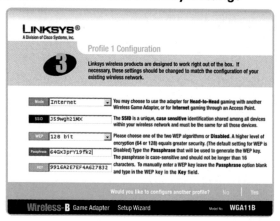

Step 7 Two dialog boxes are displayed. These are normal; not very graceful, but normal. Click **OK** for both dialog boxes.

Step 8 Unplug the Ethernet cable connecting the game adapter to the wireless router. Power off the adapter (unplug it) and then power it back on.

Step 9 Press the blue button on the side of the game adapter repeatedly until the display on the front reads **P1** (see Figure 13-26). The wireless channel LED indicator light on the front of the wireless game adapter should be lit.

Figure 13-26 Select Wireless Profile P1

Connecting a Video Game Console

After you verify that the wireless game adapter is properly communicating with your wireless network, you can move on with setting up the rest of the online gaming system:

Step 1   Unplug the Ethernet cable to the game adapter (if it's still connected) and move the game adapter to the location in your house where you want the video game console to be. Because it is wireless, it can be placed anywhere there is an electrical outlet (and TV) nearby.

Step 2   Plug one end of an Ethernet cable into the port on the back of the wireless game adapter. Plug the other end into the Ethernet port on the back of the video game console, as shown in Figure 13-27.

Step 3   Connect the power cable to the wireless game adapter. After connecting the cables to both the game adapter and the video game console, remember to plug in the video game console to the electrical outlet.

Step 4   Turn on the video game console. After it boots, you should see both the LAN and wireless channel LED lights on the front of the wireless game adapter light up. If not, check the cabling and try powering off and on the game adapter. Also, try changing the X -ll switch setting.

Now we should have the game adapter joined to the wireless network, and the video game console connected and ready to access the network. The default settings may work and the game console may just connect at this point.

Figure 13-27 Connect the Game Console to the Game Adapter

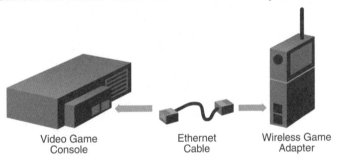

Video Game   Ethernet   Wireless Game
Console   Cable   Adapter

Connecting to an Online Game Provider

Now that the wireless game adapter is on the network and your video game console has been connected, you need to set up the online game service. This will vary greatly depending on the particular service.

Here's a short example for Xbox Live service. First, we need to set up and verify the network settings:

Step 1   Power on the Xbox. In the main window, scroll using the arrow pad until **Settings** is highlighted and then press the green **A** button (see Figure 13-28).

Figure 13-28 Xbox Main Menu

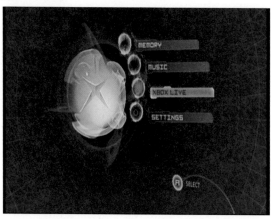

Step 2 Afer choosing **Settings** choose **Network Settings** (see Figure 13-29).

Figure 13-29 Xbox Network Settings Menu

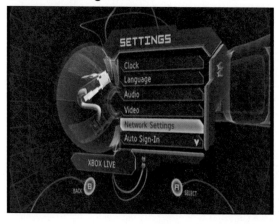

Step 3 There are four Network Settings submenus (see Figure 13-30). Choose **IP Addresses**.

Figure 13-30 Xbox Network Settings Submenus

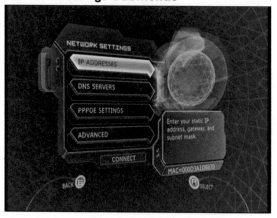

Step 4   Set Configuration to **Automatic** (see Figure 13-31). Click **B** to go back one menu.

Figure 13-31 Setting IP Address to Automatic

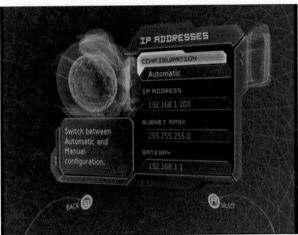

Step 5   Follow similar steps to set

■   DNS Servers to **Automatic**

■   PPPoE Settings to **Off**

■   Advanced to **blank**

Step 6   After you verify the settings, select and click **Connect** (see Figure 13-32).

Figure 13-32 Test the Connection to Xbox Live

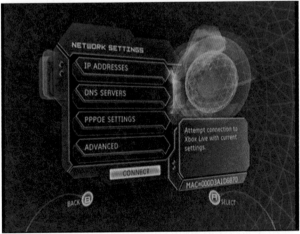

Step 7   The Xbox tests the connection by accessing the Xbox Live server. All four status indi-cators should appear as green (see Figure 13-33).

Figure 13-33 Connection to Xbox Live Is Successful

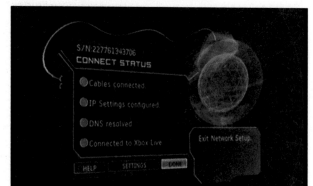

Now that we have set the network settings for the video game console, you can move on to setting up an account with the online gaming provider (we use Xbox Live for this example). Before continuing, you need to purchase a subscription to Xbox Live either from a retail store or online. The subscription comes with a code number that you need to enter during the setup process.

When you have completed the account setup, you are ready to jump into online gaming. Whenever you power on your Xbox game console, it automatically connects to the Xbox Live service. Now put in your games and go play!

We, the authors, do not assume liability for any marital or family problems or carpal tunnel syndrome caused by the (excessive) use of this technology.

Note: If you have trouble getting your gaming system online, check your firewalls. You might have to temporarily disable one or more security measures. Just remember to turn them back on when you are done.

Networking Your DVR

For those of you who, like us, have become TiVo or digital video recorder (DVR) junkies, we are about to show you something wicked cool you can do with your TiVo and your wireless network.

In case you have been living in a cave and have not heard of TiVo or DVR yet, here is a 30-second version. TiVo and DVRs allow you to record your favorite TV shows or movies to watch later. Big deal, VCRs can do the same thing, right? Well, not exactly. See, TiVo and DVR boxes are able to sit in between your television and the content provider (cable or satellite) box. Then, you can select what you want to record from an interactive programming menu, and the DVR records it digitally and stores it on its hard disk. Depending on the size of the hard disk, DVRs can store 40, 80, or more than 100 hours of shows.

Like a show a lot? TiVo lets you record a season pass, which means every time your favorite show is on, TiVo records it. At your leisure, you can simply go into the recordings list and watch your favorite shows whenever you feel like it.

Typical DVR Setups Today

The typical setup today for a TiVo or DVR is not networked, as shown in Figure 13-34.

Figure 13-34 Typical Non-Networked DVR Setup Today

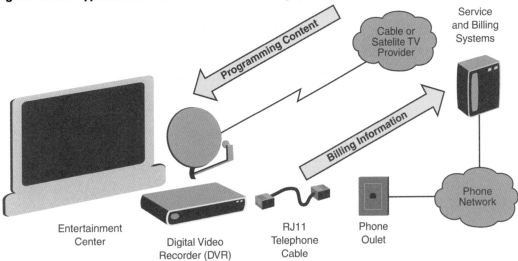

The TiVo or DVR is connected to your television, either as a standalone box or integrated into your content provider's set top box (this is an increasingly popular option).

Programming content is transmitted by the provider, over satellite or cable, to your home. TiVo or DVR sits in the middle and records content you have specified. TiVo also requires a telephone connection that its internal modem uses to "call home" for billing and subscription service purposes.

With these basic requirements met, life is grand.

Reasons to Network Your DVR

So, if your TiVo or DVR is already recording your favorite shows and keeping you from missing *The Dog Whisperer*, why worry about networking it?

Well, networking your TiVo or DVR offers several distinct advantages. Remember that DVRs record TV episodes and movies in digital form. Essentially, they are computer files, sitting on a hard drive.

So what if we told you that you could do one of the following?

- Transfer movies and TV episodes from your TiVo to a laptop to watch when you travel

- Transfer movies and TV episodes to a portable player, like a video iPod

- Burn a DVD of your favorite TV episode

- Transfer movies and TV episode recordings between two different TiVo players

- Download a video file from your PC or laptop into the TiVo or DVR to watch later on your widescreen TV

Does any of that sound interesting? Yeah, we thought so.

Further, now that you have a wireless network, you can put the TiVo or DVR anywhere in your house without worrying about a telephone jack. The DVR can just use the wireless network to do its "call home" function, over the Internet. Pretty sweet.

Networking Your DVR

It is relatively easy to connect your TiVo or DVR to your wireless home network. Figure 13-35 shows how it works.

Figure 13-35 Connecting a DVR to Your Wireless Network

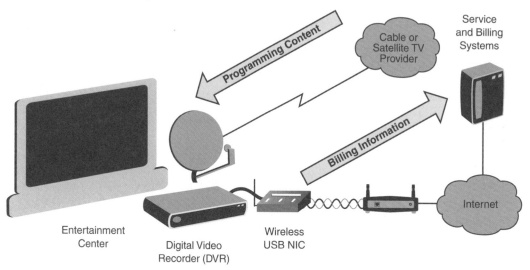

Essentially, instead of having a telephone cable connecting the DVR to a phone jack, you add a wireless USB NIC that bridges your DVR onto your wireless network.

There are a couple of very important requirements to be met before you start. First, the TiVo Home Media feature is required for networking, which means you need a Series 2 TiVo box. If you are not sure which series your TiVo is, contact TiVo and ask a representative.

 Note: If you are a DirecTV subscriber, the DirectDVR TiVo service uses integrated satellite receiver/TiVo DVR boxes. Unfortunately, DirecTV opted to disable the Home Media capabilities in its implementation, and has no specific plans at the time of this writing to include these cool functions. For more information, you can contact DirecTV at www.directv.com/DTVAPP/customer/howToReachUs.jsp.

Second, TiVo supports a specific list of wireless USB NICs, because there is a very limited user interface for you to configure them, and there is not really a way for you to load new NIC drivers. The list can be found at the TiVo support site: www.tivo.com/adapters/.

The Linksys WUSB11 is one of the supported wireless USB NICs. Check the list for the latest supported NICs.

As long as you have a Series 2 TiVo and can acquire a supported wireless USB NIC, you are all set. What are you waiting for?

Connecting your TiVo to the wireless network is relatively easy:

Step 1   Using a standard USB cable, connect a supported wireless USB NIC to an open USB port on the back of the TiVo.

Step 2   Using the TiVo menu, access the **Settings** menu. Locate the network settings. Choose **Wireless**.

Step 3   Using the TiVo remote control, enter the SSID for your wireless network, the security type (128-bit WEP), and the WEP key.

Step 4   Save the settings.

If you entered the SSID and WEP key correctly, the wireless USB NIC should connect to your wireless network.

 Note: Don't forget, if you have enabled MAC address filtering as a security measure in your wireless network, you need to add the MAC address of the wireless USB NIC before it will be permitted to join the wireless network.

More detailed setup instructions for adding TiVo to wireless home networks can be found at the TiVo support site: http://customersupport.tivo.com/knowbase/root/public/tv2013.htm.

Using TiVoToGo

After your TiVo is networked, you can start taking advantage of the connectivity and freely move your favorite TV episodes and movies around. Figure 13-36 shows a couple possible scenarios.

Suppose you have two TiVo or DVR boxes: one in the living room downstairs, and one in the family room upstairs. Suppose you have recorded your favorite episode of *CSI: Crime Scene Investigation* (possibly the best show ever to grace the screen of a television) on the downstairs TiVo.

But you neglected to remember that your spouse is hosting a function downstairs and so you are kicked out. No problem, you can just transfer the episode over your home wireless network to the TiVo upstairs, and you are once again in business.

Another very useful function is TiVoToGo. As the name implies, TiVoToGo lets you transfer episodes recorded on a TiVo to a portable viewing device to take with you, such as a laptop or video-capable iPod.

Figure 13-36 What You Can Do with Networked DVR Boxes

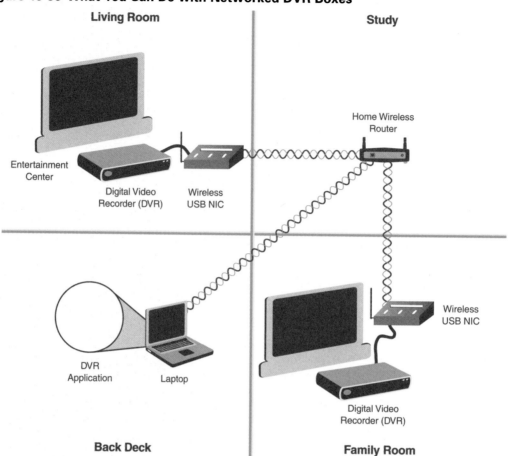

To transfer between a DVR and a laptop, you typically need to download a software application. For TiVo, this is called the TiVo Desktop. The application is free and can be found at the TiVo website: www.tivo.com/desktop.

TiVo Desktop is a very straightforward application that lets you see what is on your TiVo and laptop, and then transfer episodes back and forth. Figure 13-37 shows an example of TiVo Desktop.

More information on getting started with TiVo Desktop can be found here: http://customersupport.tivo.com/knowbase/root/public/tv2178.htm?.

Help on transferring video files from your computer to TiVo can be found here: http://customersupport.tivo.com/knowbase/root/public/tv251080.htm?.

Get your DVR networked, and enjoy!

Figure 13-37 TiVo Desktop Example

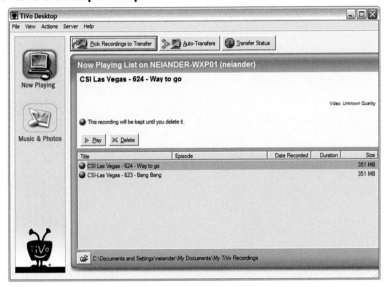

Summary

Wireless home networks are for connecting more than just your computers and laptops. They can connect wireless video cameras, video game consoles like Xbox 360, TiVo and DVRs, home automation devices, and someday refrigerators, pantries, and maybe sock drawers. We have just barely scratched the surface here of what you can do with your wireless network. But we hope we have at least given you a glimpse and got you excited about the possibilities.

Where to Go for More Information

For more information about wireless video cameras, go to the Linksys website: http://www.linksys.com.

For more information about online gaming, go to the following websites:

- **Xbox and Xbox 360**—http://www.xboxlive.com

- **PlayStation 2 and 3**—http://www.playstation.com/

- **PlayStation PSP**—www.us.playstation.com/PSP/OnlineGaming

- **Nintendo Wii**—http://wii.nintendo.com/home.html

For more information about networking your TiVo, go to TiVo customer support: http://customersupport.tivo.com/userWelcome.asp?path=2&faq_node=Network.

For more information about voice over IP (VoIP), check out our book *Internet Phone Services Simplified* (Cisco Press, 2006).

Wireless to Go

One of the biggest advantages of wireless technologies is the ability to easily take it on the road with you. Public Internet access was rare before the advent of Wi-Fi mostly because of cost and convenience. Allowing patrons of a coffee shop, airport, or bookstore to access the Internet meant expensive cabling retrofits to put Ethernet ports in, and—even if a lease holder were willing to put up the expense—there are only so many ports you can put where patrons can get to them.

Wireless, of course, removes the need for network cabling and provides vendors the same flexibility as home users of wireless. With virtually no need to cable outside access and power, a shop owner can provide Internet access to every patron in the store and even those sitting outside. No cables and no expensive retrofits are needed. In most cases, the actual Internet access is provided by a regional or national service provider who charges individual users directly.

What Is a Wireless Hotspot?

A *hotspot* is an area served by a Wi-Fi wireless access point to provide Internet service. Figure 14-1 shows the basic elements. A *hotspot provider* is the owner of the Internet service, and it can be a very large commercial operator, such as T-Mobile, or a small privately owned hotspot, such as a neighborhood shop. Some cities and communities are also starting to provide Wi-Fi service in downtown areas for use by citizens. Depending on whether the service is a free or pay service (which requires a subscription), the hotspot provider may have a membership database, which contains information about who is permitted to use the service.

Figure 14-1 Wireless Hotspot and Its Basic Elements

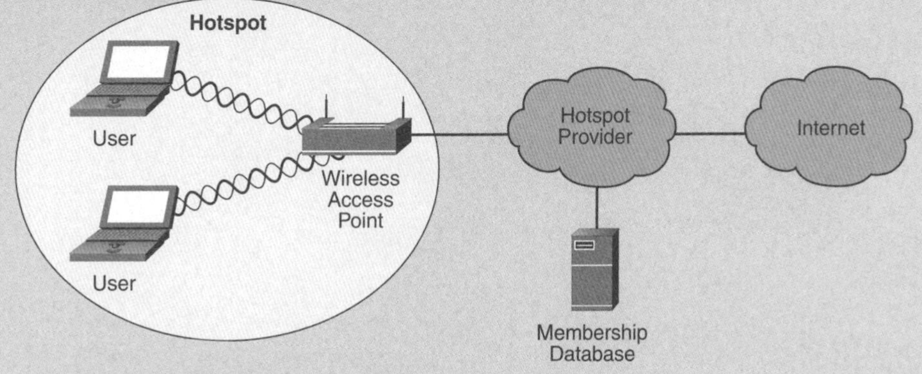

Connecting to wireless hotspot networks is similar to connecting to your wireless network at home, with some distinct differences:

- At home, we know the SSID of the wireless system; with a hotspot, we need to discover this crucial information. To make this easy, hotspots typically broadcast their SSID.

- For a home network, we want to provide access to *only* our computers, so we turn on very strong security measures. By their nature, hotspot networks are very open, using no encryption; otherwise, how would we be able to connect?

- Our home network is free to access (but you still need to pay your ISP), whereas hotspot networks may be free or may require a membership or subscription to use.

- We know that our home network is our own and can be trusted. We have to be far more careful with hotspot networks because, by their nature, we may not always be certain who is operating them. Currently, no regulations exist regarding who can and cannot operate wireless hotspots.

- Having secured our home wireless network, we know the users are "friendly." On a hotspot network, we have no idea what other people are also using the hotspot, whether they are "friendly" or are the source of a potential hack attack.

How to Find Wireless Hotspots

The first step to using wireless access while you're away from home is to find a hotspot. Hotspots are relatively easy to find (and it gets easier every day).

There are a few different ways to find out where wireless hotspots are, including

- Doing an online search
- Downloading a list to your PC
- Scanning

If you know you will be looking for a hotspot before you leave your home or office, your best bet is to do an online search prior to heading out. There are several sites that allow you to enter an address, airport code, or even a ZIP or postal code. For example, the search tool at JiWire, http://www.jiwire.com, allows you to sort by proximity, location, or by service providers (who pay for preferred placement on the site).

If you plan on using hotspots regularly, you may want to download a program to your laptop that contains a list of hotspots (regular updating is required). This can be of great benefit if you need to find a hotspot after you have already left home.

A third option for finding a hotspot is to do a scan for a hotspot at the moment you need one. To do so, you need a program that will go out and "sniff" for a wireless signal. Depending on the wireless NIC that you are using in your laptop, it may come with a scan function in the NIC's management utility (the Linksys products do). Windows XP has this functionality built into its wireless NIC management. There are also several programs available for free download with built-in scanning capability.

Table 14-1 lists some good resources and tools for finding Wi-Fi hotspots.

Table 14-1   Resources for Finding Wi-Fi Hotspots

Resource	Online Search	Download Location Database	Download Wireless Connection Manager	Website
Boingo	Yes	Yes	Yes	http://www.boingo.com
JiWire	Yes	Yes	No	http://www.jiwire.com
T-Mobile HotSpot	Yes (T-Mobile locations only)	Yes (T-Mobile locations only)	Yes (T-Mobile locations only)	http://hotspot.t-mobile.com
WiFi 411	Yes	No	No	http://www.wifi411.com

Note: Lists of hotspots in tools such as these may or may not be up to date. If you know where you are staying or going to be in advance, it's also helpful to check that location's website to see what they offer. For example, most hotels list on their website whether or not they provide Wi-Fi Internet access.

Wireless Hotspot Options and Costs

In general, hotspots are either free sites or pay sites. Free sites are typically offered by businesses such as hotels, coffee shops, and restaurants to attract customers. Pay sites are more numerous and widespread. Many business-like hotels are using them to extract an extra $10 from your wallet. Pay sites are also growing rapidly due to the entry of large wireless cell phone companies, such as T-Mobile, Cingular, and SBC. Four basic types of hotspot services exist, as shown in Table 14-2.

Table 14-2   Types of Wireless Hotspot Services

Type	What They Are	Where You Can Find Them	Examples
Free	A free connect-and-go hotspot service that is becoming rare these days.	Small neighborhood businesses, public libraries; provided to attract customers	Public library, local communities (increasing trend)
Free with registration	It's free, but you provide your name, address, e-mail address, and maybe answer a survey.	Hotels, coffee shops, restaurants; provided to attract customers	Schlotzsky's Deli, Bear Rock Cafe, Panera Bread, Holiday Inn Express
Subscription	You pay a monthly, annual, or per-usage fee to use the service, much like your cell phone.	Hotels, airports, coffee shops, restaurants, business service shops, planes (soon)	T-Mobile (at Starbucks, Borders, Kinkos), SBC (at UPS Store), Wayport (airports, McDonald's), Cingular (airports)

Table 14-2   Types of Wireless Hotspot Services

Type	What They Are	Where You Can Find Them	Examples
Roaming	Same as subscription service, except you are roaming on another provider who has an agreement with your provider.	Same as subscription	Same as subscription

Ironically, the initial popularity of wireless network hotspots was the idea of free Internet access. Despite attempts at an organized citizen-led mosaic of free hotspots, it seems inevitable that the sizeable market opportunity is just too attractive for the traditional telecommunications companies to pass up.

The upside is that to make money, these companies will invest the cash to put hotspots everywhere you need them. Soon, any place that people can stand or sit for more than 60 seconds will be a hotspot.

One growing trend worth mentioning is that many local communities are starting to invest in city-wide wireless hotspot networks. Most have two aims: provide high-speed access for public-sector agencies such as police, fire, and so on, and provide access to citizens themselves.

If you fall into the category of a regular hotspot user, and you either can pick the hotspot location where your preferred provider has an access point or can always access from the same locations (such as your local airport), your best bet may be to get a monthly or annual subscription. If you are a casual hotspotter, you will probably be better off with a per-day or other pay-per-use option.

 Note: Accessing a network that was unintentionally left open (such as your neighbor's) isn't very nice. On the other hand, there are many "unwired city" initiatives where local governments are providing free access. It's no problem to use free access when it is made available on purpose, but not when someone just forgot to set up security. It's usually easy to tell the difference.

Discovering and Connecting to Wireless Hotspots

Because hotspot locations want to advertise their willingness to accept your business, they broadcast their SSID and do not require an encryption key to connect. But you do need to discover or be told what the SSID is for the hotspot so that you can tell your wireless NIC how to connect to it.

You can use several methods to discover the hotspot's SSID, depending on the Windows operating system you use, the capabilities of the wireless NIC in your laptop computer, and the hotspot service to which you want to connect. In general, there are three possibilities:

- The wireless NIC management utility that ships with the NIC, such as Linksys WLAN Monitor

- Windows Wireless Network Connection utility

- A third-party wireless connection manager, such as Boingo or T-Mobile's Wireless Connection Manager software

As discussed in Chapter 8, "Wireless NIC Setup," you are likely using Windows or the manufacturer's utility to manage your wireless NIC. These are also fine to use for connecting to hotspots. If you connect to hotspots a lot, you may want to consider using a connection manager from Boingo or T-Mobile (if you subscribe to one of them) for convenience. We cover connecting to a wireless hotspot with each of these possibilities in the sections that follow.

Connecting to Hotspots Using Linksys WLAN Monitor

If you are using the Linksys WLAN Monitor to manage your NIC, the following steps show how to find and connect to a hotspot:

Step 1   Launch the WLAN Monitor utility by double-clicking the icon on the desktop or by choosing **Start > Programs > Linksys > Wireless Notebook Adapter**. Click the **Site Survey** tab (see Figure 14-2). Click the **Refresh** button to perform a survey of what wireless networks are available.

Figure 14-2   Perform a Site Survey

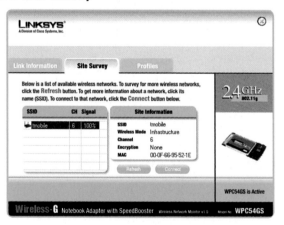

Step 2   Click the hotspot that you wish to connect to. In our example, we found a T-Mobile hotspot. Click **Connect**. You should see the connection made to the hotspot (Signal Strength and Link Quality show green, as shown in Figure 14-3).

Figure 14-3   Successful Connection to Hotspot

Step 3   You can save this hotspot into your profiles so that the next time you use it, connection happens automatically. Choose **More Information > Save to Profile** (see Figure 14-4).

Figure 14-4   Save the Hotspot in Your Wireless Profiles

Step 4   A dialog box appears asking for a name for the new profile (see Figure 14-5). Enter a description you will remember, and click **OK**.

Step 5   The new profile just created now appears in the Profile list (see Figure 14-6). Now, whenever you encounter a hotspot with this profile, the wireless network adapter will automatically connect to it.

Figure 14-5   Enter a Name for the New Wireless Profile

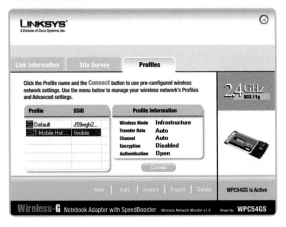

Figure 14-6   New Profile Is Listed

Note: Generally, after you create a profile for one hotspot on a provider's network, this allows you to connect to all the other hotspots on that provider's network. You do not need to create a new profile each time you connect to a hotspot in a different location, only when you use a new provider for the first time.

Connecting to Hotspots Using Windows XP

If you are using Windows XP to manage the NIC in your laptop, the steps for connecting to a wireless hotspot are as follows:

Step 1   Choose **Start > Control Panel > Network Connections**. Note the red X on the Wireless Network Connection icon. This is normal, because we have not yet established a connection to the wireless hotspot network. Click the **Wireless Network Connection** icon in the right section of the window and then click **View Available Wireless Networks** on the left. (See Figure 14-7.)

Figure 14-7   Perform a Site Survey with Windows XP

Step 2   Click the hotspot that you want to connect to (tmobile in this example), and click **Connect** (see Figure 14-8).

Windows may prompt you to verify that you want to permit a connection to an unsecured wireless network. This is normal, because the hotspot is not running encryption such as WEP or WPA. Acknowledge that you want to allow the connection.

Figure 14-8   Select an Available Hotspot

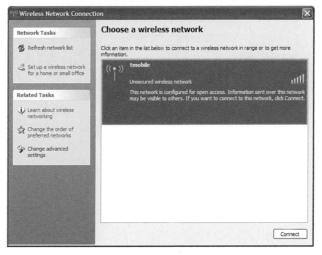

Step 3   In the Wireless Network Connection window, you can verify that you are connected successfully to the hotspot. (See Figure 14-9.)

Figure 14-9   Successful Connection to the Hotspot

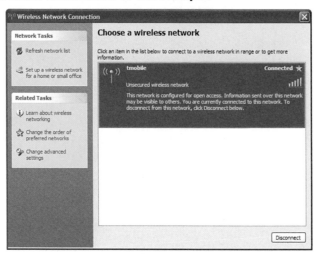

Step 4   Windows XP typically adds the hotspot to the Preferred Networks list upon successful connection. To check this, in the Network Connections window, choose **Change Settings for This Connection > Wireless Networks**. You should see the hotspot in the Preferred Networks section (see Figure 14-10). Click **OK**.

Figure 14-10 Verify Hotspot Is Added to Preferred Networks

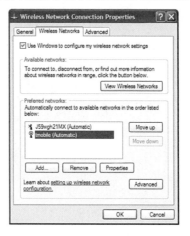

 Note: Being in the Preferred Networks list in Windows means that your laptop will automatically connect to the wireless network in the future if encountered. This can be convenient if you use hotspots often. If you would prefer not to connect automatically, remove the entry from the Preferred Networks section.

Connecting to Hotspots Using Boingo

A third possibility for connecting to hotspots, which can generally be used on any of the Windows operating system versions (98, 2000, Me, XP), is to use a connection manager software program that is provided by the hotspot system provider you have a membership with. For example, if you sub- scribed to a T-Mobile or Boingo hotspot service, using the provided connection manager software can make location of and connection to hotspots literally just a click of a button.

Boingo Wireless operates through a collaboration of many different hotspot providers who choose to affiliate with Boingo Wireless and list their hotspots in the Boingo database. Figure 14-11 shows the connection manager program that Boingo provides.

Figure 14-11 Boingo Connection Manager Program

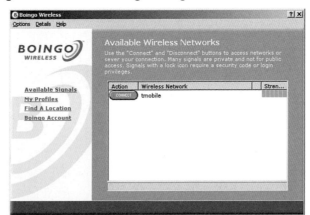

The Boingo application automatically detects wireless hotspots you encounter. To connect, you sim- ply click the **Connect** button for the hotspot network you choose.

Boingo also provides a searchable database of hotspot locations. You can use the Boingo application if you have a paid membership with Boingo, or you can use it for free (limited functionality) as a general connection manager application, whether you are connecting to Boingo-affiliated hotspots or someone else's.

Passing the Membership Test

At this point, you have accomplished getting your laptop to talk properly with the wireless hotspot access point. But you are not yet to the point of being able to access the Internet. The next step is the *membership test*.

Whether using a free site or a pay site, the membership test is almost always started the same way: by launching your Internet browser. When your browser first attempts to access the Internet, you will be redirected to the membership page for that service. For free services, this web page may ask you to fill out some information about yourself and possibly hit you with a quick survey. For pay servic- es, you typically must enter your user ID and password to prove that you have a valid subscription to their service.

Following are two examples: one for a free service, and one for a pay service.

Example: Connecting to a Free Service at Bear Rock Cafe

The following is an example of using the hotspot service at a Bear Rock Cafe. In this example, access is free with registration. The registration process lets you create a user ID and password for easy repeat access in the future.

Step 1   Use your chosen connection manager program to connect to the hotspot. In this example, we used the Boingo free connection manager (see Figure 14-12). We can see that the SSID is wiresnap. Click the blue **Connect** button next to the wiresnap network.

Figure 14-12 Using Boingo to Connect to the Hotspot

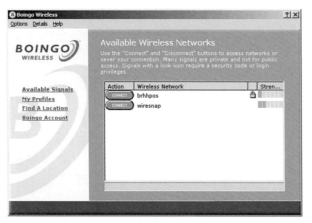

Step 2   Launch your Internet browser (such as Internet Explorer) and type in any web page address (see Figure 14-13).

Figure 14-13 Launch Internet Browser to Trigger the Redirect

Step 3   You are redirected to the membership test page, prompting for the user ID and password (see Figure 14-14).

Figure 14-14 Hotspot Membership Login Page

If you have already registered previously, you can enter the user ID and password and immediately log in.

If you have not already registered previously, you can click the **Create Your New Account Now link** . To register for a free account, you provide your name, address, e-mail address, and age. You also create a user ID and password.

After logging in to the free service, you can then use the Internet.

Example: Connecting to T-Mobile Service at Borders Book Stores

This section provides another example of using the hotspot service, this time at a Borders store. In this example, T-Mobile owns and operates the Borders hotspots as a pay subscription service. (This example assumes you have already signed up for service with T-Mobile.)

 Note: It is never a good idea to sign up for a new hotspot subscription service over the hotspot. Remember, you are in a public location on a public network, and you do not want anyone to obtain your personal information or credit card number. Plan in advance where you are going, determine what hotspots you may want to use, and sign up from home or office.

Step 1   Use your chosen connection manager program to connect to the hotspot. In this example, we used the T-Mobile-provided Connection Manager (see Figure 14-15). The Connection Manager program indicates (with bars of service, much like a cell phone) when there is a T-Mobile hotspot in range. Click **Connect**.

Figure 14-15 T-Mobile Connection Manager

Step 2   Launch your Internet browser (such as Internet Explorer) and type in any web page address.

Step 3   You are redirected to the membership test page, prompting for the T-Mobile login credentials (see Figure 14-16). Enter the user ID and password that you chose when you signed up for a T-Mobile HotSpot account.

Figure 14-16 T-Mobile Login Page

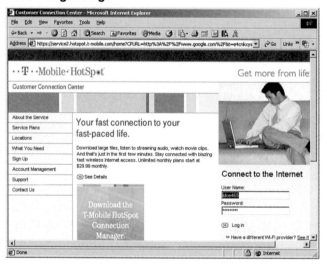

Step 4   A login confirmation box appears. Shrink this down to your taskbar and save it. When you are ready to log off, go back to this little box and click **Log Off** or simply click **Disconnect** in the main T-Mobile Connection Manager window.

After you pass the membership test, you can finally move on to using the Internet. Make sure to read the following section for some important security tips.

What Not to Do When Using a Wireless Hotspot

Okay, so you never thought you would actually need to use a hotspot when you suddenly find that you need to take a cross-country trip or go to visit family for a week and, to your horror, discover that they do not have broadband access in their home. We discuss how to deal with this so-called family of yours later, but in the mean time, you need to find a hotspot and reconnect.

Unfortunately, many people start using hotspots without advanced planning, which leaves them extremely vulnerable. Hotspots are convenient and kind of cool in a nerdy way, but you must protect yourself if you are going to use what is, by design, a very open and unsecure medium. Unlike a home or business network, a hotspot is wide open to allow maximum use through the provider's network.

In this environment, security is second to access, so you need to take some precautions. Using a hotspot is a bit like being out in public: You don't go leaving your credit card lying around, speaking loudly about a confidential topic, or handing out spare keys to your house.

Keep these commonsense things in mind when using hotspots:

- Be aware of what hotspot you are connecting to. Use known, reputable services like those listed previously. Sometimes you get what you pay for; free sites are very attractive, but if they are provided by individuals and not businesses, you should eye these with great suspicion.

- Do not shop online or enter your credit card information into websites over a hotspot connection. Exercise caution when reading e-mail, using instant messaging programs (chat), and other forms of personal communication. Assume everything you read or type might be read by others sitting next to you.

- If you use a pay hotspot service, change the password to your account frequently. Someone can grab the user ID and password "off the air," and then use your subscription on your dime. When you are typing passwords, take a quick look around to make sure no one is looking over your shoulder (or over your fingers).

- Make sure your laptop is running a personal firewall program (such as ZoneAlarm) and an antivirus program (such as Norton AntiVirus, McAfee VirusScan, or Trend Micro PC-cillin). For a more thorough discussion on security, pick up a copy of *Home Networking Security Simplified*.

- Turn off ad hoc wireless networking. Chapter 9, "Wireless Security Setup," discusses how to do this. Turn off all file sharing while using your computer in a public place. In the off chance that someone does access your computer, don't make it easy on them by sharing your entire C: drive. (You should never do this anywhere, ever.)

- If you have the need to use hotspots frequently, ask your provider about using a Virtual Private Network (VPN) software program. These programs encrypt all communications between your laptop, through the hotspot access point, and up to the Internet. Boingo Wireless provides a VPN service included with a pay subscription. Eventually, all service providers should do the same. If you already have access to a VPN service through your employer, use it!

Note: One of the biggest security issues with PCs is laptop theft. A big problem using hotspots can be the logistics of a bathroom break. Having to disconnect and reconnect can be a pain. Taking the laptop with you to the bathroom is an option, but obviously that creates some other "logistics issues."

The bottom line is, if you are in a public place, treat your PC the same way you treat your wallet. Don't walk away from it, or it will walk away from you.

Following these simple steps should keep you plenty safe while using public hotspots, especially because the vast majority of folks don't take these measures, and hackers hit the easy targets first. We do realize that some of this might be a pain, but if you have ever lost data on a hard drive, or had your identity stolen (and had to deal with fixing your credit), you know that the pain of prevention is far, far less than the pain of getting burned by a hacker or thief.

So go out there and surf the Internet while sipping a cappuccino-coffee-hot milk thingy—you hip thing you—but protect yourself and your PC first.

Setting Up Your Own Portable Hotspot

Wireless networking is pretty addictive. After you start using it, you will find very quickly that when you have to switch back to a wired connection, you feel like someone just leg-cuffed you to a ball and chain.

Fortunately, availability of wireless connectivity is increasing at a dramatic pace. But still, there are a significant number of places where it is not available. For example, many higher-end business hotels are installing wireless networks throughout their hotels, including room access. However, others are installing wireless only in common areas such as the lobby, and rooms are still wired-only.

This can be fine. After all, do you really need wireless in your hotel room? Can you not just sit at the desk and use the wired connection? Well, maybe. But we are telling you, when you start using wireless, you will quickly forget how to plug in an Ethernet cable.

So what do you do if your favorite hotel, travel destination, family member you visit, and so on, does not have wireless access? The answer is: get a Linksys Wireless Travel Router.

How Wireless Travel Routers Work

Wireless travel routers essentially work just like your home wireless router, but they are more portable. When you use an Internet connection in a travel location, such as a hotel, what occurs is shown in Figure 14-17.

Figure 14-17 Wired Internet Access from a Hotel Room

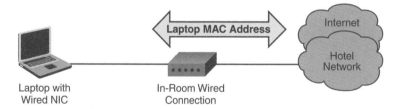

Laptop MAC Address

Internet

Hotel Network

Laptop with Wired NIC

In-Room Wired Connection

You connect your laptop to a wired Ethernet connection that is connected to the Internet through the hotel's network. You launch your Internet browser and are redirected to a membership page (very much like a wireless hotspot). After verifying your information, and possibly charging you a fee, your access is opened up and you can access the Internet.

How does the hotel network know that it is your laptop it needs to allow through to the Internet? It is based on your laptop's MAC address. As long as the hotel network sees that the traffic is coming from that MAC address, it is permitted and forwarded on to the network.

So now if we want to convert the wired connection to a wireless connection using a travel router, what needs to happen is shown in Figure 14-18.

We can simply connect the travel router to the wired connection instead of connecting the laptop to the wired connection. Then, the laptop can connect through the wireless router and onto the hotel network.

Figure 14-18 Wireless Travel Router in a Hotel Room

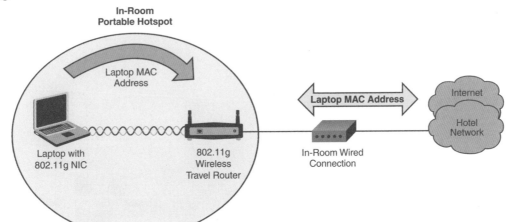

One very important point to remember is that the hotel network permission is based on the MAC address of our laptop. So, a critical function of the travel router is to be able to "clone" the laptop's MAC address and make the hotel network think that it is the laptop. It turns out that the Linksys Wireless Travel Router makes this extremely easy to do.

Note: Do not worry, the MAC cloning performed by the travel router is a perfectly legal thing to do. Essentially, it is just passing along the MAC address of your laptop's NIC to the hotel network.

After you establish a connection to the wireless router with the laptop, you can simply launch an Internet browser, get redirected, and enter the authorization or payment information, just as if you were connected over the wired connection. Very, very easy.

Setting Up a Wireless Travel Router

Before you travel, you want to set up the wireless travel router while you are still at home. This section explains the steps you need to take. Use the same laptop computer you plan to use when traveling, with a wired connection during the setup.

This example uses a Linksys WTR54GS Wireless-G Travel Router:

Step 1   Start an Internet browser and type the router's default address, **192.168.1.1**, into the Address field and hit **Enter**. When prompted for the username and password, leave the username blank and enter **admin** for the password.

Step 2   Click the **Setup** tab and the **Basic Setup** subtab, and set up the basic router setup information, as shown in Figure 14-19. Set the following parameters:

- Incoming Internet Type: **Wired**

- Internet Connection Type: **Automatic Configuration – DHCP**

Step 3   Click **Save Settings**.

Figure 14-19 Wireless Travel Router Basic Setup

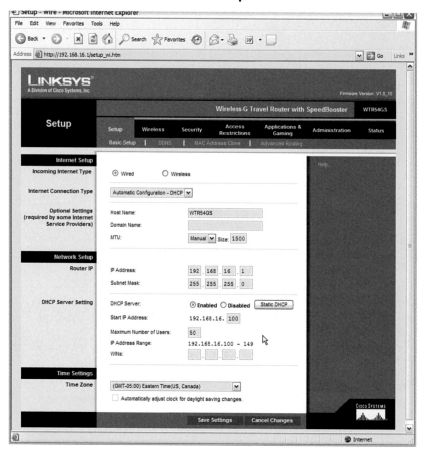

Step 4   Click the **Wireless** tab and the **Basic Wireless Settings** subtab, as shown in Figure 14-20. Create an SSID for your travel router (see Chapter 6, "What to Buy," on how to choose SSIDs). For this example, we chose d92JdlPq. It is also a good idea to disable the SSID broadcast at this point. Click **Save Settings**.

Step 5   Click the **Wireless Security** subtab, as shown in Figure 14-21. We strongly recommend that you use either WPA or WPA2 wireless security, not WEP. For this example, we chose WPA-Personal, and created a WPA key of 3kD$df501nc0waZ. It is also a good idea to "tighten up" the key renewal period. The example here shows 300 seconds, or 5 minutes, for renewal. Click **Save Settings**.

Figure 14-20 Choose an SSID

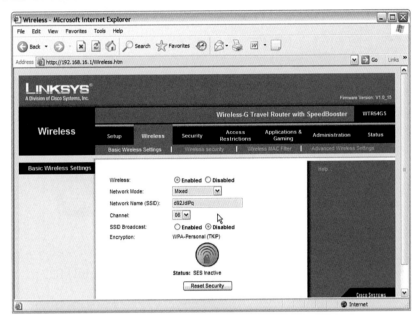

Figure 14-21 Turn on Wireless Security

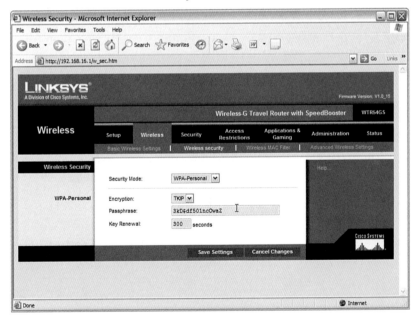

Step 6 Click the **Setup** tab and the **MAC Address Clone** subtab, as shown in Figure 14-22. Click **Enabled** and then click the **Clone My PC's MAC** button. You should see the MAC Address field change from all 00s to the MAC address matching the wired NIC in your laptop. Click **Save Settings**.

Figure 14-22 Enabling MAC Address Cloning

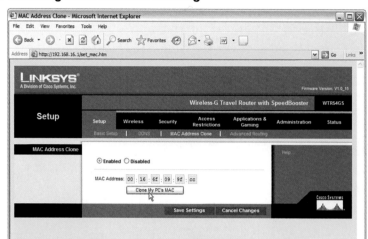

Step 7   Make sure to change the router's administration password.

Setting Up Your Laptop to See the Travel Router

Next, we need to create a wireless profile in the laptop for the wireless travel router. If you are using Windows Wireless Network Connection utility, choose **Start > Connect To > Show All Connections**. Select the wireless NIC and then click **Change Settings for This Connection**. Click the **Wireless Networks** tab and then click **Add**.

In Figure 14-23, we set the SSID to d92JdlPq, WPA-PSK as the network authentication method, and TKIP as the data encryption type. Then, we need to enter the WPA key twice, once in the Network Key field and again in the Confirm Network Key field. Take extra care to type in the WPA key exactly as we set it up on the travel router, paying attention to upper- and lowercase letters. For this example, we typed in a WPA key of 3kD$df501n0waZ. Click **OK** to save the settings.

Figure 14-23 Adding the Travel Router Profile in Windows XP

If we typed everything in correctly, the laptop should be able to connect to the wireless travel router. If it does not, then follow the troubleshooting suggestions in Chapter 10, "Troubleshooting: I Can't Connect at All."

Verify at home that you can connect to the wireless travel router with the laptop. You may even want to temporarily connect the travel router to your home broadband connection (through a wired connection on the home wireless router) to verify that you can reach the Internet on the laptop.

How to Use a Wireless Travel Router

When you have set up the travel router and laptop, using the travel router is very easy. Here is how:

Step 1   When you arrive at the location in which you need a portable wireless connection, plug the router into an electrical socket. The Linksys WTR54GS Wireless-G Travel Router has a plug built into the router instead of a cord, which is a very nice travel feature.

Step 2   Connect the Ethernet cable from the hotel's wired Internet connection to the port on the travel router marked "Internet."

Tip: Pack your own Ethernet cable in the bag with your travel router. You cannot always count on a cable being in the hotel room.

Step 3   Turn the laptop on and use Windows XP (or your chosen wireless NIC manager) to connect to the wireless travel router.

Step 4   Launch your Internet browser. You should be redirected to the hotel's authorization page, such as the example shown in Figure 14-24. Enter the authorization code you received from the front desk, or click the appropriate pay option.

Figure 14-24 Hotel Connection Authorization Page Example

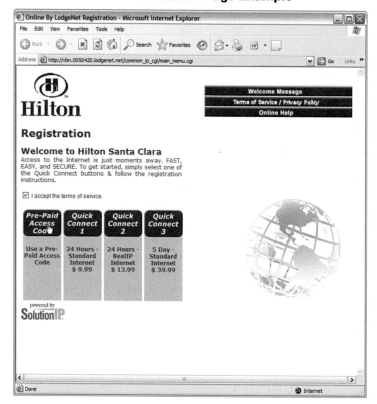

You should now be able to access the Internet over wireless within your hotel room. Coolness.

Summary

Wireless networking is addictive. When you use it at home, you will feel naked when you do not have wireless Internet access when you are away from home. Fortunately, there are many wireless hotspots where you can get connected when you travel. If you travel to a location that does not have a wireless hotspot, you can create your own portable hotspot with a wireless travel router. It's easy, and it's fun.

Where to Go for More Information

Microsoft provides an article titled "Tips for Working Securely from Hotspots" by Armelle O'Neal: www.microsoft.com/atwork/stayconnected/hotspots.mspx.

About.com offers an article titled "Top 10 Ways to Find a Hot Spot" by Catherine Roseberry: http://mobileoffice.about.com/od/locatinghotspots/tp/locatehotspot.htm.

For more information about JiWire, visit www.jiwire.com/.

For more information about T-Mobile HotSpot, visit http://hotspot.t-mobile.com/.

For more information about setting up security in your home network, check out our other book, *Home Network Security Simplified* (Cisco Press, 2006).

The Future of Wireless Networking

The future of technology is always difficult to predict. Usually you get some pretty generic statements that do not really tell you anything, or wild predictions that are usually wrong and provide little insight for those trying to figure out if the $400 worth of stuff they just bought is going to be useless a year from now.

In this chapter, we try to give you some points to think about regarding where this technology is going in the near future (which we see as being 2 to 5 years out). We hope to avoid being too generic or making any wacky predictions. We see wireless networking evolving as follows:

- Wireless networks will be faster.

- Wireless networks will go farther.

- Wireless networks will be in more places.

- Wireless networks will move with you.

- More devices will connect to wireless networks.

This chapter explores each of these, including how it will affect your network and the stuff you just bought.

Wireless Networks Will Be Faster

There is no doubt that wireless users are addicted to speed. With perhaps the sole exception of security improvements, speed is where most of the R&D and engineering dollars get spent in companies that provide wireless equipment. The interesting thing is that most people's high-speed Internet connection is slower than the slowest wireless standard currently on the market (which is being phased out because consumers are demanding the faster standards).

Paying for extremely high speeds doesn't make sense unless you are using wirelessly enabled computers where the connections are faster (perhaps at the office or Internet cafés) or if you are using bandwidth-intensive applications within your network, such as music or video servers or head-to-head video or computer games. The funny thing is that most wireless users are not doing this, but folks are addicted to speed whether they are on the road or on their own network.

So, how fast will wireless home networks get? We are already up to 100 Mbps. That is as fast as most corporate wired computer networks have been for a couple of years. The next big jump would

then be to 1 Gbps (that's a billion bits per second), which is where corporate wired networks are moving today. But we don't think that home wireless networks will go that far any time soon (nor do they need to). They may double or triple in speed but we think that's about it. Given that most people have a hard time using up 54 Mbps with home-based applications, 300 Mbps should be a lot. Remember that if your downloads or uploads bog down, it's your broadband connection, not your wireless router, that is the choke point.

Another aspect of speed that will improve is latency, which is the delay of signals to and from the router. This improvement will have a big impact on the performance of online gaming and streaming video applications.

Wireless Networks Will Go Farther

Another aspect that is improving all the time with wireless networks is the range of wireless equipment. Most of the wireless routers claim that the usable distance is about 150 feet (for B, G, and A networks), but this is rarely achieved except in lab environments without obstructions such as floors or walls between the router and the computer. In the real world, the range is quite a bit less than that, and signal strength at that range is so low that the speed would noticeably drop. Even worse, the power drain would suck your laptop battery dry in no time.

The good news here is that the range is getting much better, and will continue to do so as more improvements come along, such as the 802.11n standard. The range will get a boost as computer manufacturers begin to embed 802.11n technology into the computer itself. This type of technology addition will improve range without decreasing battery performance. In others words, the distance that your computer will work away from your router will increase much faster than the rate your battery will drain due to the added power requirements of the wireless transmissions. If you are plugged in, even better.

So how far do we think it will go? The N standards claim a range of about 600 feet today (which we expect means about 300 to 400 or so in the real world). As the technology improves, we think the usable range (without signal-sucking obstructions such as metal framed buildings) could approach 800 to 1000 feet, which is great if you want to do e-mail from the neighborhood pool. By the way, this range will make turning on your security options even more important, because war-drivers who would usually sit in front of your house in a car will be able to access your network from around the block.

Wireless Networks Will Be in More Places

The general availability of wireless has been increasing for years from coffee shops to hotel rooms to airports. When it first appeared, it was always a pay-for-service model, but now many places are offering wireless connections for free. Now the race is on, as more and more places offer wireless access, and more and more of both the new and existing hotspots offer free access.

For any business that offers other types of services (such as hotels or coffee shops), the free wireless access is the hook that gets you to buy their coffee at a 5000 percent markup while you browse the

Internet. For business travelers, the choice between a hotel without wireless access and one with (even if the cost or quality of the hotel without is better) is almost an automatic decision.

The list of places offering wireless service is also growing to include RV parks, vacation resorts, and apartment complexes and underserved rural areas (no more dialup for those of you in the country). In addition, the phenomenon is growing in many countries, which is great if you are in Vietnam or Sri Lanka and want to check your e-mail. A good place to check for places with free wireless access is the Wi-Fi-FreeSpot Directory, at http://www.wififreespot.com.

The really interesting trend, though, is citywide free Wi-Fi, also known as muni Wi-Fi (short for municipality provided Wi-Fi). Several cities, including San Francisco, Portland, Chicago, and Philadelphia, are in various phases of planning or implementing citywide wireless networks. According to an article written by Michael Grebb at Wired.com, many city officials view free city-wide wireless as a form of public works, much like libraries and public schools. Others view city-wide wireless as a way to operate existing city services more cost effectively, such as meter reading, public safety, and city planning.

So, how far will it all go? The idea of coast-to-coast wireless is interesting, but it's a long, long way off. We do think that we will see a significant number of cities (both large and small) implement free wireless access in the next few years, despite the cost and complexity of implementing a network of that size. Some cities may offset the cost by asking people to agree to viewing advertising content while on the system. We think that within 3 to 5 years, many cities will either have it deployed or will be taking a serious look at it.

Wireless Networks Will Move with You

Most people think that wireless capability gives them the ability to be "mobile." To be specific, though, wireless in its current form allows portable access rather than mobile access. This means that you move to where you want to go and then you use your computer on the wireless system. When you want to go somewhere else, you disconnect your computer, move somewhere else, and then connect again. Many view this working model as "portable" or "nomadic" wireless access.

Our prediction is that in 3 to 5 years truly mobile wireless will start to become available. This means that while riding in a train, bus, or car (as a passenger only, please), you will be able to get connected and stay connected as you move from one place to another. The distance you can go and stay connected will be limited (usually to a city or along train routes between cities) but it will be a huge improvement, especially for long-distance commuters taking trains into major metropolitan areas.

One of the big difficulties that must be solved is roaming. Much like your cell phone, your computer will need to switch from access point to access point as you move between different coverage areas. The good news is that many of the technical issues here have long been solved by wireless companies. The bad news is that wireless ISPs (also known as WISPs) have a different cost structure, so some business issues (including roaming fees between companies) need to get sorted out. At this point, it's a toss up as to who will win: the current ISPs who have the speed and access or the mobile carriers who have the roaming (and billing) parts down. Chances are there will be consolidation in the form of mergers and acquisitions and both will win in parts.

By the way, some airlines (such as Germany's Lufthansa) offer Internet access on their flights today via satellite link, and more are expected to follow.

More Devices Will Connect to Wireless Networks

Probably the most significant change impacting wireless networks will be the number and types of devices that connect to it. A number of new devices have already come out, but these are network-specific types of gear like print servers and such.

In the next wave, we see all types of devices connecting to the network, including some obvious devices such as TVs, stereos, and digital recording devices (DVRs), but also appliances, home security systems, and electronics that can control home lighting, sprinkler systems, air conditioning, and answering machines.

Connecting these devices will have some pretty important implications on security and processing requirements for your wireless router. Because most routers are underutilized today, the processing power required should not be an issue. Even if processing power were an issue today, it wouldn't be an issue in 3 to 5 years given the pace of technology. Security is particularly important because in this scenario a hacker could really mess with you.

Having a handle on how this technology really works is also important. If you think it was annoying when the clock was blinking 12:00 on your VCR for 5 years, just wait until you have to upgrade the firmware on your toaster. That said, as manufacturers make it easier to connect, secure, and use this technology with tools such as EasyLink Advisor, adoption will increase.

Summary

This chapter provided not so timid but not too crazy predictions on where wireless networks are going. The capability for everything we mentioned in this chapter exists today. The issue is that the technology is too expensive. Technology costs are dropping all the time, however.

The real determining factor with wireless (and all technology for that matter) is its usefulness to the average consumer or business user. It is a rare event when a technology is broadly adopted within 5 to 10 years of its discovery. In fact, the history of fax machines, cellular phones, and the Internet suggests that the new technology adoption time frame is closer to 25 years than to 5. There are a lot of great "solutions" out there waiting for the right problem to come along. The day that the public demands wireless networking that is faster, goes further, exists in more places, moves with you, and connects to more stuff is the day someone will be standing there with a box that does it.

Where to Go for More Information

The Michael Grebb article for Wired is called "Cities Unleash Free Wi-Fi." You can find it at Wired.com: www.wired.com/news/technology/technology/wireless_special/0,68999-0.html.

Appendixes

Appendix A MAC Address Filtering

Appendix B 802.11n Wireless Channels

Appendix C 802.11 Additional Revisions

We end the book with a few appendixes. You do not need to read these unless you are curious about MAC address filtering, 802.11n wireless channels, or revisions to 802.11.

Appendix A, "MAC Address Filtering," shows you how to add MAC filtering to your wireless network security. MAC filtering can be a bit difficult to implement and maintain, so we chose not to make it a core part of the security steps you should take. Instead, it is offered as an optional security measure.

Appendix B, "802.11n Wireless Channels," contains a discussion on how the 802.11n standard uses wireless channels. If you want to set up a wireless network based on the 802.11n standard, it uses wireless channels differently from 802.11b or 802.11g.

Appendix C, "802.11 Additional Revisions," contains a list of other, lesser-known 802.11 standards. Most of them do not affect home networking, but they are included for completeness.

MAC Address Filtering

Just like a wired NIC, a wireless NIC also has a MAC address, which is a unique identification for every single NIC manufactured, much like a social security number or a set of fingerprints. It is possible to use MAC addresses as a security measure for your wireless network.

Because you know the MAC address for each wireless NIC you have purchased and planned to use on your network, it is possible to "lock" those into your wireless router and instruct it to let *only* those wireless NICs access your network. Then, if someone should try to access the wireless network using a laptop with a different NIC (that is, a different MAC address), the wireless router will deny access, even if the correct SSID and encryption key are provided.

Sounds great, right? Yes, but there is a trade-off. MAC address filtering can be difficult to manage and even harder to troubleshoot. Every time you add a new wireless NIC or another wireless device to your network, it won't work until you add the MAC address for it to the network. You receive no warning or reminder that you need to do so; the new device just won't work.

Another disadvantage occurs when a visitor, like a relative, comes to your house and wants to join your wireless network during her stay. You have to find out the MAC address for her wireless NIC and add it to your wireless router's permission table. Again, if you forget to do this, you and your visitor could spend hours trying to figure out why the laptop simply can't see your wireless network.

 Note: MAC addresses can also be "spoofed" by hackers and clever users, so it's not a bulletproof solution, but it does add to your overall security if you choose to implement it.

Overall, we believe that the wireless security measures outlined in Chapter 9, "Wireless Security Setup," will make your wireless network secure enough about 99.77 percent of the time. If you want to spend the time (and potential frustration) to nail down the other 0.23 percent with MAC address filtering, this appendix is for you.

Enabling MAC Address Filtering

To enable MAC address flitering, you do not need to do anything on the computers with wireless NICs (or wireless devices) on the network. For the wireless router, it takes a couple steps.

First, make sure all the computers with wireless NICs (and devices) are configured for the wireless network (see Chapter 8, "Wireless NIC Setup") and the other security measures have been successfully turned on (see Chapter 9).

Then, access the router using your Internet browser as you have done before and perform the following steps:

Note: You will want to perform these steps from a computer that has a wired, not wireless, connection to the router. As soon as you do Step 1, your wireless NICs will not be able to access the wireless network any longer, until you complete Steps 2 and 3. However, you won't be able to do those steps because you have, as the saying goes, "sawed off the branch you were standing on" in Step 1.

Step 1   Click the **Wireless** tab and click the **Wireless MAC Filter** subtab (see Figure A-1). (On some Linksys products, this is labeled Wireless Network Access.) Click **Enable** and select **Permit Only**. (On some Linksys products, this is labeled simply Restrict Access.) Click **Save Settings**.

Figure A-1   Enabling MAC Address Filtering

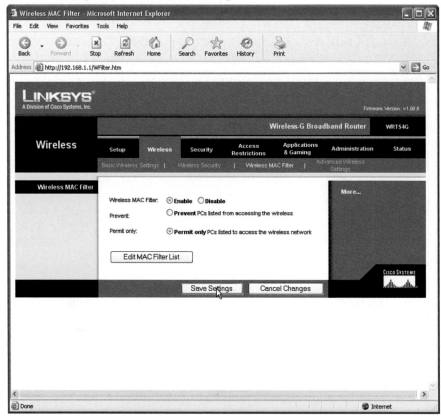

Step 2   Click the **Edit MAC Filter List** button. The MAC Address Filter List dialog box appears, but it is empty until we add addresses (see Figure A-2).

Figure A-2   Viewing the MAC Address Filter List

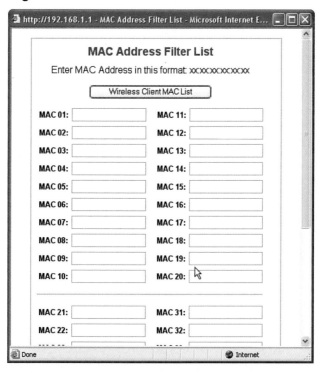

Step 3   Click the **Wireless Client MAC List** button. A list displays all the computers (by NIC) and their associated MAC addresses (see Figure A-3). Check each entry's check box in the **Enable MAC Filter** column. Click **Update Filter List** and then click **Close**.

Figure A-3   Adding a New MAC Address to the Filter List

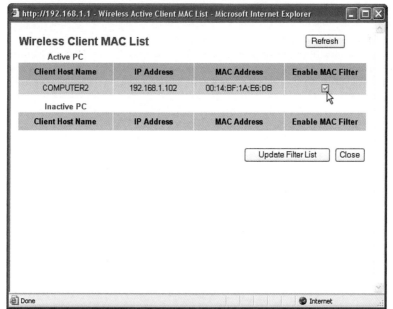

Step 4   Back in the MAC Address Filter List dialog box (see Figure A-4), click **Save Settings**.

Figure A-4   Save the New MAC Filter List

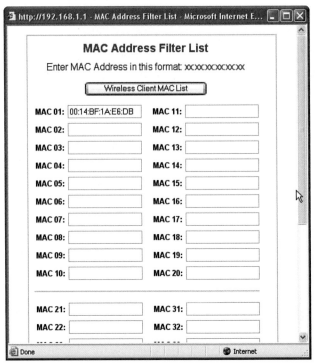

Now the wireless network is "locked" to permit only our NICs to gain access. Check each of the computers with a wireless NIC to make sure it still can connect to the wireless router. If any of the computers can no longer connect, it is possible the MAC address for that computer did not make it into our "lock down" table.

 Note: MAC address filtering only works for computers or devices trying to connect via wireless. A computer with a wired connection to the router will be able to connect even if the MAC address has been placed on the MAC Address Filter List.

Troubleshooting Tips for MAC Address Filtering

If any of the computers do not re-establish communication, check these items:

■ Make sure the number of entries in the MAC address table on the wireless router is the same as the number of computers with wireless NICs in your network.

■ Disable the MAC address restriction, reboot the computer that is not connecting properly, and see if it re-establishes a connection. If it does, repeat these instructions and add the "missing" MAC address from the computer.

■ If all else fails, manually enter the MAC address for the computer's wireless NIC. You can find the MAC address usually on a sticker label attached to either the NIC itself or the package it came in.

■ Remember that if you upgrade your NIC or plug-in card, you need to update your MAC list with the new address because the list has the MAC address of the card and not the computer.

802.11n Wireless Channels

The 802.11n standard uses the same band (2.4 GHz) and channel plan (channels 1 through 11) as the 802.11b and 802.11g standards. However, 802.11n has two possible modes of operation: standard channel and wide channel. In the standard channel mode, 802.11n uses a single channel, very similar to 802.11b and 802.11g. In the wide channel mode, 802.11n uses a secondary channel to gain additional speed.

With the Linksys Wireless-N Broadband Router (WRT300N), you have the ability to choose between standard channel and wide channel modes. If you choose standard channel, then you are asked to select a wireless channel from 1 to 11, the same as 802.11b or 802.11g. In this case, the router acts like an 802.11g router, using only the single channel. In this mode you will not get the extra speed advantages of 802.11n wide channel mode.

If you choose wide channel, you are presented with the option to choose a wide channel as the primary channel and a standard channel as the secondary channel, as shown in Figure B-1.

Figure B-1   802.11n Wireless Channel Selection with the Linksys WRT300N Router

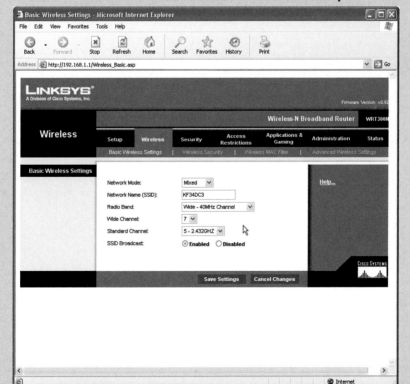

The Linksys WRT300N implementation of 802.11n restricts wireless channel selection to certain possible "pairs" of channels, as shown in Table B-1.

Table B-1   802.11n Primary to Secondary Channel Map

Channel	Possible Channel Pairs						
Primary (Wide)	3	4	**5**	6	**7**	8	9
Secondary(Std)	1 or 5	2 or 6	3 or 7	4 or 8	5 or 9	6 or 10	7 or 11

The default is wide channel mode, with channel 5 as the primary channel and channel 7 as the secondary channel.

When the 802.11n router is set to wide channel mode, wireless clients associate with the wireless router on the primary channel, and this channel is used during normal single-channel communications. When both the wireless router and the wireless NIC have 802.11n capability, they can additionally take advantage of the secondary channel to increase the data rate.

802.11 Additional Revisions

The following list outlines additional revisions to the 802.11 standard. Most of these revisions do not directly impact the home networking user.

- **802.11c, "Operation of Bridge Procedures"**—The 802.11c specification provides guidance for companies developing access points or hotspots.

- **802.11d, "World Wide Regulation Compliance"**—The IEEE created the 802.11d update to promote the widespread adoption of 802.11 by ensuring compliance with the regulations of more countries than the original standard. When the original 802.11 specification was written, only a few countries had regulations in place for wireless LAN transmissions. This amendment ensures that the rules for wireless LANs (WLANs) meet the restrictions of multiple countries. This specification was ratified in 2001.

- **802.11e, "QoS Enhancements"**—Quality of service (QoS) is a method for prioritizing certain types of traffic (for example, voice and video) that are prone to quality issues when delay occurs.

- **802.11f, "Access Point Roaming"**—802.11f provides rules for vendors to follow to ensure that computers that roaming (or switching) from one access point to another works, even when the access points are from different vendors. This enhancement was ratified in 2003.

- **802.11h, "802.11a Enhancements for Europe"**—802.11h addresses additional European regulatory requirements for the 802.11a standard. This was necessary because of the potential for 802.11a to interfere with satellite communications (which have priority on the frequencies in question). This enhancement was completed in 2003.

- **802.11i, "Security Improvements"**—802.11i is a security enhancement that makes it much more difficult for hackers to decipher wireless encryption keys. The original specification used static keys, which meant that hackers using automated programs (which could try millions of key combinations) would eventually stumble on the right key code. Once that happened, the user's security would be compromised. The updated standard (completed in 2004) addresses this issue and allows for dynamic key updates.

- **802.11j, "802.11a Enhancements for Japan"**—Much like the h update for Europe, the j update addresses regulations for the 5-GHz frequency band in Japan.

- **802.11k, "Radio Resource Measurement"**—802.11k provides rules for system management on commercial or enterprise network infrastructures.

- **802.11l (not used)**—The l standard was skipped due to possible confusion with the I standard (I and l look alike).

- **802.11m, "Documentation Upgrades"**—The 802.11m specification will update the documentation of the entire 802.11 standard.

- **802.11o (not used)**—The IEEE skipped 802.11o to avoid confusion with 802.11O (zero).

- **802.11p, "Wireless Access for the Vehicular Environment"**—This specification extends the 802.11 standard for use in moving vehicles and may be adopted in 2008.

- **802.11r, "Fast Roaming/Fast BBS Transition"**—This specification describes fast roaming support via Basic Service Set (BSS) transitions.

- **802.11s, "ESS Mesh Networking"**—This specification describes Extended Set Service (ESS) mesh networking for access points.

- **802.11t, "Wireless Performance Prediction"**—This specification describes wireless performance prediction (WPP) testing standards.

- **802.11u, "Interworking with External Networks"**—This specification describes internetworking with external networks such as 3G/cellular.

- **802.11v, "Wireless Network Management"**—This specification describes device configuration.

- **802.11w, "Protected Management Frames"**—The 802.11w specification provides security enhancements.

- **802.11y, "Contention Based Protocol"**—This specification describes interference avoidance.

2.4 GHz

Operating frequency shared by cordless telephones, wireless home networks (WLAN or Wi-Fi), and (unfortunately) microwave ovens and other devices that can cause interference.

5.8 GHz

Operating frequency for newer cordless telephones and wireless home networks (WLAN or Wi-Fi), with less interference (yet) from other devices.

802.11

IEEE working group and standards dealing with wireless networking.

802.11a

An IEEE wireless networking standard that specifies a maximum data transfer rate of 54 Mbps and an operating frequency of 5 GHz. Not compatible with 802.11b, 802.11g, or 802.11n.

802.11b

An IEEE wireless networking standard that specifies a maximum data transfer rate of 11 Mbps and an operating frequency of 2.4 GHz. Forward compatible with 802.11g and 802.11n.

802.11g

An IEEE wireless networking standard that specifies a maximum data transfer rate of 54 Mbps and an operating frequency of 2.4 GHz. Backward compatible with 802.11b and forward compatible with 802.11n.

802.11n

A fairly new IEEE wireless networking standard that specifies a maximum data transfer rate of 100 Mbps (and higher) and an operating frequency of 2.4 GHz. Backward compatible with 802.11b and 802.11g.

A

ad hoc mode

Refers to a wireless network that is computer to computer, without a wireless router.

Advanced Encryption Standard (AES)

A very secure encryption algorithm used as part of WPA2 wireless security encryption (and is also used for other types of data encryption).

B

bandwidth

The measure of how much data can be sent over a network connection, for example between your router and the broadband provider's network, at a point in time.

bit

Short for "binary unit"; this is a single digit of information, which is a 1 or 0.

broadband

A term used to describe high-speed Internet service. The term comes from the fact that a broad range of frequencies is used to attain high information exchange rates.

browser

A program used to access content on the Internet.

brute-force attack

Defeating a password or encrypted data by successively trying a large number of possibilities; for example, exhaustively trying password combinations using a dictionary attack program.

byte

A standard-size "chunk" of computer language or network information. A byte is made of 8 bits.

C

cable

A wire with connectors to connect two devices together. Also, the type of broadband service you get from your cable TV provider.

cable modem

A device that provides a broadband Internet connection to your home network by transmitting over the cable TV network.

chat

Instant messaging session where often there are three or more people involved.

D

delay

The length of time required to transmit packets from their origination point to their destination. Sometimes called latency.

denial of service (DoS) attack

An attack on a computer system or network that causes a loss of service to users, by consuming the bandwidth of the network or overloading the processor and memory of the computer system.

DHCP (Dynamic Host Configuration Protocol)

Protocol used by routers and similar network equipment to automatically assign IP addresses from a pool rather than assign permanent IP addresses to users.

Domain Name Service (DNS)

Fast computers at your ISP that can translate URLs (web links) into their actual IP addresses.

downlink

The connection and information flow from the service provider to your computer.

DSL (digital subscriber line)

A high-speed Internet connection that uses unused frequencies on phone lines to deliver very high data rates with the use of a specialized modem.

DSL modem

A device that provides a broadband Internet connection to your home network by transmitting over the public telephone network.

dynamic DNS

A service that tracks the dynamic IP address of your broadband connection and associates it with your own URL.

dynamic IP address

An IP address that is assigned by a device in the network (such as a wireless router for a private home network or a device at the ISP for public networks), which can change each time an address is requested. *See also* static IP address.

E

e-mail

An application used to exchange notes and files between two or more people. An e-mail address is identified by the username and the service provider, such as bob@network.com.

encryption

The manipulation of data to prevent accurate interpretation by all but those for whom the data is intended.

Ethernet

A protocol that defines the rules for computer communication over certain types of network cables and other physical media. It is the dominant protocol in use for both home and businesses.

F

firewall

A physical device or software program that prevents unwanted access into a private network from an outside location.

G

Gb (gigabit)
1 billion bits.

GB (gigabyte)
1,073,741,824 bytes.

GHz (gigahertz)
Measurement of a radio frequency equating to 1 billion cycles per second.

H

hack
A clever or elegant modification to computer software to gain unauthorized access or otherwise cause computer software to malfunction.

hacker
A person able to exploit a computer system or gain unauthorized access, usually by creating or modifying computer software.

hotspot
A wireless network available for use in a public place such as a coffee shop or airport.

HTTP (Hypertext Transfer Protocol)
The computer network protocol used to retrieve information from web pages written in certain "markup" languages.

I

IEEE
Institute of Electrical and Electronics Engineers, commonly pronounced "eye triple-e," is a group of professionals from many companies, governments, agencies, and so on that gets together to standardize different technologies.

infrastructure mode
A topology for deploying wireless networks in which a centralized "base station" (such as a wireless router) provides a common access point through which all computers and devices communicate.

Internet
The worldwide system of computer networks. Although many private networks connect to it, the Internet is public, cooperative, and self-sustaining.

IP (Internet Protocol)
Defines the communication rules for devices on the Internet. Communication within this protocol is based on the assignment of IP addresses.

IP address
Numerical address by which computers, web servers, and devices are known on the Internet. IP addresses have little bearing on geographic location.

ISP (Internet service provider)
A company that provides access to the Internet for residential or business use.

J–K-L

kilobit (Kb)
1000 bits. This is a standard transmission-rate unit for dialup modems when referred to over a portion of time such as kilobits per second (Kbps).

kilobyte (KB)
1024 bytes.

LAN (local-area network)
A small network within a house, department, or business.

loss
A measure of communication link quality, by measuring the number or percentage of packets that are lost between their origination point and destination.

M-N

MAC (Media Access Control) address
The unique physical serial number given by the manufacturer to every networking device used for network communication.

MAC address locking
A security measure for wireless networks whereby access through a wireless signal is restricted to specified MAC addresses, and others are rejected. Also called MAC filtering.

megabit (Mb)
1 million bits. When measured over time, this is the standard transmission-rate unit for high-speed modems, such as 2 megabytes per second (Mbps).

megabyte (MB)
1,048,576 bytes.

modem (modulator demodulator)
Device that translates computer language for transmission over a network media (phone line, cable, DSL, and so on) and back again.

Network Address Translation (NAT)

The technology by which a home router translates the private IP addresses used by computers on your home network into a single public IP address assigned to your broadband modem, providing the ability for multiple computers to share a connection, and also providing a degree of privacy because the computers on your home network are not able to be accessed directly from the Internet.

NIC (network interface card)

Provides the connection for a computer to either a wired or wireless network. Can be installed internally in the computer (PCI), connected externally to a USB port, or plugged into the PCMCIA slot of a laptop.

O-P

packet

A message containing data that is transmitted between an origination and destination in a network.

passphrase

Used much like a password, typically, to seed an ecryption key.

peer-to-peer

Another term for ad hoc wireless networking, whereby two computers establish a connection directly to each other without a wireless access point.

ping

Utility program on most PCs that can be used to test a network connection.

Point-to-Point Protocol over Ethernet (PPPoE)

Communication protocol commonly used on DSL broadband connections to communicate between your DSL modem and the DSL service hub.

Q-R

registry

A database that stores settings and options for the Microsoft Windows operating system, containing information and settings for all the hardware, software, users, and preferences of the PC.

RJ11

The connector on the end of a telephone cable, typically four wires, thinner than an Ethernet jack.

RJ45

The connector on the end of an Ethernet cable, typically eight wires, wider than a telephone jack.

router

A networking device that makes "intelligent" decisions regarding how traffic is moved across or through a network.

S

Skype

Popular free Internet-based voice chat service.

SSID (service set identifier)

A term used for the name of a wireless network.

SSID broadcast

An advertisement by a wireless router announcing its network's assigned SSID. Disabling SSID broadcasting can be one wireless networking security measure.

stateful packet inspection (SPI)

Examining each packet that flows through a firewall to make sure that the packet is both in response to a legitimate request by a computer on the home network and the correct packet in the expected sequence of packets.

static IP address

An IP address that is assigned by the ISP (or installed on a private home network) and that does not change. *See also* dynamic IP address.

T

TCP (Transmission Control Protocol)

A subset of the Internet Protocol (IP) set of rules to send data in the form of message units between computers over the Internet.

Temporal Key Integrity Protocol (TKIP)

A wireless encryption protocol that periodically changes the encryption key, making it harder to decode. Commonly used in WPA.

throughput

The amount of data moved successfully over a network connection, from one place to another in a given time period.

TiVo

A digital video recorder service that allows digital recording of live TV. Warning: The authors have found TiVo to be highly addictive.

U

uplink

The data flow from the computer to the service provider (and then to the Internet).

URL (uniform resource locator)

The official term for a link to a website or other material on the Internet; also known as the web address.

USB (Universal Serial Bus)

An interface that allows other devices to be connected and disconnected without resetting the system. Also a serial communication standard that allows high-speed data communication to many devices.

V

VoIP (voice over IP)

A protocol for transporting voice conversations across a data network. Also known as IP telephony.

VoIP chat

Using the Internet for voice conversations and phone calls, where there is typically no number to call but you reach others through their "handle," much like instant messaging. Online gaming systems, such as Xbox Live, often provide a voice chat feature for players to communicate during games.

W-X-Y-Z

WEP (Wired Equivalency Protocol)

Encryption security standard for 802.11-based wireless home networks.

Wi-Fi

A common reference to wireless networking; playing on the 1980s term for a high-fidelity (or Hi-Fi) stereo, Wi-Fi refers to wireless fidelity.

WiMax

A future wireless standard in the works that promises outdoor wide-area wireless networking, much like your cellular phone does today for voice.

WLAN

A wireless local-area network. *See also* LAN.

WPA (Wi-Fi Protected Access)

More recent encryption security standard for 802.11-based wireless home networks, considered more secure than WEP.

WPA2 (Wi-Fi Protected Access 2)

Latest encryption security standard for 802.11-based wireless home networks, considered more secure than WEP and WPA.

INDEX